# Readings in Account Planning

**Hart Weichselbaum, Executive Editor**

©2008

Published by The Copy Workshop
A division of Bruce Bendinger Creative Communications, Inc.
For further information, contact:
The Copy Workshop
2144 N. Hudson • Chicago, IL 60614
773-871-1179 • FX 773-281-4643
www.adbuzz.com • thecopyworkshop@aol.com
ISBN-10: 1-887229-36-1
ISBN-13: 978-1-887229-36-4

We dedicate this book to the amazing and wonderful
Alice Gagnard Kendrick, Ph.D.


Alice of Dallas connected us.
Without her, this book would never have come to pass.

# How I Learned To Be an Account Planner

## By Hart Weichselbaum

*Dr. Weichselbaum is president of The Planning Practice, an ad and brand planning consultancy based in Chicago. He was head of planning at The Richards Group for 13 years, has been an adjunct faculty member at DePaul University's Kellstadt Graduate School of Business, and was a founding member of the organization that became the Account Planning Committee of the 4As. He is executive editor of this book.*

In 1986, a few years out of graduate school, I moved to Dallas and looked for a job. Because I knew a bit about research design and statistics from my graduate work, a friend suggested I visit the ad agencies in town. He said they sometimes hire people to do market research.

My first interview was with a guy named Stan Richards, then and now, owner of The Richards Group. Stan told me he was trying to hire something called an "account planner." I didn't know much about ad agencies at that time, and Stan was pretty vague about what planners do. Frankly, I had no idea what he was talking about. But eight years of higher education prepared me for the challenge. I went straight to the library and looked it up in the card catalogue. *(That's what we did in the old days. You know, BG — before Google.)*

My research turned up some random articles in *AdWeek* and a few others in academic journals. I discovered that many London agencies had account planners and that the planner's job was to represent the consumer in the creation of advertising... more or less.

So in my second interview with Stan Richards, I told him my career plan had always been to find to a job where I could represent the consumer in the creation of advertising. For some reason, he hired me. That's how my education as an account planner began.

In retrospect, I realize I actually had a few things going for me in becoming a planner.

- First, I liked advertising. (I grew up watching about forty hours of TV a week and knew most of the jingles.)

- Second, I liked talking to people and hearing what they had to say. (During grad school, I worked the closing shift at a bar in Boulder and met and talked with people from all walks of life.)

- And, third, not only was I numerate, but my academic training had made me skeptical of most market research. (Over the years, that skepticism has come in handy.)

As it turned out, these were desirable traits for a young planner-to-be. But I still didn't know much about how advertising was made, much less how account planning worked. At the time, there weren't any training programs in the US and certainly no account planning courses at colleges and universities.

Fortunately, I had a few lucky breaks in my quest to become a planner.

The first occurred a year into my job at The Richards Group. One day, we were visited by a British headhunter who had seen the success of Brit planners at Chiat/Day and had the smart idea that other US agencies might benefit from having a Brit planner or two. As a parting gift, the headhunter left a kind of how-to book about account planning called *How to Plan Advertising*.

That book was a revelation.

I don't think it's too much of an exaggeration to say that most of what I knew about writing creative briefs in those formative years came from reading a chapter in that book.

Two more years into the job, I had another lucky break.

I'd heard that planners in the UK belonged to an organization called the Account Planning Group, which had regular meetings and pretty good parties. Naturally, I approached Stan Richards about sending me to London to find out more. Although he's always been a great proponent of planning, Stan has never been much of an advocate for professional development (especially if it meant paying for a business-class ticket to London). So he proposed that we have our own conference in Dallas. (You might say Stan had the original idea for a North American planning conference.)

I invited the three dozen US planners I'd heard of, and to my surprise nearly all of them agreed to come. The rest sent their sincere regrets. Talk about pent-up demand!

We met for two sunny days in February. Jon Steel came, and so did Nigel Carr, Daniel Baxter, Catrina McAuliffe, and Irina Lapin. It was another revelation. All these smart people had lived through the same experiences I was having. We talked about creating an agency culture for planning, finding, and training new planners, and whether the preponderance of British planners in America was good or bad. At night, we drank margaritas and ate cabrito at a Tex-Mex restaurant. (The planner from JWT-San Francisco threw up!)

The next day, we decided that the experience had been sufficiently worthwhile that we ought to do it again. The name Account Planning Group-US (APG-US) seemed logical, so that's what we agreed to call it.

Not only did I instantly gain a personal network of working planning directors upon whom I could call for advice and empathy, but the meeting in Dallas also launched the annual APG-US conference, which has continued to be a great source of inspiration and enlightenment for me in the ensuing years. (It's now run by the American Association of Advertising Agencies. You must attend if you ever have the chance.)

Working at a great agency was another part of my education. I learned to hire people who were smarter than me (another piece of good advice), and I got to work with highly capable creatives, account people, media people, clients, and talent.

I mention talent because Tom Bodett, the voice of the famous Motel 6 radio campaign, is an example of an intuitive planner — someone with deep and useful insight into others — whom I've met many times in my career. Tom had been working as a carpenter in Homer, Alaska, when he was hired to do the ads for Motel 6. Many of his most important lessons about planning used metaphors from the frozen North. For example, Tom was the one who taught me the "Moose Principle" of advertising.

Tom told me that where he lived there was hardly a day he didn't see a moose standing in the river or on the road near his log cabin home. But when moose hunting season began, the moose suddenly disappeared. His explanation: moose know they are a "target audience." They don't like being treated that way, and neither do consumers. Tom believed that people want to be talked to the way they talk to each other. And the twenty-year success of the Motel 6 campaign (and Tom) is evidence that people respond when your advertising treats them with respect.

A lot of things have changed since I started out. One of them is that learning to be a planner has become somewhat easier. Now you can take a course or read any of several good books about consumer insight, brand planning, qualitative research, and how agencies practice planning. And now there's one more resource – this one.

Much of the literature of planning is still scattered hither and yon. What we've tried to do is collect some of the best of these articles. We've also included a chapter or two from other excellent books. These chapters will give you a taste of what those books have to offer, and if you want to continue in your journey of learning to be a planner, you'll probably want to read the rest of the chapters as well.

I should mention that there are some excellent websites and blogs that list and review books relevant to the planning discipline. I recommend John Griffith's planningaboveandbeyond.com and russelldavies.typepad.com and, of course, adbuzz.com (The Copy Workshop's website).

I'll have a bit more to say as you work your way through this collection. You're about to go on a fascinating journey to gather insights from some very smart people. Enjoy the trip.

# Readings in Account Planning

## Table of Contents:

# Section I: Origins

The four readings in this section present a good description of the history of planning in the US and UK and, at the same time, begin to describe what planning is and what planners do.

Account planning is truly a "revolutionary" development (to use Bruce Bendinger's word) in the way ad agencies are constituted. The distinct role of planner did not exist in agencies before the 1960s.

Today, planning is established in virtually every agency of any size in the world. But in the '70s (in the UK) and the '80s (in the US), planning was a novelty that disrupted the status quo. These four articles describe some of that turmoil.

# The Account Planning Revolution

## By Bruce Bendinger

*Bruce Bendinger is, among other things, the creative force behind The Copy Workshop, publisher of this book. In an earlier life, he was a semi-legendary creative (Leo Burnett's youngest VP) and consultant, with clients ranging from Apple Computer, Archway Cookies, LensCrafters, Popeye's Chicken, a President of the United States, and numerous ad agencies and consulting organizations. Need to know more? Go Google.*

*"The planner has a point of view about the consumer and is not shy about expressing it."*

Stanley Pollit, BMP

THIS PIECE, WHICH MAY BE FAMILIAR to a few of you as Chapter 16 of *Hitting the Sweet Spot*, was originally the beginning of that book, written in 1992. Account planning was building up a head of steam in the US, and, thanks to a pile of files from Professor Esther Thorson (then of the University of Wisconsin) and a bagel breakfast with Dr. Joseph Plummer, I was on the trail.

It led me to Dr. Lisa Fortini-Campbell – and the end of the rainbow, *Hitting the Sweet Spot: How Consumer Insight Can Inspire Better Marketing and Advertising.* The book and the insights are hers – certain bits and pieces of textbook housekeeping are mine – including this particular chapter.

As a matter of fact, Lisa had decidedly mixed emotions about how planning was being implemented in the US. A few years earlier, she had an experience where an agency she worked for had basically swapped the "Research Department" sign for a trendier "Account Planning" sign on the door, and did little else. She found herself participating (briefly) in a situation far below her high standards.

In general, Lisa looks at the spectrum of consumer insight as a larger playing field. She has primarily focused on how companies behave as marketers. On the agency side, we call it planning. On the marketing side, they call it consumer insight.

This chapter, such as it is, met with her approval. Or at least Lisa was kind enough that she didn't object. If you've already read the book and this chapter, well, you can send it on to a friend living in ignorance.

It's a summary of Account Planning's origins and early days. More and better things have been written since, but this gives you a pretty good sense of how it all got rolling.

— Bruce Bendinger

One of the newest roles in advertising is that of account planning. The account planner's job is to bring to life the philosophy of Consumer Insight within an ad agency.

The account planner is a person who actively works to understand the consumer and explain him or her to the other members of the agency team.

Some have described the role as adding passion and intuition to traditional agency research. Others say it's simply consumer research done the way it should be done.

In many cases, the account planner has proven to be an important addition to the traditional agency team. This was particularly true in England, where account planning has its origins.

Today, the account planner is a valuable partner at many agencies in many countries. Often, the planner is a valuable member of agency management.

In the US, account planning began at Chiat/Day/TBWA, which has used it extensively since the early '80s.

Jay Chiat attributes much of his agency's success to the way they've used account planning to provide their creative department with the insights needed to create exceptional work – and their work *has* been exceptional.

After introducing the concept to C/D/TBWA, Jane Newman, an account planner, became head of their New York office.

Tom McElligott chose a former C/D/TBWA account planner, Rob White, as one of the partners at his new advertising agency, McElligott Wright Morrison White. White is now president of Fallon, Minneapolis.

At other agencies, account planning is known by many other names, such as Consumer Insight and Strategic Planning. At the root is a commitment to understanding the consumer and explaining the consumer to other members of the agency team.

The account planning function and its variants have changed the way agencies develop advertising.

Its impact has been truly revolutionary.

## A Brief History

To understand how account planning began, it's helpful to understand the British advertising business in the late '60s and early '70s.

The nature of the British advertising business – with less reliance on more expensive quantitative research, more use of qualitative data from smaller samples, and fewer layers of client approval – made the environment more receptive to this change in approach.

At the time, there were also numerous smaller agencies breaking away from larger British firms, and these new agencies needed to organize more efficiently (a large research department was a luxury few could afford).

One example was Boase Massimi Pollitt (BMP), a small agency that included Stanley Pollitt, a former Cambridge boxer turned media director.

In 1965, Pollitt introduced the concept when he was at Pritchard Wood & Partners. The agency researcher, he said, was to act as 'The Account Man's Conscience':

*"He was charged with ensuring that all the data relevant to key advertising decisions should be properly analyzed, complemented with new research, and brought to bear on judgements of the creative strategy and how the campaign should be appraised."*

It was the first formal attempt to integrate people directly responsible for understanding consumers into what had, up to that point, been a very intuitive process of creating advertising in Britain.

The result? Disaster! Pollitt had identified the need, but picked the wrong people for the job. (This is still a common problem.) However, the idea itself began to catch on. And other agencies tried to work with the concept.

Some of the first agencies to develop this function were Collett Dickerson Pearce and the London office of J. Walter Thompson, which renamed its Marketing Department the Account Planning Department in 1967.

In 1968, Pollitt joined with two partners and formed BMP, and planning was made an integral component of the agency's philosophy and practice. They were the first "new breed" planning agency with as many account planners as there were account executives.

This significant change in the way accounts were handled was also the result of a number of other pressures that were occurring at about the same time.

## Other Causes of "The Revolution"

During this period, British clients were becoming more marketing-conscious and more interested in the purchasing habits of their consumers.

Agency marketing departments began to suffer from redundancy as, more and more, account executives and clients thought of themselves as marketers. There was increasing reluctance to defer to people with a similar title.

Client marketing departments were developing their own quantitative research functions, which made many agency services in this area increasingly redundant. More importantly, there was increasing reluctance to use or pay for these "extra" services.

Yet, there were many functions that remained both necessary and helpful – particularly a concern with information from the marketplace.

Agencies realized that there was a real need to retain specialists skilled in the handling of information about the consumer and the marketplace.

In some ways, it was becoming even more important, with ever greater amounts of information being generated and with client decision-making becoming more layered and complex.

Meanwhile, there was great discontent with the way research was used as part of the advertising process.

In many agency operations, the research function was often used quite late – testing already developed advertising as opposed to using research as a part of the development of advertising.

Certainly this is something many researchers have advocated for years – and the advertising business has many examples where early insights provided by research have been responsible for the creation of effective advertising.

But there were all too many examples of research being used as a "win/lose" decision tool in testing developed advertising. Usually this was related to the testing of storyboards or rough "animatic" commercials.

Research was used as a provider of early input. The initial focus group was commonly used, but the process usually came to a halt at that point.

This misuse of research was a constant source of friction, particularly with creative departments. As creatives became more key in British agency management, this point of view became, not surprisingly, a management point of view.

Tom Luke, account planner at Campbell-Mithun-Esty, notes, *"Planners will continue for some time to cope with creative directors who carry their 'bad research' experiences with them.*

*"Many researchers have no idea of how disgusted and vindictive a young copywriter or art director can be when their ad is shot down with questionable research.*

*"When that young creative person eventually becomes head of a creative group or agency, they make their attitudes known and sometimes law."*

"Keep the researchers at bay" is a cry oft heard at many creative shops. But when a creative person trusts that research is supportive and nurturing of great creative advertising, they can then begin to see the benefit of a relationship with a planner.

Needless to say, the most successful account planners have been those who could handle these conflicts and turn them into productive relationships.

Finally, there was not only discontent with research departments, there was significant discontent *within* British research departments.

In an effort to be "objective" or "neutral," research departments in British agencies often seemed to retreat to the security of established techniques and standardized norms.

Agency research people were not "advocates," nor generally a part of the agency team. All too often, they showed up, dumped the bad news on the table, and left the meeting.

This also forced people to focus on research techniques, such as a certain method of storyboard testing, rather than the specific task at hand, which might lend itself to a more useful approach to understanding the consumer.

Instead of transmitting useful information to the agency creative department, which was now being forced to worry about questionable research scores on storyboard testing, they were kept apart until it was time to tell the creatives whether they had "won" or "lost."

And, since many clients paid for copy testing but little else, if one was in research and did not have a storyboard to test, well, there often wasn't much that one could do – a frustrating situation.

Researchers knew there were many things that could be done if they were released from the statistical straitjacket of copy testing and allowed to roll up their sleeves and really understand the consumer.

Yet the focus of research became technique rather than analysis and interpretation of the information. There was data and information, often in abundance, but seldom insight or inspiration.

This was aggravated by the fact that many important meetings went on without a research person in attendance. They were brought in and out according to whether there was a problem or a research budget.

So it is perhaps not surprising that many researchers did not relish the role they were relegated to — and that much of the push for account planning came from within the ranks of the agency research department.

Each of these circumstances was a powerful force contributing to the account planning concept:

- Changing client needs
- Changing use of the marketing function
- Changing creative/agency management point of view
- Discontent within the research department

The result was truly a revolution.

## Early Controversy & Early Success

As mentioned, account planning began at JWT/London, where it was an outgrowth of the marketing department, and at BMP, where it developed out of the media department, primarily because Stanley Pollitt was BMP's media director.

BMP enjoyed great success, and that success reinforced the trend. Planners themselves promoted this "new way" of doing advertising, as well.

In 1978, The Account Planning Group was formed "to support and promote the account planning function within advertising agencies," although this came after the fact.

By the mid-1970s, account planning was a well-accepted function in British agencies and was in the process of being adopted by a small West Coast agency named Chiat/Day.

It was, however, not accepted without some degree of controversy. In addition to a reluctance on the part of agencies to add another decision maker, there were differing schools of thought on the matter.

At BMP, the planners were involved closely in the development of creative ideas, as well as strategy and campaign appraisal. One of the planner's jobs was to extract "an early indication of consumer response."

Collett's (Collett Dickerson Pearce) had an equally well-articulated philosophy, with the planner functioning as a strategist rather than a researcher, and kept somewhat at arm's distance from the creative.

At JWT, the account representative coordinated the planning group and used planners to set both campaign *and media* objectives. There was also on-going measurement of how the work was performing in the marketplace.

It has been noted with some amusement that JWT, in those days, had a particularly well-dressed and well-bred group of account people. They just weren't much good at *thinking.* JWT literally hired some people to do the thinking, though they were not well-dressed enough to send to "JWT's rather elegant clients" of the era.

This additional use of planners has since caused much confusion and consternation among US agencies.

As Rob White noted in a 4A's paper, "Planning and Its Relationship with Account Management," "*This close working relationship should not be confused with interchangeable roles. There is, and must be, a clear delineation of responsibilities between planner and AE.*"

Where you draw that line depends on the specific agency operational philosophy – or, in a few isolated cases, the relative IQ of those involved.

Here are a few definitions.

This one is attributed to the late Stanley Pollitt of BMP: "*The account planner is that member of the agency's team who is the expert, through background, training, experience, and attitudes, at working with information and getting it used — not just marketing research but all the information available to help solve a client's advertising problems.*"

Another definition: *"Simply put, account planning serves to channel the consumer's viewpoint to the agency's creative staff during the entire process of making an ad campaign."*

And here's ours, with a salute to Stanley Pollitt: *"Planners are involved and integrated into the creation of marketing strategy and advertising. Their responsibility is to bring the consumer to the forefront of the process and to inspire the team to work with the consumer in mind. The planner has a point of view about the consumer and is not shy about expressing it."*

While each definition expresses the idea somewhat differently, you'll notice some common threads.

1. The account planner is well versed in *data* and *information* of all types.

2. The product of the planner's work is *insight* into the consumer.

3. The planner's responsibility to the rest of the agency team is to *inspire* their work with those insights.

Data, information, insight, and inspiration — these steps help define the role of the account planner.

Finally, it should be noted that not everyone could be a planner — at least not a good one. Just as Pollitt's first experiment ended in disaster, many in the US were not up to it. Education and training became continuing concerns. And, as US agencies were to discover in the '80s, just "bolting on" a bit of planning didn't work. It had to be *integrated* into the process. Not every agency was equipped to make that big of a change in the way they did business.

But one US agency was most definitely able to make it work — Chiat/Day, now Chiat/Day/TBWA. Jay Chiat wanted to make his agency special, and he viewed account planning as key to achieving that goal.

He felt that planning was crucial to British creative work, which, he believed at the time, was superior to most American advertising. Chiat also most certainly had a point of view on traditional research. He said, *"Research is ancient history, it's archeological. It's what already has been done."*

Planning, on the other hand, is about discovering and inspiring something new. Chiat's commitment to planning was a major reason why it worked at Chiat/Day. As one person said, "Jay Chiat did not decide to experiment with account planning. He decided to *have* account planning." This is viewed by many as a key factor in Chiat/Day becoming one of the most successful agencies of the 1980s.

## The Account Planner at Chiat/Day

Here's what Chiat/Day thinks about account planning:

- It is a means of achieving superior creative work that is based on sound marketing and relevant strategic thinking.

- It is a means of ascertaining the effectiveness of the particular advertising in the marketplace and applying the lessons learned.

- It is based on three fundamentals.

   A. To work, advertising must first be noticed.

   B. To work, advertising must deeply understand, empathize with, and speak the same language as the consumer.

   C. To be leading-edge, advertising must be on the leading edge of social change.

Chiat/Day/TBWA believes these fundamentals can be achieved only through direct contact with the target consumer, via the account planner.

And here is how they define the planner's role:

**1. Planners cover the traditional full service agency research function.** In addition, planners personally conduct ongoing qualitative research, which gives both the agency and the client continuous and invaluable insight into the mind-set of the consumer.

**2. Planners are marketers.** In addition to research skills, planners have marketing expertise, which allows them to understand the implications of the consumer mind-set for the whole marketing mix.

**3. Planners are line managers.** This is an important point. They are accountable, particularly in relation to the effectiveness of the advertising.

At C/D/TBWA, account planning is not a staff or service function where people come and go as needed. Planners are involved all the time, working in tandem with both account management and creative.

This approach involves research-trained people in the process of making ads more fully than the traditional "staff" structure. It also forces them to take more responsibility for the final work.

**4. The planner's principal "product" is the creative brief.** The "creative brief" is a term used more often at British agencies. Basically, it is a document that "briefs" the creative department on the particular advertising problems at hand. But a good creative brief is more than that.

At its best, it is a carefully constructed document aimed at focusing the creative department on a consumer message that is relevant and motivating. It provides the creative department with vital Consumer Insight.

## A Few Examples

Here's how account planning and Consumer Insights helped make effective advertising at Chiat/Day for Bazooka Bubble Gum. Planners discovered that kids perceived Bazooka as old-fashioned because it wasn't soft.

This new insight aided the creative staff in developing the campaign theme *"Are you tough enough for the hard stuff?"*

Said Chiat, "Through account planning, we've taken a perceived defect and turned it into a benefit."

The work of account planners has also contributed to the visibility and success of many of C/D/TBWA's other accounts – from Pizza Hut to Eveready to Nissan Motors.

Here's how Dave Ropes, who was head of marketing for Pizza Hut when it was at Chiat/Day, described it:

*"The planner is like having your heavy user in the strategic and creative meetings.*

*"You have a guy sitting across from you being your target, emulating how the heavy user would react to something. What we're talking about is an on-line agency research source,*

*rather than a staff research function that comes in and out only on a problem and doesn't totally understand your business."*

# Additional Controversy
## Research vs. Account Planning vs. Account Service

One of the thorniest issues in making account planning work in American agencies has been distinguishing it from traditional agency research.

Traditional agency researchers and account planners seem to have had the most difficulty understanding each other. While account planners must be versed in and capable of working with every research tool and source of information, account planners have tended to emphasize direct conversations with consumers over impersonal survey results.

Thus, account planners have been charged with a lack of rigor and discipline and with overreliance on their individual intuition to develop consumer insights.

In many cases, the sides have squared off, with "qualitative" account planners in one corner and "quantitative" researchers in the other – neither willing to budge.

But the true difference between planners and researchers has more to do with the role they play in the development of advertising than with the tools they use.

1.  Account planning is a fundamental and creative part of ad development – an integral part of the agency team.

2.  As such, it is involved on a continuous basis with an account – very much in harness with account management, creatives, and the client.

3.  Account planning is particularly important in creative development *before* the creative team puts pen to paper. The account planner is involved in the development of strategy and the creative brief where, after all, the information available to creatives is so much more useful and reliable (and much less inhibiting) than it is at the later execution/pretesting stage.

4. The account planner is, unapologetically, a person with a point of view – not hiding behind the objective "voice of a thousand households," but with an outlook developed from all the data, of course, and also from his or her own experience and views about advertising. The planner is someone who can inject stimuli and stimulation into the creative process. The planner is an "advocate."

5. Importantly, the planner is someone who does not leave the meeting after the information is presented, and is actively committed to translating the data and information into actionable insights and inspirations.

Many traditional agency researchers would argue that this is, in fact, the role they have always taken.

In Joe Plummer's words, account planning is just "research done right." And, in many cases, this is true.

But, all too often, researchers have remained detached and dispassionate, either feeling discouraged from that role or feeling that their own demands for objectivity prohibit them from "getting so involved."

## Learning to Make Account Planning Work

Because account planning represents such a strong shift in the way advertising is developed at most US agencies, it's a role that has often been difficult to incorporate in an existing agency.

Realistically, most large agencies don't have the luxury of starting up fresh with a planner as a partner.

There is also a view that there is something "uniquely British" about account planning. As a result, US implementation has been quite spotty.

Dave Berger, former director of research at FCB, notes that, when asked to describe the "moment of insight," it consistently emerged as part of an internal debate in which the planner participated.

Berger notes that this tradition of debate is uniquely British and extends even to Parliament, where the Prime Minister must debate members of the opposition as a matter of course.

American traditions, meanwhile, are more bureaucratic and hierarchical. The friction of free-flowing debate, while it certainly happens within agencies, is often subordinated to other organizational concerns. So someone whose job it is to bring an argument into the meeting is not apt to be penciled into the organization chart at American agencies.

As planner Rob White noted, after an unsuccessful period at a major advertising agency, *"They wanted planning, but they didn't want the consequences of planning. You don't rock the boat in client service, where layers and layers of management say you can't do something because it's been done another way for 30 years."*

## Different Definitions, Different Titles

There are many differences in the way agencies are organized and many differences in titles and job descriptions – often there are different titles for identical functions and identical titles for functions that may vary greatly between agencies.

For this, and other reasons, account planning now has many different titles and many different definitions. In fact, some of the following information is sure to be out of date as you read this.

Many agencies have reorganized and refocused their research departments, adding the planning function. Some agencies call it "consumer" or "strategic" planning.

Since account planning developed as part of relatively new agency structures, established agencies that wished to add or even test the function had to reorganize – usually a painful and risky process. It was often more efficient and less risky to reorganize at the next level down, at the account level.

Here, the planner is a member of an agency account team, which includes an account executive and a creative group.

In general, each account has its own team and its own account planner. On smaller accounts, the planner may have numerous account responsibilities, similar to other members of agency management.

Here are some examples of agency terminology related to account planning: Wells, Rich, Greene called its planners *marketing directors.* NW

Ayer has *AyerPlan*. J. Walter Thompson/West has *strategic planning directors*.

BBDO/LA gives the research director planning responsibilities using a "team" structure. At DMB&B, the planners report directly to the creative director. They have found good planners from fields as diverse as art history, anthropology, and dream research.

A related development at British agencies (with a few examples in the US) is the growth of "brand groups," which broadens the agency team concept (account executive, account planner and creative group) to include a media manager, and, sometimes, the client.

The agency team is also similar to the organization of many student agency groups: "campaigns" classes, student agencies, and ad competitions – such as the AAF/NSAC Contest.

So, if you're a new agency, or a student agency with few research resources, you may have a few advantages in making account planning work for you.

Whatever it's called, account planning generally represents an active shift from providing information and being a "score-keeper" to providing Consumer Insight and becoming an active part of the development of the advertising itself.

## The Future of Account Planning

As the account planning function becomes more common, we will surely have ample examples of "bad account planning" to put things into better perspective.

Chuck Overholser of BJK&E described the two possible extremes of the contributions of planners:

*"When she is good, she contributes a deeper, more insightful understanding of consumers and how they react to stimuli. She tells how the market really works in flesh-and-blood terms, and relates this information to the market problem. The planner, unlike the traditional researcher, is an invaluable personal intermediary between consumers and creatives — the catalyst between information and the creative world. The result is advertising which enthralls the consumer, creates a sympathetic closeness to the product, and makes people want to buy."*

On the other hand...

*"When she (or he) is bad, she uses suspect, invalid data which she manipulates and controls. She gains the trust of creative people by helping them get ideas and selling their favorites. She's not trained in traditional survey research methods and thus may lose sight of the benefits that are important to the brand's target segments. She makes very little use of experimental methods to test advertising for clarity of communication or power to shift beliefs and attitudes about the brand. The result is advertising which, although entertaining, is often ineffective in the marketplace."*

There will be a wider range of examples in the US as more and more agencies and marketers use a more active search for Consumer Insight as part of the advertising process.

In this context, we can be certain that the account planning process will become an increasingly important part of the way agencies make advertising.

Equally certain is that, for the most part, it won't be called "account planning."

"Planning" is a confusing descriptor. Many people, at both the client and the agency, are involved in some sort of planning. The exclusive use of this word attached to one person's job is confusing at best and offensive at worst.

The word "account" is less limiting, but it has been used by account service in the same way that media, creative, and research have been used by their respective departments.

Finally, more and more agency people in every agency function will find themselves working for, and searching for, Consumer Insights as part of their job. As Gabe Massimi, Stanley Pollitt's partner, said, *"Leo Burnett was a great planner by instinct."* So are many of the best and brightest minds in advertising.

In every job, as marketing and advertising demand greater insights to gain competitive advantage in the marketplace, the search for Consumer Insight will grow from a new job called account planning to a major reworking of the way we develop advertising. And we will need people trained in the discovery and expression of Consumer Insight.

Call it "account planning," call it "research done right," or whatever it's called tomorrow – it all drives toward the discovery of Consumer Insight. And in the future, to some extent, all of us will become account planners.

# How I Started
# Account Planning in Agencies

## By Stanley Pollitt

*Stanley Pollitt was co-founder and Joint Chairman of Boase Massimi Pollitt Univas and is generally acknowledged as one of the originators of the planning concept. Here, he discusses the emergence of a new breed of admen, which he first introduced in 1965. This article appeared in* Campaign Magazine *in April of 1979. Pollitt died all too soon at the age of 49.*

"ACCOUNT PLANNING" AND "ACCOUNT PLANNERS" have become part of agency jargon over recent years. I've been able to track down about ten agencies currently using them.

There's even a new pressure group called the Account Planning Group.

Unfortunately, there is considerable confusion over what the terms mean, making discussion of the subject frustrating. It's worth tracing how the terms came to be introduced in 1965, how planning has evolved and what it means at BMP.

Market research in agencies has changed substantially over the past few years. Planning emerged as a particular way of dealing with this. In the fifties, advertising agencies were the main pioneers for market research. Except for a few of the very largest advertisers, it was the advertising agency that devised total market research programmes, often from budgets in the advertising appropriation.

Main agencies had either large research departments or research subsidiaries like BMRB and Research Services. It was a reflection of the broader consultancy role advertising agencies played. They were partly torchbearers for a new marketing perspective on business.

In the sixties, this changed dramatically and rapidly. More consumer goods companies were restructured along marketing lines. Included within this new "marketing" function was a closer responsibility for market research.

Companies let up their own market research departments, devised their own research programmes and commissioned research themselves. They looked to their agencies for more specialist research advice on specifically advertising matters.

This again was part of a wider – and I believe, a healthier – trend. Agencies were moving out of general consultancy and concentrating more specifically on the professional development of ads. This meant a substantial reduction in agencies' revenue from market research – especially from commissioning major surveys. Agencies cut the numbers of market research people they had.

The old research subsidiaries, and some new subsidiaries formed out of departments, became increasingly separated from their agency parents. They had to fight competitively for general research work in the open market and worked for more non-agency clients, thus losing any previous connections with, and interests in, advertising.

A small rump of researchers stayed in the agency to cope with the diminishing number of clients still wanting a total research service and to provide some research advice for other departments. This is still largely the case with most agencies today and leaves something of a research vacuum there.

At just this time there was a considerable increase in the quality and quantity of data that was relevant to more professionally planned advertising – company statistics, available consumer and retailer panel data, etc. And facilities for analyzing data were becoming more sophisticated and more cheaply accessible.

This posed a paradox: as more data relevant to sharper advertising planning was coming in, more and more people qualified to handle it were leaving the agencies.

At this point in 1965 I found myself, essentially an account director, suddenly acquiring responsibility for research and media at the then Pritchard Wood Partners. I had a free hand to try to resolve the paradox. And this was how the idea of "planning" and "planners" emerged.

It seemed wrong to me that it should be the account man who decided what data should be applied to ad planning and if a researcher was needed. Partly because account men were rarely competent to do this – but more dangerously because, as my own account man experience had shown – clients on the one hand and creative direction on the other made one permanently tempted to be expedient. Too much data could be uncomfortable.

I decided, therefore, that a trained researcher should be put alongside the account man on every account. He should be there as of right, with equal status as a working partner. He was charged with ensuring that all the data relevant to key advertising decisions should be properly analyzed, complemented with new research, and brought to bear on judgments of the creative strategy and how the campaign should be appraised. Obviously all this was decided in close consultation with account man and client.

This new researcher – or account man's "conscience" – was to be called the "planner." I felt existing researchers in the agency – the rump – were being misused.

They were closeted in their own little back rooms, and were called on at the account man's whim, dusted down, and asked to express some technical view about an unfamiliar client's problem.

PWP was not an untypical agency. It had a separate media research unit where researchers were beavering away to determine how many response functions would fit on the head of a pin: a market information unit which sent market analysis through the internal post, which if read were never systematically applied to solving the main advertising problems; a general researcher who was called in spasmodically and, inevitably, superficially to give instant advice on particular research problems; and finally, a creative researcher who would occasionally be called in to conduct creative research to resolve political problems either within the agency or between agency and client.

He would usually be called in too late, when a great deal of money and personal reputations had already been committed to finished films or the commercials were already on air.

It seemed to me that these researchers should be taken out of their back rooms, and converted to being an active part of the group involved with the central issues of advertising strategy. They were to be the new "planners".

This experiment proved disappointing. I found the existing agency researchers had grown cozy in their back rooms. They did not want mainstream agency activity.

They had grown too familiar with relying on techniques as a crutch, rather than thinking out more direct ways of solving problems themselves. They had grown too accustomed to being academic to know how to be practical and pragmatic. They mostly disappeared into research agencies.

As my first planning manager, I chose Bob Jones, who had precisely the pragmatic — but thorough — base we wanted. We decided the only way to find this new type of researcher was to breed them ourselves from numerate but broad-minded graduates. Peter Jones – first planning director at BMP – and David Cowan, our current director of planning, were the first mutations at PWP.

Since then we've "bred" from 22 trainees – 15 are still with us – and adapted five agency or company researchers – three are still with us.

That was the first phase of "planning". Difficult to define precisely, but it was concerned with making sure that research was a central part of the way all the main decisions were taken.

Planners were people who were willing and able to take up this central role – people who were practical, pragmatic, confident, and more concerned with solving problems than selling techniques.

When we set up BMP in 1968 we were already able to structure this on the account manager/account planner team basis (JWT had adopted the planning idea in 1967 and coined the term "account planner". I borrowed it from them).

From the outset at BMP, we added an important new dimension to the planner's role which has almost come to be the dominant one. In addition to the development of advertising strategy and campaign appraisal, we started to involve planners more closely in the development of creative ideas.

It is impossible for anyone not directly brought up in advertising agencies to understand the immense importance a good agency can attach to getting the advertising content right. It can become a mission and a never-ending struggle for standards of excellence.

At BMP the way we have aimed to get it right is through a sensitive balance between the most important ingredient – the intuition of talented creative people – and the experience of good account people and clients, and with an early indication of consumer response, which the planner is there to extract.

Traditional market researchers are heavy-handed when trying to deal with creative work. The nightmare world of sixties advertising, when a number of now discredited mechanistic techniques were being used, is a good reminder of this.

What we set out to do was to guide account planners to be able to be honest and clear about consumer response without stifling creativity.

All creative work – and we mean *all* creative work – at BMP is checked out qualitatively with a tightly defined target market. Commercials are checked out in rough animatic form, typically with four discussion groups of about eight respondents each. Press advertisements are checked out in individual depth interviews with some 20 respondents. Target market samples are recruited by our own network of 80 recruiters – the majority outside London. Account planners are the moderators of the groups or depths. To give some idea of scale, we conducted some 1,200 groups last year, which arguably makes us the largest qualitative research company in the country.

This may not sound particularly unusual. Some elements of qualitative research on rough and finished creative work is commonplace in most agencies. But I would argue that the scope and thoroughness of account planning at BMP makes it not readily – or maybe sensibly – transplantable to other agencies. It does require a particular agency environment with a number of elements present at the same time.

First, it means a total agency management commitment to getting the advertising content *right* at all costs. Getting it right being more important than maximizing agency profits, than keeping clients happy, or building an agency shop window for distinctive-looking advertising.

It means a commitment and a belief that you can only make thoroughly professional judgments about advertising content with some early indication of consumer response.

I would guess a majority, not only of creative directors, but of account directors, would find this hard to swallow. For planning to work it needs the willing acceptance of its findings by strong creative people. John Webster and his creative people have grown up with the system. John would say that "planning" is very far from perfect – but like "democracy" it's better than the alternatives.

If advertising is to be rejected or modified, it is better that this should be the result of response from the target market than the second guessing of account men or clients.

Secondly, it means a commitment by agency management to "planning" absorbing an important part of agency resources. For a "planner" to be properly effective, both in marshalling all the data relevant to advertising strategy and in carrying out the necessary qualitative research, he can only work on some three or four brands.

You need as many "planners" as "account men". It is interesting to compare some industry figures in this respect – in the top eight agencies billing between £35m and £65m, the average number of researchers involved in advertising and creative planning is about eight. In the next 12 – billing between £15m and £30m (excluding BMP) – the average number is four. Last year, with less than £20m, we employed 18.

It involves a financial commitment and the even more difficult commitment to find and train qualified people.

Thirdly, it means changing some of the basic ground rules. Once consumer response becomes the most important element in making final advertising judgments, it makes many of the more conventional means of judgment sound hollow. You cannot combine within this same environment decisions to run advertisements because account directors or creative directors "like" them or because US management believes UK consumers respond in some way that the hard research evidence contradicts.

This obviously limits the territory in which the agency can operate. Evidence of consumer response can act as too much of a constraint on some clients and agency people. If it helps to limit the territory for the agency to operate in, it also helps establish a clear identity and a remarkably consistent sense of purpose within the agency.

This second phase of account planning has involved it more directly in the sensitive and (rightly) carefully guarded area of creative ideas development.

Politically fraught a minefield though this is, account planners at BMP seem to be coming through it well.

"Account planning" described in this way is very much a central part of the agency. As such, it is not a simple task to convert to it.

Although I am sure we will be hearing the terms "account planning" and "account planners" more widely used, I doubt whether they will carry the significance and meaning that they carry at BMP. "Bolt-on" planning, as *Campaign* rather unkindly referred to one recent change in an agency, is not a really practical exercise.

# Growing Pains:
## How planning came of age in the U.S.

### By Robert Lauterborn

*We think Bob Lauterborn is a very cool guy. At GE, he developed their Focus Strategy System — one that's still useful today. At International Paper, he was the client for one of the great print campaigns of the 20th Century. He has been on the board of various associations — ANA, BMA, ARF, BPA, BBB, NARB, and a few more we've probably missed. He is a co-author of* Integrated Marketing Communications, *one of the most influential books in advertising and marketing. Currently, Bob is the James L. Knight Professor of Advertising at the University of North Carolina at Chapel Hill. In addition to teaching, he and his wife Sylvia travel around the world, where Bob shares his knowledge with wit and good humor. This article, based on interviews with planners and other influentials, was written specifically for this book. Thanks, Bob.*

THIRTY-FIVE YEARS AGO in General Electric's house agency we devised an approach to creative work called Focus that organized the process into three action steps: Analyze the Receiver (our word for the person whose behavior we wanted to affect), Strategize a Proposition (not the late Rosser Reeves's USP; rather, a UBP — a unique *buying* proposition), and, finally, Dramatize the Proposition (put such a sharp point on it that it penetrates the Receiver's mind and creates action). Prescient as that may have been, we still had only the most primitive notions about how to accomplish the first step. We had no idea that at the exact same time, on the other side of the Atlantic, a couple of Brits — Stanley Pollitt and Stephen King — were working separately on a solution to precisely that problem.

Ten years later a young woman named Jane Newman, the ink barely dry on her Green Card, came to my office at International Paper to explain this thing called Account Planning and I fell in love. (With the process, although I've always had a soft spot for Jane, too!)

Jane had just been hired by Jay Chiat, and it was Chiat/Day's stunning win of the $150 million Nissan account in 1987 that ignited planning in the United States. Asked why he chose a bunch of people with rope-soled sandals who worked on a beach in Venice, California rather than a proven Midwestern rust belt agency to handle a *car* account for goodness' sake, Nissan's vice president of marketing said: "All the other agencies came and told us about the car business. We know the car business. Chiat told us about the car *buyer*." Planning suddenly mattered.

Growth was exponential, albeit from a small base. The first Account Planning Group meeting I went to was in Santa Monica. One of the organizers, maybe Damian O'Malley, asked the few dozen attendees what they'd observed the first night there. "It's amazing how many people in the bars had British accents," one attendee deadpanned. Ten years later, the AAAA's reports that it has nearly 10,000 planners on its books and most of them are homegrown Americans, trained first by the early immigrants and increasingly by the portfolio schools and a handful of US academics.

But there have been a few shadowy moments along the way. Not all the planning bulbs that were screwed in glowed brightly. Some fizzled; others flared but burned out quickly. Not all the light they shed made the desert bloom. And some left behind parched earth.

This chapter — based on personal interviews done over three years with 27 account planners and a dozen agency execs — is about the unplanned side of planning: what can go wrong (and therefore, according to Professor Murphy, will); why it goes wrong; and how to prevent such problems in the first place, which is a lot better than trying to fix them later.

Issue number one has to do with how planning plugs into the host body of the agency. Or doesn't. When Chiat/Day alum Bill Hamilton became creative director at Ogilvy & Mather in New York in the late 1980s, the then-advertising columnist for the *New York Times*, Phil Dougherty, asked him what his first move would be. Bill answered, "to bring in account planning." Uh-oh, I thought — that quote's going to be posted all over the account service floor. O&M research director Jennifer Stewart had tried to introduce planning a couple of years before, and the account management people revolted. It might have seemed like a no-brainer there, given David Ogilvy's respect for research gained in his years with Gallup & Robinson. But research was one thing and planning was another. "They're trying to take away the best part of my job," a senior management supervisor said back then. The second time around, either luckily for, or thanks to, Bill Hamilton, the culture didn't prove quite so resistant.

Maybe people finally realized that "bringing in planning" didn't mean taking away anything; it meant adding. The idea that an account person could do anything but a fraction of the planning job is absurd on the face of it. The account person is the general manager of a significant piece of business in an agency. He or she needs to understand the client's business, its engines of profitability, the competitive framework, the issues of the category, the politics of the client organization, and more. He or she also has to understand the economics and politics of the agency, organizing and managing agency resources to do great work for the client, flawlessly and profitably. And then sell the work. And be the point man or woman in the ongoing CRM program. That person is going to do planning besides? Um, not on your Nellie. It's a tribute to the carapace of self-confidence an account person needs to have that he or she even thought so. (Or to the paranoia of the breed, one bruised planner opined.)

A lot of the early tension in many agencies was a product of flawed or non-existent organizational thinking, not unlike what's happening in the current corporate fad for CMOs. Agencies decided they had to have a planner or two, but didn't devote a lot of thought to why, where planning would be placed in the organization, how planners would work with creatives, media, account service people, or any of the other precursors of success. Studies show that the average tenure of today's first wave of CMOs has been only about 23 months, for some of the same reasons. Companies decided they had to have one, so they either hired someone from another company or appointed someone from within (often a person with the wrong orientation or skills — we'll get to that later). Job descriptions, when there were any, were generalized boilerplate. Relationships with other departments were not thought through. Objectives were vague and there was seldom agreement on how "success" would be defined and measured. Early planners were often in the same "no-win" situations.

Another issue was where planners belonged organizationally. In creative? Logical, but impractical. Planners are creative, but they're not "creatives." There's a world of difference. Account service? See above. That's a non-starter. In the research department? Ah, talk about worlds of difference. In the early days, agencies in account reviews where they knew Chiat/Day was a competitor changed the tabs in their leave-behind books from "Research" to "Account Planning" – but changed nothing else. All the same people were suddenly transferred at least on paper from the Research Department to the Account Planning Department. All the wrong people. All account planners are researchers, but most researchers are not account planners. Researchers tend to be statisticians, more interested in designing the elegant sample than in applying the results. Generally speaking, researchers are more interested in numbers than in people. Researchers are all about data. Planners are about insight. Agencies that actually made that sleight-of-hand transformation in fact, not just on paper (and there were more than a few), were invariably disappointed that nothing changed. They didn't see a lot of benefit. "Duh," we would say in hindsight.

So where does planning belong? Media provocateur Erwin Ephron made an eloquent case, a few years ago in *Ad Age*, that planning belonged in the media department. Indeed here's how one planner described how planning functioned in her agency: "We merge with media and account service to pursue together what we think is the most critical issue today: How to get to customers."

It's obviously true that insight into how people use media – their Personal Media Networks, in DDB Needham's parlance – is a critical element of planning. I remember one planner constructing a glorious chart that illuminated not only the pattern of media that prospective car buyers followed along the path to a decision, but the intensity with which they interacted with the various media at different stages. That's true insight; insight that media people obviously need. But it's only one part of the insight planners bring to the process. It's nice to feel wanted, but few planners would feel fulfilled tucked away in a media department.

Maybe planning should be its own department? Ah, there's where a lot of agencies went wrong. They set up a separate, and often optically unequal, fiefdom and compounded the perceived unfairness by "taxing" the other agency citizens to support these new princes and princesses. No wonder there was resentment.

Does size matter?

> "Larger agencies tend to get sterilized in relationships – my job, your job – whereas in smaller agencies, you're not so insulated from each other," observed one planner who'd experienced both situations. "In smaller agencies, you work together no matter what the organizational structure is."

Maybe it all comes back to culture.

> "Planning isn't a function; it's a management philosophy."

> "Planning isn't a department, it's a way of thinking."

> "Planning shouldn't be a silo. Everybody in the agency needs to be a planner."

> "Maybe it's more like a faculty than a department."

Oops, that latter view might be misinterpreted in a lot of agencies. Can you imagine the reaction of some of the "Benevolent Dictators" Bart Cummings described to a planner's vision of himself or herself as the bringer of enlightenment to the masses mired in the Dark Ages of agencies before planning? Communicated consciously or unconsciously, that attitude would have been more than enough to activate the ejection button in a lot of shops, and I'll bet it did.

However an agency organizes, it's how the individuals relate to each other and work with each other that determines acceptance or rejection, the consensus said.

> "There may be a planning group and it stands to reason that they have a lot in common with each other, but ultimately their success individually and as a group is a product

of how well they're integrated and the relationships they develop with everyone else in the agency."

Oops, again. Mix messianic young Brits supremely sure they're bearers of Ultimate Truth with pragmatic Old School veterans of the agency wars and you've got the makings of a Big Bang, which happened here and there in the early days. Not all the imported planners were equally good at "the relationship thing." Scarred survivors describe how some planners not only didn't assimilate; they alienated the cultures they were dropped into. Unfortunately, besides earning themselves one-way tickets home, some set back the adoption of planning in their horrified host agencies a decade or more.

> "We didn't need a qualitative vs. quantitative nerd who turned everybody off."

> "We got a bloody politician who said one thing to us inside the agency and something quite different to the client."

> "Too clever by half. She was too concerned about her image to ask the naïve questions that often get to the truth."

> "He fancied himself a creative. He didn't want to know about the business realities."

> "Arrogant. Condescending. Overeducated. Overimpressed with himself. And over here (as they used to say about Americans once)."

Ouch. Some bruised feelings there. So how did most agencies avoid the chemistry problems and cultural clashes?

> "Internal credibility is very important; a planner can't be dogmatic or prescriptive. There's a fine line between empowering creatives and trying to shoehorn them."

> "We have a 'casting profile' for planners. We want true believers, of course – people with a passion for how planning can improve the work we do for our clients. But we also want people whose aspirations go beyond running a

planning department, to weaving planning into the fabric of the agency."

"Curiosity is the number one characteristic we look for, and not just curiosity about the consumer – curiosity about the category, the client, and the agency and how it all fits together."

"Functional objectivity is a key quality – someone who wants to be involved in all sorts of stuff, not just research."

"We look for someone who's worked on the client side or for a research company. We definitely don't want someone who's only ever been a planner."

"An appreciation for the business imperatives is a must. I'd love to find a planner who's actually run a business and met a payroll, but that's probably a fantasy on the order of a weekend with Nicole Kidman."

Agencies once-burned learned to look for certain personal characteristics in planners as well.

"Maybe there ought to be a Planner Test, like there's a test for copywriting talent at most agencies."

"Active listeners. They don't just record the answers, they follow the flow, seek discovery, tap the richness of the conversation, find patterns."

"Compassionate."

"Courageous. Someone who's not afraid to stand up and say, 'This is how it is.'"

"Confident. Wants to be at the table."

"On the Myer-Briggs scale, we look for an ENTP."

"Good planners have a 'bedside manner' with clients."

"A great planner is someone who has the magical ability to articulate sound, compelling, intelligent strategy to the client, but also someone who can inspire creatives and in the end, sell their work – structure and present a case."

"You're useless if all you can do is connect to the creatives. You need to be able to post-rationalize intuitive findings in left-brain terms. Creatives jump down the pole in the firehouse; you may have to build a staircase for the client."

Even when they'd found and hired the perfect planner and all was peace and love inside, agencies sometimes found the concept of planning difficult to explain to some clients and even harder to get them to pay for it.

"Early on, we couldn't sell it. We lumped it in with the creative."

"For a quote/unquote 'planning agency' it's even tougher. Clients suspect you're just selling it to give planners something to do."

"For a long time, we billed only for out-of-pocket expenses; we ate the time."

"We just made it part of our fee. Agencies find it hard to charge separately for strategic management input."

"The irony is, consulting firms come in and charge $500 million for what agencies gave away."

For too many years, agencies did give away research to clients, burying its costs in ever-escalating media commissions. That good old 15% (*requiescat in peace*) solved a lot of problems, or maybe more accurately it allowed agencies to avoid directly confronting clients about awkward subjects. Unfortunately for US agencies, the advent of planning coincided with the demise of the commission system and the rise of consultants who forced transparent billing. No matter how passionately agencies might embrace planning, they now had to transfer that passion to left-brained advertising and marketing managers and their gimlet-eyed purchasing departments. So what do agencies say to doubting, reluctant, or accountability-stressed clients? Tough question.

"What makes it tougher is that the name is wrong, and 'brand planning' isn't much better."

"Don't call it planning; just talk about it as a process. Don't talk about the function; just talk about the company and the work."

"Planning is positioned wrong. It's sold as a way to improve creative. How it should be positioned is as a way to understand your business. Getting to senior management is the key."

"It's easier to get paid for planning on a new product; then maybe you can get it accepted for existing products."

"You must have agreement on the business's long-term goals before you can do planning and develop strategy. We try to identify core brand issues and how consumers relate to brands. After demonstrating the process we ask, 'Would you agree there's value in this?' We sell it as an upfront cost."

"It's how we work. Love us, love our planning."

"You don't sell it. You just do it."

OK, once it's in place, then what? How do you keep planning sold? Inside the agency as well as among clients?

"Proving your recommendations makes you more credible; but often you don't have time to do the quantitative validation."

"Actually, acceptance of planning is accelerating as the pace of technology maturation quickens."

Ah, but pace is part of the problem, it seems.

"Time (or rather, the lack of it) is the enemy. And it's getting worse. As time to market compresses there's more volatility, windows of opportunity are narrower, competitive situations pop up out of nowhere."

"Problem in most cases isn't that clients say, 'We don't want planning.' What they say is, 'We need this in two weeks.' "Speed kills. But on the other hand, speed also focuses. So if they say, 'We need this in two weeks,' you say, 'OK, this is what has to happen. Everybody is operating on compressed timetables and you can help them."

"The issue isn't time, you know. It's being able to come up with the brilliance and insight you need."

But there's another problem. Not all clients are equally enlightened. Not all clients may want to be helped, much less dazzled.

"The reality is, too many clients don't *want* to be educated. They change objectives, change strategies, make it up as they go along. Planning would force them to be more disciplined, to actually think about what they're doing. They use time as an excuse, but the reality is that many are simply avoiding the intolerable labor of thought."

"There are times when the client rejects planning findings that conflict with his or her feelings about 'the way things are.' Sometimes clients would actually rather act on flimsy knowledge, flawed impressions, limited personal experiences with customers, salespeople's advice, et cetera, than change their thinking — or somebody else's, to whom they may report. Sometimes you just have to sigh and move on."

So, did planning complicate the client/agency relationship? Despite the initial fears some agency execs had that introducing a new element would prove disruptive to the process and that adding a strange player to the mix would compromise existing relationships, agencies quickly learned that planning was a plus.

"At the very least, planning gives the client another bright person on the business."

"A star planner can be a great asset, just as a star creative or media person can."

"Client/agency relationships were changing. More and more, we were being treated like vendors. Consulting companies like McKinsey were usurping our old place at the strategic table. Planning gave us a new weapon to fight back with."

"Clients, especially in technical companies, need something better than 'Trust me' as a basis to take decisions. Planning research cloaks what we might have intuitively recommended anyway in respectability."

"Client/agency relationships are all about credibility and trust. Planning contributed to that, we found."

"Clients can't say 'You don't understand our business' anymore. We do. Sometimes better than they do themselves."

"Merging planning's insight with the client's numbers adds another dimension to the relationship and gives us both more to work with. Clients have data they don't know what to do with. They do quantitative. Planning gives those numbers meaning."

"Sometimes clients have a hard time not being subjective, even though they may know deep down what they ought to do. Planning helps them turn that corner."

"Planning breaks down fences and helps build a genuine partnership between the client and the agency. We work with the managing directors and marketing directors, not just the ad directors. We work on segmentation strategies, new product development, media strategies, marketing plans, even business plans. In the case of smaller clients that don't have formal marketing departments, we become it!"

"Planning helps make sure the stuff we do *work*. With clients having to deal with diminished budgets, while being more and more harassed by their management to demonstrate accountability, you can't overstate the value of that, to them and to us."

What a 180-degree turn agency execs have taken from the early days of planning, when they viewed the process with suspicion (if not outright hostility) to where many, if not most, have become passionate advocates.

> "Planning looks to the future with a longer-term focus. Rather than 'Swell, we solved the current ad problem,' it's about 'Are we headed in the right direction?'"

> "Planning helps you understand how people interact with a brand. Besides planners, who's thinking about this?"

> "We work parallel with current issues, solving short-term problems while building towards brand. We keep feeding what we learn about the brand into short-term projects, to minimize dissonance. Planning is the key to managing the process."

> "I'm happiest when I'm providing strategy advice on a corporate level, not just on a product."

> "Planning sets the stage and plots out the script. It's vital to new business; the key to our agency's growth."

> "Planning unifies the agency's efforts around what's right for the client."

> "When done right, it's always effective."

If I were starting my own career over, I'd be a planner. I guess I always was, temperamentally; there just wasn't a position description for it. I advise my students who have the attitudes and instincts and aptitudes we talked about earlier to think about planning as a career. And there will be jobs for them, say the leaders. We've come a long, long way since the time of the struggles.

> "There is an explosion of demand for planners. It's a critical position in an agency with disproportionate impact on growth and success."

> "He who understands the customer best wins."

# What is Account Planning?
## (And What Do Account Planners *Do* Exactly?)
## A Revised Millennium Definition

## By Merry Baskin

*Merry Baskin is one of the few planners who has been both an "Ad Tweaker" (six years as Head of Planning at Chiat/Day New York, where the planning department was modeled on BMP, and then nine years as Head of Planning at JWT) and a "Grand Strategist." Prior to both of these, she was the planner on British Airways at Saatchi from 1983 to 1986. She revamped the APG in time for planning's 30th birthday, and her contributions appear in a number of APG planning books. A staunch believer in planning craft skills, she has trained and inspired countless planners, both here and overseas. She is currently a principle of the Baskin Shark Brand Planning Consultancy in London. Merry originally wrote this article in 2001 to provide a definition of account planning for the new millenium. She updated it in 2007 in advance of the 40th anniversary of Account Planning.*

## A Bit of an Update

IT HAS BEEN ALMOST 40 YEARS since the first account planner walked the earth. Since then, account planning has developed into a job function that exists not only in the advertising agencies but in client marketing departments, direct marketing agencies, design consultancies, PR firms, media independents et al. It has long since existed outside its London, England birthplace, extending to the US and Canada, Australia, Scandinavia, Chile, Brazil, Argentina, Western and Eastern Europe, Hong Kong, and China. And those are just the countries that have approached us about starting their own APG.

In 1978, Jeremy Bullmore, the Creative Director at J. Walter Thompson London, who worked alongside Stephen King at the agency, was invited to speak at the inaugural meeting of the Account Planning Group.

He spoke of the problem of explaining, first to the creative department and later to clients and potential clients, exactly what an account planner does. Particularly, the challenge of explaining what an account planner is for, without simultaneously conveying serious doubts about the adequacy of the rest of the agency team. He closed by challenging the audience "to let me know, with some urgency, just as soon as you've agreed on a comprehensible definition of what an account planner actually does."

In the mid '80s, Sev D'Souza (of the then fabulously named Still Price Court Twivy D'Souza ad agency) attempted a much needed and much referenced definition of account planning. It has been distributed to our membership and resided on our website since its inception. The time has now come, given planning's ascent up the ladder of evolution, to have a stab at updating that definition. It is high time we identified the various sub-species that exist, and predicted the key craft skills and genes that will ensure our successful commercial survival beyond the year 2000.

Merry Baskin
Baskin Shark
APG Chair 1998–1999
Co-Editor: *A Master Class in Brand Planning: The Timeless Works of Stephen King*

Grateful acknowledgements to fellow planners' wisdom I have cribbed; including Janet Grimes, Chris Forrest, and Jon Steel.

# A Brief History of Account Planning
## Where it Started and Why

Stephen King of JWT and Stanley Pollitt of BMP are the undisputed forefathers of account planning. In separate agencies, but at pretty much the same time, they started a revolution in the advertising world which has spread from the UK to other countries and from ad agencies to management consultancies, direct marketing, PR, design and client research departments.

In 1964, Stephen King, dissatisfied with the workings of both the media and marketing departments within his agency, developed a new system of working (the T-Plan or Target Plan) which concentrated on combining consumer research and insights to create more effective, creative advertising.

Stanley Pollitt in 1968, was concerned at the enormity of discretion given to account management in the writing of the creative brief, and felt that they were using data either incompetently or expediently. He wanted a research person at the elbow of the account man. For Stanley, the voice of the consumer was of paramount importance, and using consumer research to clarify the issues and enrich the advertising development process was an essential component. When BMP was formed, each of its three accounts was managed by an account director and a (line function) account planner.

Both Stanley and Stephen shared a desire to reorganise the media planning, market research and marketing departments. Stephen initially by a process, and Stanley via a person. Both were led towards the creation of a new department and a new discipline.

*"I hope that the coming anniversary of account planning isn't going to mean another orgy of 'who first started it?' articles. There wasn't an It, it's impossible to tell and it's about the least interesting element of the whole thing."*

—e-mail from Stephen King to Jeremy Bullmore in 1998

## The Origins of the Job Title

The name 'account planning' was coined by Tony Stead at a JWT away day in 1968, attended by media planners and account people from the marketing department.

> *"Tony Stead thought of the name 'Account Planner'. We started by not knowing what on earth to call it. We thought of 'Brand Planner' and we used that as a code name for quite a while. Then people said that 'brand' suggests that we were only involved in small packaged things so Tony said "Why don't you call them Account Planners?" And that was that. That was at a meeting of one of our Away Days in July '68. There was a lot of discussion going on and by the time it had emerged we had a department of 23 people. It was very easy to cast because it was taking people from the Marketing Department and a very few key people from the Media Department. Some of the Reps felt a bit threatened by the new Department, but Reps always feel threatened, it's part of their job description. We had a pretty bad first six months with Planners — who are inclined to gloom at the best of times — feeling that it was all a disaster. But it picked up. . . Planning seems to have lasted rather well".*

—Stephen King interview, *Fifty in 40: The Unofficial History of JWT London*, Tom Rayfield, Dec. 1996

Delivered with characteristic understatement, planning has indeed lasted rather well, in spite of its unhelpful name. So this explains how we have been saddled with one of the most obfuscatory job titles ever since. Our North American friends in adopting the discipline have strived to better it with the likes of 'Brand Planner' and 'Strategic Planner' (preceded by the usual Senior Executive Vice President tosh, of course) but none of these appear to have stuck. Perhaps we rather enjoy the mystique of having a job title that implies crystal ball gazing without a clearly defined handle?

## The Evolution of Marketing

A brief note on the nature of marketing in those days: From the '50s, 'Marketing' and 'Marketing Plans' were in fact executed by the agency (who also did everything else). Ad agencies pioneered market research; they created test kitchens for npd, devised TV programming (think Compton's P & G soap operas), PR ladies who lunched in hats, etc.

The '60s and '70s brought dramatic changes as more and more clients restructured along marketing lines, such that nowadays the majority of clients have their own marketing and market research departments in house. These days they look to their agencies for specialist advice on advertising or whichever specific communications channels they specialise in rather than as (media neutral) marketing consultants.

More fool them, some planners might say. For that broader brush communications vision to express a core brand idea is where planning has been heading for some time, and the accountability that planning can bring to the party has now slipped further down the agenda as marketing has ceased to feature at the board room level. Which is unfortunate. And also a topic for another day.

## What is Account Planning for (Daddy)?*
### And why you should have some

Most problems benefit from being tackled systematically. Almost every communications agency (and their clients) benefits from a disciplined system for devising communications/advertising/commercial strategy.

> *"Any systematic approach to planning advertising has to do more than simply provide controls and disciplines. It must actively stimulate imagination and creativity too"*.

—Stephen King, *JWT Planning Guide*, 1974

We need a process that enhances an agency's ability to produce outstanding creative solutions for our brands that will be effective in the marketplace. It is the planner's job to guide or facilitate this process via the astute application of knowledge, otherwise known as consumer and market understanding. From the real world, outside the myopic, navel-gazing self-absorbed, self-rewarding industry we love and work in. Only Planners (not Heineken) can do zees. And why can only planners do this?

Planners are in a unique position because they (should) have a detailed understanding of the audience and the market context through research

---

*Title stolen, with pride, from Jeremy Bullmore's Inaugural Address at the first APG meeting in 1978.

expertise *and* an appreciation of how this can be applied to their client's business. Planners must provide the crucial bridge between the two worlds in order to get customers to engage profitably with the brand. If researchers are data gatherers, then planners are knowledge applicators. Planners must insightfully interpret and illuminate the data, and develop intuitive hypotheses from it – not simply regurgitate it in an indigestible form for the rest of the brand group.

So, at the core of the Planner's task, is the need to understand the consumer (and how they perceive the brand and the market) in order to unearth a key insight for the communication solution (Relevance). As nontraditional media has mushroomed and new media communication channels have multiplied, it has become increasingly important for communication to cut through the clutter and the cynicism and connect with its audience (Distinctiveness). And Planners also need to prove its worthiness, to demonstrate how and why the communication has performed (Effectiveness).

With the burgeoning of digital communication the planner's job has become much more like that of a social anthropologist. Whereas a key insight, proposition, or message has been the development plank of most communications, how we "engage" with people through digital means is far more about observing and predicting behaviour and much more like product design. Instead of trying to influence behaviour through changing how people think, we are increasingly bypassing this process and moving straight to interaction and behaviour. This requires yet another set of skills – we are now facilitating product design, engineering engagement into the brand idea itself, not just its communications.

Finally, the planner is there to bring upstream thinking to the brand's ongoing development. For brands must move forward, or they die!

## What Roles does Planning Fulfil?

Thinking about the portfolio nature of the planner's working day, we've made a list of the various job functions and skill sets a planner often needs to fulfil.

## Market Researcher

Many account planners have evolved from market researcher origins. Jane Newman (undisputed Queen of Planning, USA) used to say that account planning 'subsumed' the agency market research function. We believe quite strongly that market research craft skills (and adherence to MRS [Market Research Society] Code of Practice principles) are the backbone of the planner's platform. If you can't devise, conduct, analyse, report on and monitor surveys objectively, how can you possibly hope to judge their usefulness or commission them appropriately? The planner should never assume that the researcher is the sole expert. Elements of questionnaire design, the way a question is phrased, for example, can fundamentally affect the outcome of the study. Black box modelling techniques may be so much impressive theory but they can critically enhance or destroy projects. Planners need to be able to ignore, challenge or exploit such things from a perspective built on understanding or on at least something more solid than assertion and prejudice.

## Data Analyst

The planner is charged with ensuring that all data relevant to the brand's communication decisions be properly analysed, complemented with new research where appropriate, and then brought to bear on judgements of the creative strategy and evaluation of the communications. This is more than just knowing your way around computer tabs from a pre-test, but also sales data, share data, trend data, demographics, etc. Knowing how to interrogate data and find a story through it rather than be intimidated by it is the challenge. Common sense, intuition, numeracy and clarity of thinking all help. Think of yourself as an 'incisive detective solving the crime' rather than a plodding copper on the beat 'conducting house to house enquiries, asking people where they were on the night of 12th'.

## Qualitative Focus Group Moderator

Qualitative research (and the ubiquitous focus group) has taken on an increasingly significant role in everyone's lives. "Let's do a couple of groups and see what they say and then we'll adjust our policies to suit", says Tony Blair, former Brand Manager to the nation. Moderating your own groups is by far the best way of coming to grips with your target audience, putting yourself in their shoes and seeing the world from their perspective. It also gives the planner a confidence and an authority he or she wouldn't otherwise be entitled to. It means you are both a psychologist and an interpreter.

## Information Centre

Knowledge is the bedrock of the planner's craft. Knowing where to go to find stuff out is key. However much time pressure is brought to bear on your working day, planners should always make time to feed their heads. This generation of planners just don't know how lucky they are to have the World Wide Web. I remember in my day we had microfiche in the local library… (mutter mutter).

## Bad Cop (to account management's good cop)

Despite the fact that planners are outnumbered by account management by 4 to 1 (source: IPA survey 2000) we tend to work in pairs. Very often, it makes sense to adopt the bad cop/good cop routine with some clients and some creatives in order to deliver some bad/challenging/alternative/unexpected news without ruining the relationship. Since the news is usually grounded in objective fact, the planner should deliver it as constructively and simply as possible. Occasionally, of course, you get to play good cop, too – depending on your agency culture and your client relationships!

## NPD Consultant

One of the most fun aspects of working on multinational packaged goods brands is the fact that they are still investing in new product development. Being in at the birth of a product through to its positioning, naming, testing and (rarer than hen's teeth) successful advertising launch, can be one of the most interesting and formative experiences for a planner. Don't forget that it was Stephen King who invented pretty much every aspect of Mr Kipling, right from when RHM came to the agency and said, 'our flour mills are producing a surplus, what shall we do with it?'

## Brainstorming Facilitator

What better way than the brainstorm to hothouse creativity or to get everyone on the team singing from the same song sheet so the brand and its communications can move forward? More challenging and more exhausting than the average group discussion because you'll (hopefully) be dealing with the chairman and the brand manager and the creative director in the same session. It's also more rewarding. Make sure you have some good warm-up exercises up your sleeve.

## Target Audience Representative/Voice of the Consumer

It's the oldie but goldie. The planner's 'cocktail party' job definition. Their job is to ensure that an understanding of consumer attitudes and behaviour is brought to bear at every stage of communications development via continuous involvement in the process. Many of the places we work and the colleagues we work with are not representative of the sorts of people and places where our communications are aimed, so it's a good idea to be an empathetic sort, and to be curious about everything and everyone.

## Soothsayer/Futurologist

Let's face it, our job title does have a hint of crystal ball gazing within it. This aspect of the planner's craft is to have a genuine interest in and capacity to generate knowledge about trends and anticipate social movements that their colleagues can actually use to grow their brands. And then of course, there's always the Henley Centre and Faith Popcorn. Planners can drive the future by finding gaps and creating interest in things the punter may not have thought of, but may be interested in. Faster horse, anyone?

## Media/Communications Planner

Some might say that this job is the next evolutionary phase of the account planner. Certainly, as new media emerge and the myriad of digital and interactive opportunities broaden, integration across media becomes every agency's growth strategy, and understanding how consumers consume communication their mission statement. It is therefore increasingly more important for the planner to understand the strategic role and effectiveness of different media, by target and by category, and know when and how it is relevant to use them to achieve the brand's objectives. Studies have shown that people are now moving seamlessly between on- and off-line, using combinations of resources to make their decisions – understanding how they work together and how to assess their effectiveness is becoming more and more difficult. And more important for the planner to try and resolve.

## Strategic Thinker/Strategy Developer

If the creative brief is one of the planner's tangible product outputs, developing the brand communications strategy is the precursor task. Strategies help us get to the 'right' marketing/communications brief. It ensures the whole team is aware of the assumptions being made and aids evaluation of the work's effectiveness. The planner identifies the key issue and determines the role for communication against a specific target. It is the 'How could we get there?' proposition question in the Planning Cycle, once you have already figured out 'why are we advertising?' and the 'what are we trying to achieve?' bits. There is as much need for creativity in strategy as there is in media and execution, and a really creative strategy can make a substantial, definitive impact on the commercial outcome of a campaign. AA's (Automobile Association) '4th Emergency Service' and BT's (British Telecom) 'Its good to talk' are great examples of powerful strategies.

## Writer of the Creative Brief

The brief is widely considered to be the planner's main product – or 'key tangible deliverable' to the creative development process. One of the myths is that all planners do is transcribe the client's marketing jargon into baby talk so the creatives can understand it. There's considerably more to it than that of course; clarity, brevity, and fertility being the hygiene factors of a good creative brief. And as the creative brief has the power to spark ideas – and ideas is what our business is all about – then that is a pretty important role.

Nowadays we also have to consider many new internal audiences – not just "creatives" but technologists, programmers, project managers, event organisers, editors. This means the briefs have to be multi-functional and, more importantly, agreed upon by many more people. The planner's job here is not just to produce the brief, but to facilitate the process.

## Think Piece Polemicist

There are aspects of the planner's job that sometimes entail sitting in a darkened room with a towel round your head, mulling over deep thoughts. These times may be accompanied by a passion or a fascination for a certain theme. Write it down, rant about it from conference platforms and blogs, get it published. Original thinking is a powerful tool and, when persuasively and compellingly delivered, can have real impact on the business you are working on and the people you are working with.

## Social Anthropologist

Our world is changing at an amazing rate, with technology and information moving at a breathtaking pace. Advertising has always been a young person's profession and nowadays it is even more important for creative people to be in touch and *au fait* with rapidly evolving cultural and social trends to ensure their idea's relevance to the target audience. In the time it's taken me to write this, surfwear has probably gone out of fashion, and my Sony VAIO has been superseded by yet another "wafer-thin" mobile phone that thinks it's a laptop. Monitoring cultural and social trends is a specialist task, and the findings need to be fed in early to brand and creative development. Differentiating between mere "fashion" and genuine cultural trends is not something for the inexperienced – many people can tell you what's in and what's out, but planners should be able to tell you why.

## Insight Miner

This section probably deserves its own book, but deriving insight from knowledge is one of the most important skills a planner can possess. These insights about the client's business can come from a variety of areas.

- the consumer
- the client's culture
- the marketplace/category
- the competition

- the brand (past, present, future) values
- the product qualities
- the advertising and communication conventions of the category

Mining all these areas (whether sporting a virtual helmet with a lamp on the front or not), peering into nooks and crannies without losing sight of the big picture in order to identify a key insight that can transform a client's business, is a real skill.

*"At the heart of an effective creative philosophy is the belief that nothing is so powerful as an insight into human nature, what compulsions drive a man, what instincts dominate his action, even though his language so often can camouflage what really motivates him."*

—Bill Bernbach

## Knowledge Applicator

Not wishing to sound like a cosmetic brush (or worse), there are those who believe most passionately that in this new information age it is in the applying of (rather than acquiring and regurgitating) knowledge that the planner truly comes into their own. To paraphrase Jon Steel, finding things out, filtering them, rethinking them laterally and then using that knowledge to help creative people come up with a (better) idea easier or faster means that the planner is doing their job properly and making a difference. Not making a difference in this way is a hindrance and you should move out of the way and let everyone else get on with it.

## What Planners Don't Do (Well)

Opportunity here for some cheap gags about bag carrying (account man's job) and the general administrative disfunctionality of the account planning breed.

In general, planners are not very well organised. Tidy minds tend to move in a linear fashion, rather than laterally. And while some may feign incompetence so they don't get stuck delivering proofs to clients at 11pm, it's not advisable to ask a planner to do the following:

- go to client meetings on their own (they'll get lost)
- write the contact report (their minds wander)

- act as a shill for the creative work (unless it's grounded in consumer knowledge otherwise integrity and objectivity are compromised)
- write timetables (many of them do not possess a watch but use their mobile phone, which they have left in the back of a cab, as a timepiece)
- set deadlines (there might just be some other nugget out there that I've still to unearth)
- have anything to do with invoices!

## The Ideal Account Planner – Recruitment Spec

The following is an excerpt from a recruitment brief from my days at Chiat/Day in the US. Were I to be setting up a department from scratch, I don't think I would change much of it, except perhaps to substitute the word "communication" where it says advertising. With thanks to Rob White and Jane Newman.

### Key Characteristics

Curiosity about what makes people act and think the way they do; capable or real insights into motivation; someone who understands that what people say is not necessarily what they believe or do; someone who is detailed enough to examine a problem from different perspectives without losing sight of the big picture; logical and analytical, yet capable of lateral thought; views research as a means to an end; not technique-oriented; pragmatic approach to problem solving.

Ability to conceptualise and think strategically; ability to clearly identify problems (getting to the nub of it); capable of taking a commercial and making a reasonable judgement/guess on its intended effects (role of advertising, target consumer, desired responses); intuitive about people, brands and advertising; able to portray a target consumer without immediately stating demographics; an understanding of advertising as only one tool in the marketing mix, its potential uses and its limitations; an ability to see alternate strategic routes for a given problem/brand.

Numerate. Able to visualise the meaning of numbers and generate hypotheses, or draw conclusions; an eclectic user of information, with a desire to draw on all sources rather than just the most recent; someone who accepts nothing at face value, and challenges assumptions until the whole picture (sales, quantitative, qualitative, competitive info, etc) makes sense.

Advertising orientation; passionate about the subject, "I've always been interested in advertising"; above all, someone who enjoys talking about advertising.

Presentation skills; able to argue a point of view coherently and concisely; not afraid of big or senior audiences; able to 'win' an argument without making the protagonist (client) feel like a loser; quick-thinker; able to speak authoritatively, without seeming dogmatic or inflexible.

People skills; a team player; someone who can appreciate and use inputs from others; someone who knows when to push and when to relax.

Great personality! Must be able to see the funny side of it all; to be a participant, not an observer; involvement must be genuine, not forced; must to able to deal with pressure, unpredictable circumstances (like jumping on a plane to Wichita at a moment's notice), an informal, loosely structured work environment, and (occasional) criticism; not territorial nor defensive nor paranoid.

## The Ideal Craft Skills and Experience of an Account Planner

Finally, there is an aphorism, to which I subscribe, that there is no such thing as a "junior planner". Joseph Heller would approve. The problem is that the planning role (in most agency cultures) is imbued with such credibility and authority that whatever a planner says can be construed as pearls. And as with most professions, the more experience you have (in terms of not just breadth of categories worked in or years on the clock, but also craft skills accumulated), the more useful and productive you can be. The following therefore is a list of ideal experience and craft skills for a full-grown adult planner.

## Market Research Practitioner – Bedrock
- Conversant with the key methodologies and practitioners.
- Understands how to use the research tool; its potential and its limitations.
- Qualitative skills – able to translate research objectives into a discussion guide, experienced moderator, comfortable dealing with parties on both sides of the one way mirror. Good facilitator (brainstorms, away days, etc)
- Quantitative skills – Well versed in basic quantitative terms, philosophy, methodologies and protocols, has experience of tracking studies, A&Us, test markets, and quantitative advertising research. Able to write questionnaires and read data tables. Knows how to tell good studies from bad (can kick the tyres on a survey).

## Brands
- Has been involved with decisions about brands, as opposed to decisions about research. Has understanding of brands and their brand values.

## Advertising and Communications
- Has direct experience in the development and production of commercial communications, preferably not just 30-second ads.

## People Management
- To have had client contact experience at Marketing Director level (minimum).
- Able to present points of view or research findings to this level of audience.
- Team catalyst – not just a good team player, but able to "lead" teams via persuasion, facilitation, and inspiration, rather than command and control leadership.
- Comfortable working with a broad church of types – junior to senior, creatives to media, design to digital, senior clients to secretaries, teenagers to businessmen.
- Able to train, motivate, appraise, and "bring on" juniors, not simply delegate their menial jobs to them.

# Section II: Ideas

The practice of account planning is based on a few fundamental ideas about the communications process. (By the way, "advertising" here means all the different ways commercial organizations communicate with their customers: TV, public relations, direct mail, search advertising, etc.).

The following readings contain provocative thoughts such as these:

- Advertising does much more than simply persuade people.

- Brands serve functions beyond identifying the manufacturer.

- Brands are a special language for expressing the range of needs that products and services satisfy.

- Attention and persuasion are under the consumer's control, not the advertiser's.

- The creative brief is an effective way to summarize one's strategic thinking and give direction to the creative team.

- Measuring the impact of advertising is really quite difficult, even in the best of circumstances.

These four seminal readings will introduce you to these key concepts.

# How Advertising Works:
## New Steps on the Advertising Timeline

### By Mike Hall

*Mike Hall, an ex-Leagas planner, founded Hall & Partners on Stephen King's principles and theories of how communication works. In 1991, he developed the "Framework" model for identifying the different ways advertising works to build brand relationships. Hall & Partners have updated the original thinking by looking at the way digital and integrated media work (Admap, Terry Willie, 2007).*

### All You Need To Know?

IN 1923 AN AMERICAN ADVERTISING AGENT, Claude Hopkins, wrote ads.

They were press ads, because TV had not been invented. They were in black and white because color printing had not been invented. They invited response by mail order, because telephones, although invented, were not generally available. They were about products, because the concept of brands had not been invented. Inevitably, Claude predicted: "We now know 90% of how advertising works, and very soon we shall know the other 10%."

Quite rightly, he's a faint and forgotten footstep on the advertising timeline. But we shouldn't forget the lesson he failed to learn — just when you've worked out how advertising works, somebody comes up with a new idea.

### Circumstances Change

Hopkins had a theory about how advertising works, and it was invalidated not because of any inherent flaw but because circumstances change. I'm going to look at all the ways that advertising works, and to explain these I'm going to take you down the advertising timeline.

### 1950s Innovation

Let's move along that advertising timeline to the 1950s. It was a period of great innovation after the Second World War, especially in the US, where hundreds of factories had converted from producing munitions to household goods like televisions, and people looked for new products that would improve their quality of life.

### How Your Grandmother Washed Dishes

Now take the mundane event of washing the dishes. Your mother or grandmother washed dishes by hand and used this product – washing crystals. They were a soluble chemical that dissolved slowly in very hot water. Unfortunately they had a side effect: they made your hands red and raw. So one company, Procter & Gamble, invented a product called Ivory Flakes, and they advertised it on the new medium of television, so that as many people as possible would see it. And the promise was, "for hands that do dishes as soft as your face".

### A Theory of Advertising Is a Theory of Brands

Behind this advertising is a theory of how advertising works. But the really important thing we should never forget is that behind a theory of how advertising works is a theory of how brands work. And when you think about brands in a new way you inevitably use advertising in a different way from before.

### Key Differences from Now: Few Brands

The way brands were thought of in the '50s and early '60s was dictated by the fact that there were very few of them. You chose between a couple of different washing crystals maybe, then along comes Ivory and you *switched brands*.

### Passive Consumer

The manufacturer played the role of inventor and provider, and the individual was given the label of "consumer". Although we still use the term today, it's out of date because it implies a passive, receiving, responding role. But that's what people were like then, and it's not a criticism: they enjoyed a continual process of discovery, as trusting beneficiaries of a stream of manufacturing invention.

### Advertising Announced New Solutions

And a really important point to note is that *products solved problems*. So people wanted to find out, to hear about these new things. And the role of advertising was to tell them and show them.

### A Single Universal Model

This is a theory of how advertising works, and taking the lead from dear old Claude, it was adopted at the time as a single universal model that applied to all advertising. If any of you have majored in advertising or read any marketing text books you'll have seen different variants of this model. They were given acronyms like AIDA and ACCA.

### Persuasion: Step-by-step Argument of Functional Superiority

I call it the Persuasion model. Technically it's called a linear progression model, less technically a step-by-step model, and in the ACCA version the first step is to establish Awareness of the brand (hence the formula of mentioning the brand name in the first 10 seconds of the commercial). The next step is Comprehension of the brand's Unique Selling Proposition — because all brands had USPs in those days — and after people had understood the message they believed that your brand performed better than other brands, and this Conviction led to Action: they switched brands, which directly increased sales. It's a rational argument about the brand's functional superiority, advertising that persuades people with a "reason why".

### Persuasion Isn't Wrong, but It's Only Right Sometimes

What I'm about to show you is not that Persuasion advertising doesn't work or that other models of advertising are better, but that *sometimes* it doesn't work and in *some* circumstances you can use advertising in a different way to greater effect.

### Advertising Changed, and Research Thinking Was Left Behind

Because times change. And people change. And brands change. But 30 years later, when I was a Planning Director at Leagas Delaney in London, I realized that thinking hadn't changed, and research hadn't changed to inform new thinking. But the interesting thing was that at a practical level advertising *had* changed. Advertisers and agencies were using advertising in very different ways and nowhere more than in the US, led inspiringly by Bill Bernbach. But what was lacking was a coherent theoretical framework that explains how this new advertising was working. So I set out to discover it, by interviewing marketing directors, creative directors, planning directors and managing directors about what they were using advertising to do. And I'm going to show you not just what we discovered, but just how the advertising timeline led us to where we are today.

## A Model of Advertising Is a Set of Assumptions

Before I take us back to the '60s, let me make clear what a theoretical model of advertising is. It's no more and no less than a set of assumptions. It's not strictly a scientific theory, because in science if you replicate the same process in the same circumstances you must get exactly the same result, or the theory is invalidated. If you put two molecules of hydrogen with one of oxygen and you get wine, it's not a miracle, it's the invalidation of a scientific theory!

## Scientific Method Is the Best We Can Get

In advertising you never have the same circumstances and even the second exposure of the same ad is not an exact replication of the process. So the best we can achieve is scientific *method*. And that means testing your assumptions against what actually happens or in probability *will* happen. A theoretical framework of how advertising works is an explicit classification of the different sets of assumptions advertising people make.

## Questioning the Single Universal Model

Those assumptions reflect the different relationships people have with different brands. So let's go back to the mid-1960s, when brand relationships were changing – the time when advertising intellectuals like Stephen King of JWT London started to observe that one universal theory of how advertising works – the Persuasion model – was not enough.

## 1960s: When Diversification Led to Active Choices

It was an era of diversification rather than innovation alone. The post-War boom had spread from the US around the world. People were offered not just better products in the markets they knew, but new markets they could now afford to enter. People didn't just make *purchases*, they made *choices*. As Judie Lannon wrote, they moved from being a passive to an active consumer.

### Advertising: from Push to Pull

As a result, marketing shifted from the product push to the consumer pull, from supply to demand. Advertising had to adapt, because now it had not just to inform, but to appeal. At which point Bill Bernbach famously and pithily said: "Telling isn't Selling". And one of the developments of this was what I call the Involvement model of advertising.

### Involvement: A Relationship Built on Identifying with Non-product Values

The main assumption behind Involvement-driven advertising is that the target market's relationship with the brand will be built most effectively by its buying into brand values rather than product values. Values such as pride, male bonding, caring, fun, excitement, contemporaneity. Open a can of beer, a box of detergent, a car door, or a health insurance policy and you don't find them. But if they're somehow attached to your brand, they can be a basis for preference when its functional characteristics don't differ or don't matter. And the "somehow" by which they get attached to your brand is advertising: the theory is that if they get involved in your ad values, people get involved in your brand values; and this brings them closer to your brand, so they're more predisposed to consider buying it.

### The Difference between Persuasion and Involvement Advertising

As the late great Charles Channon, another of advertising's intellectuals, once put it, the difference between a Persuasion and Involvement strategy for advertising is that the one argues that your brand *works better*, while the other makes your brand *mean more*. Involvement-based ads get people involved in different ways (and I'll return to that later) but none of them is primarily trying to argue functional superiority, even though each of them – like all great advertising, I think – is rooted in a product truth.

### Fragmentation Is the Great Theme of Our Era

And so the 1980s and 1990s in our advertising timeline. The '80s saw the biggest boom since the post-War period. It has mainly been an era of brand proliferation, as anybody knows who has seen their brand's market share erode. Fragmentation is the great theme of our era: fragmentation of media that led to concepts such as vertical targeting; fragmentation of product fields that led to niche marketing; and fragmentation of whole markets that blurred boundaries between such huge things as food and drink. In a recent survey in the UK, teenagers were asked to name their favorite foods and in the top ten came McDonald's, Coke, Pot Noodles, Mars, and fruit. So much for product fields.

### Differentiation Based Less on Performance

Brand differentiation has become increasingly less based on performance: do you know an automobile that is *un*safe, *un*reliable, or *un*comfortable? A dishwashing detergent that's *un*kind to hands or *won't* clean grease off plates; a spirit that you *can't* mix, *doesn't* give you a buzz, or *isn't* a sociable drink? If so, it's probably a niche brand with a small, devoted and profitable following.

### Brand Switching Replaced by Brand Repertoires

When people know they're going to be using a product field for a reasonably long time, and there are plenty of brands to choose from, they'll move between brands. Brand loyalty needs to be refined, and it's not been replaced by random acts of brand promiscuity. Rather, brand switching has been replaced by brand repertoires.

### A Brand's Advertising Is Unique

The aim is to get into the repertoire. To do this, one of the things you need to do as a brand is to stand out above the masses. Advertising is one of the things that does this, because competing brands can function the same and offer the same values, but they can't have the same advertising.

### The New USP

As one agency, BBH, put it, we've moved from the era of the Unique Selling Proposition to the age of the Unique Selling Presentation.

### Salience: Making Your Brand Stand Out with Advertising that Stands Out

This gave rise to another way of using advertising, which I call the Salience framework. Here the assumption is that people will consider your brand because they have a sense that it's got something going for it. And to make the brand stand out you need advertising that stands out.

So does this mean that dear old Claude was wrong?

### Sales Response, Claude's Model, still Valid Today

Not at all. Here's the model we've recreated as the Sales Response framework. It's not a brand building model, but seeks short-term behavioral action instead of longer-lasting predisposition. And although he thought he had only another 10% to learn, would he have dreamt up a 30-minute infomercial where a sales-orientated TV program about Terminator 3 is interrupted by commercials for... you've guessed it, Terminator 1 and 2 with a bonus video of outtakes *and* a copy of the script of Terminator 3, personally autographed by *all* the stars of the movie?

### Different Models Appropriate in Different Circumstances

One of the points I want to make, that I hope you've already worked out for yourself, is that just because there are four different models of how advertising works, you don't have to choose just one of them. Not even for the same brand. Because a brand has different objectives for different targets at different times. British Airways wrote ads to a Persuasion model for its First Class seat that turns into a bed, to an Involvement model based around Club World, and to a Salience model (The World's Leading Airline) to raise its overall status. But it also uses Sales Response ads (World Offers), even if you can't clip a coupon to take up the offer.

### First Principle of Framework Approach

This all adds up to what we call the Framework® approach to advertising. And underlying it are two basic principles. The first, as I'm sure you've gathered by now, is that different advertising works in different ways. This, as I like to say, is a truism, which therefore has the benefit of being true! It's been much copied, but not replaced, because there's no substitute for the truth. I'm hugely excited by the way many planners in the US have responded to it, but there's still a way to go, because so many advertisers won't explore beyond the Persuasion model that they know. I'd contend that it's the responsibility of Account Planners to take it further — if you know you have four options, then to consider only one is to abdicate your responsibility. And of course the same is true for a research agency like ours.

### Second Principle Emphasizes Brand Response

The second fundamental principle is my personal mantra: Brand response is ultimately more important than ad response. I think Hall & Partners can claim credit for having shifted the industry from ad tracking to brand tracking, because, like you, we know that the business of advertising is building brand relationships.

### Ad Effects Lead to Ad Effectiveness

This also has implications for planners, because the question you must address in writing a strategy is not just "Will it work?" but "*How* will it work?". In other words, to achieve advertising *effectiveness* you must first understand advertising *effects*. The planner's role is to *plan* those effects.

### The Brand Relationship: A Spectrum of Commitment

How do you do this? Well, one of the things I found as a Planning Director was that, although advertising people thought in terms of brand relationships, research people did not, so throughout the '60s, '70s and '80s there was no measure of the brand relationship. We created the concept of Brand Commitment. Basically it's a spectrum, running from rejection through various levels of consideration to commitment. Obviously the precise criteria vary by market, but it holds true for every single brand in every single market, fragmented or not.

### A Strategy Starts with the Brand Relationship, Not the Advertising

When you're developing an advertising strategy for a brand-building exercise, this is where you start, not with the advertising but with the brand relationship.

### And There's Only Three

Now here's the good news. There are ultimately only three strategies:

- keeping the Committed committed,
- converting rejectors, and,
- for most brands most of the time, somehow enhancing the commitment of those people who have a relatively weak relationship with the brand.

So, when you've chosen an overall strategy, how do you decide which way to use advertising effectively? Well I think we've established that you have to consider all three brand-building models, assuming it's not about short-term tactical promotion and Sales Response.

### Deciding on Persuasion

Here are three questions to ask in relation to a Persuasion framework:

- does your brand actually work better than other brands?
- are people already convinced (in which case should you throw bad money after good)?
- do they really care?

Based on our research, we've defined these different frameworks more precisely, with the hope of helping advertising planning to become more focused.

### Two Types of Persuasion Strategy

If Persuasion-driven advertising is a functional argument about why your brand performs better, there are two types of Persuasion:

- Problem-Solving Persuasion
- Performance-Enhancing Persuasion

### Problem-Solving Less Common Today

Let us return therefore to the instances of Ivory in the 1950s. What marks that launch campaign out is that it is Problem-Solving Persuasion — it removes a negative effect. Every now and again this still happens — for example, Nextel Direct Connect. If people were not demanding portability, it was only because they didn't know it was possible. When Direct Connect was launched, it revealed two-way talking as a "hidden need" and solved it. Similarly with American Airlines' "More legroom in coach" and Quaker's "Low cholesterol" platform for oatmeal.

### Performance-Enhancing Ads about Relative Differences — but Must Offer Reward

Much other Persuasion-based advertising is based on a different strategy — what I would call Performance Enhancing. For example, one headache pill claiming 8-hour potency rather than the 4-hour efficiency of its rival. This highlights *relative* functional *differences* rather than *absolute* functional *answers*. It seems to me that the effectiveness of these strategies is inherently more limited but still sometimes appropriate. Is a 4-hour aspirin a *problem*? Do people have 5-hour headaches? If this kind of Persuasion strategy is to work, it should at least offer a *reward* if not a solution.

## A Difference that Makes a Difference

In idea-generation sessions that we run I call this "a difference that makes a difference"®. The crucial aspect of developing an effective Persuasion strategy is therefore to answer two questions about your brand: Does it differ? If so, does it matter? Otherwise you end up with a difference that's descriptive but not evaluative. We've talked to many US clients about this. Are product claims such as built-in testers for batteries, improved car tire treads, insurance policy details, and so on differences that make a difference?

## When Salience Is Right, It's a Logical Step

So you've considered your options for a Persuasion-based strategy. What other strategy can you consider? Let's turn to Salience, because it seems on the face of it so radical and scary, that to use it as a strategy your client has to be correspondingly desperate or brave. Actually they just have to be logical.

## Three Salience Models

In fact, there are different types of Salience, and only one of them is radical:

- Radical Reappraisal

- Stature

- Self-Assertion

## Conditions for Radical Reappraisal

Radical Reappraisal, as we have seen with the recent Miller Lite, "Catfight" campaign becomes a strategic option when:

- you need to convert rejectors

- you have few existing values to enhance

- you need to break away from decline or stagnancy quickly

- your target audience gets quickly bored with consistency (familiarity breeds neglect, if not contempt)

### A Stature Strategy Is Preemptive

Radical Reappraisal is not the Salience strategy of AOL, with its "No wonder we're #1", which is about Stature (which I might define as "size with meaning"). It's a pre-emptive statement of ownership like Bud-Weis-Er. It's a "Number I" strategy that doesn't use a "reason why". You don't have to be the brand leader to follow this strategy, and for brands that are seen by people as small and relatively insignificant, it's a forceful option.

### The Self-Appointed Icon Uses Salience through Self-Assertion

Salience through Self-Assertion is different again because it's a statement of confidence rather than a reflection of achievement. Absolut is an example. It makes few claims, but simply states "take me or leave me, but if you take me, take me as I am." This unapologetic move to center stage may have superficial appeal — particularly to clients — so you do need to work out why people wouldn't leave the brand, rather than take it. What will prevent this becoming "So what?" advertising? Where's the bravura or charisma that makes the difference between carrying it off and dying on stage, naked in front of your critical audience?

### The Publicity Model — Extreme Example of Talked-about Advertising

What all Salience strategies have in common is that they make the brand stand out from the crowd and have to be prepared to face a few boos amongst the cheers. One of the ways we measure its effects is as "the sort of advertising you'd talk about". And a submodel of Salience is what I call the Publicity model — advertising that deliberately seeks to get its effects less by response to the advertising than by response to the news stories it sets out to create: Calvin Klein using apparently under-age girls; Benetton showing a new born baby and a dying AIDS sufferer. These are shock tactics, but that's an executional style, not a strategy. The Camel wall painting on 42nd street and Olympus Cameras filming Naomi Campbell (made up to look 80 and reflecting back on her life) both generated column inches through an "Ooh!" factor, not an "Ugh!" factor.

### The Assimilation Model Breaks the Rules without Making a Noise

Salience seems to me the most innovative of models right now, and not surprisingly so, since it relates most directly to what many people would term "ground-breaking" advertising. And diametrically opposite the Publicity model is what I call the Assimilation model. Take Intel. Here is a brand that crept up on you. You want your computer to have it, but it has few warm values. You think it makes your computer better, but couldn't give a reason why. You never went "Wow! What's that brand up to?!" but suddenly it was everywhere and it didn't have mere presence but that special, indefinable quality of significance, that is such an important component of Salience. It's an unusual strategy but I know of at least one other brand deliberately setting out to use "non-advertising advertising" in exactly this way.

### How Do You Know if It's Working?

Perhaps because this thinking is relatively new to the US, or because there's a fairly hard-sell advertising culture, an issue that's quite often raised with the people in our office over here is "How do I know if it's working?" and this unfamiliarity is what makes agencies wary of proposing it and clients cautious of accepting it. Ultimately you're still trying to create predisposition and you know it's working if the people with a stronger relationship with the brand are also those finding the brand increasingly salient.

### Measuring Precise Assumptions

The only thing you need to be careful of is making sure you've defined your assumptions quite specifically, which is why we've developed this new thinking and hope that it will help. It's no good saying that Salience is just Brand Awareness, if you're trying to create Publicity or acquire Stature. Those are the precise things you should measure, and if you stimulate those, and they build the brand relationship, it's working.

### Involvement Is More than Liking

The same is pretty much true of Involvement. It may be a broad concept, but it's not just about "liking". Some clients, finding their Persuasion-based ads less effective than they once were, talk about "adding Involvement", and see it as inserting a smiling kid into the commercial.

### Deciding on Involvement

That's not it. We're after a distinct strategic approach, and the sort of questions you can ask to determine whether and how you should use it. The Involvement advertising questions are:

- Does the brand say something about the person who uses it (either to themselves or to others)?

- Does it have non-product values you can easily build on?

- Does the brand mean a lot to people, and what makes it do so?

- Do these values make more of a difference than product values right now?

If you find your brand fits in here then it may be time to shift the focus on to non-product values to make the brand mean more to people. But I agree that Involvement is a broad concept, so we've updated it by adding further definition to it.

### Three Types of Involvement

From our own research we've identified three Involvement submodels:

- Shared Values

- Desired Values

- Added Values

### Identification with Shared Values

Shared Values Involvement is advertising that works by a process of identification. People see it and identify with the brand's values as matching their own. They relate to it by feeling "This is me. I *am* this brand." Volkswagen's "Driver's Wanted" campaign is all about this — advertising lifestyle rather than product features — it's ad values, brand values and target market values all in one.

### Aspiration to Desired Values

Desired Values Involvement advertising works slightly differently, by a process of aspiration rather than straight identification. People's response is that this is "the other me" or "the part of me I'd like to have more of" – they relate to it as a brand they want to be like. I'd put the Nike "Just Do It" campaign in this category, and other campaigns built around a brand attitude.

### Personification of Added Values

Both Shared Values and Desired Values Involvement reflect *intrinsic* values. They stem from things inherent to the brand. By contrast, Added Values Involvement uses *extrinsic* values. And it works by a process of *personification*. It builds a fun or lighthearted or contemporary personality surrounding the brand and the advertising itself must therefore *have* these values as well as simply express them. M&M's is perhaps the most famous example of this type of advertising.

### How to Use This Thinking

So there you have the latest steps on the advertising timeline and I hope, by narrowing down into types of Persuasion, Salience and Involvement, I've made it easier for people to use. Being practical rather than theoretical to sum up, what might you as planners use this thinking *for?*

First, for writing better strategies, because you can identify the most powerful drivers for the brand.

Second, for educating clients. Clients *want* to do new things, but they'd rather be led by the hand when they're exploring new territory, with you pointing out each step of the way.

Finally, to stimulate new ideas. There's an energy and enthusiasm coming from planning in the US that makes advertising an exciting business to be working in and working with. Planning shouldn't live in the intellectual comfort zone, lazily content with simplistic formulae, and I hope you feel that what our Framework approach offers you is a discipline for creative thinking.

# Defining a Brand

## By Paul Feldwick

*Paul Feldwick is one of the leading thinkers on brands. This article will show you why. He started his career as an account executive and became one of BMP's and London's most highly regarded planners. He then went on to run the planning function at BMP. At DDB, he developed a global framework for planning advertising and helped found DDB University. He has written and lectured extensively on how advertising works and brand equity, amongst other things. His book, "What Is Brand Equity Anyway?," was published in 2002. He has been Chairman of the APG and the AQR, and is a Fellow of the IPA and MRS. This article originally appeared in* Understanding Brands.

TOWARDS THE END OF 1989 the Marketing Society held a major conference in London. Its title was 'The Immortal Brand', and its publicity made prominent use of a quote from the Group Chief Executive of United Biscuits:

> 'Buildings age and become dilapidated.
> Machines wear out.
> People die.
> But what live on are the brands.'

The visual design accompanying this theme was striking. The immortal brand was represented by a stylised, golden sun with a face on, perhaps reminiscent of an entertainment at the Court of le Roi Soleil. This rose above a classical montage of Greek temples, broken columns and Herculean statues. The metaphor is clear: the brand as deity, a sentient being whose existence transcends our merely human lifespan.

And indeed this is how we in marketing and advertising talk of brands. They have life cycles; they have personalities. In our research we personify brands, and find consumers can play the game. Unconsciously we credit the brand with some kind of absolute, platonic existence. Our mission is to discover (rather than invent) its 'core values' and abide by them. In fact, the brand is a rather primitive kind of god. If we keep its laws and pay regularly the tributes due (mainly advertising), fortune will smile on us. Otherwise, disaster.

Now most of this is a way of saying valuable and important things about branding. Brands can 'live' longer than people. The metaphor of personality has been helpful, and I will later on make extensive use of it myself. But it may be worthwhile at the start of this book to remind ourselves that it is only a metaphor. A brand may have 'personality', but it is not a person, still less a god on a cloud. You cannot talk to it and it cannot answer you back. In fact, a brand has no absolute or objective

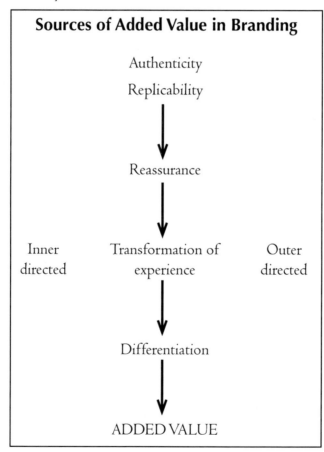

**Sources of Added Value in Branding**

Authenticity

Replicability

Reassurance

Inner directed     Transformation of experience     Outer directed

Differentiation

ADDED VALUE

existence – nor are its 'core values' written on a tablet of stone in the Gobi Desert. A brand is simply a collection of perceptions in the mind of the consumer.

What I want to do in this chapter is to start from the consumer. Why does this phenomenon called branding – about which we get so mystical – exist at all? Presumably it satisfies certain needs on the part of the consumer: but what are they? How does branding work, and under what conditions?

The tentative answers in this chapter – and I regard it only as an essay which I hope others may improve on – are rather complex. Branding can be seen as satisfying various different needs, and working at different levels and in different ways. What I will suggest in fact has happened is that brands originally begin as a badge or promise of certainty in an uncertain world, and that this offers simple and functional benefits to any consumer. But because a brand offers this kind of certainty, it also becomes a kind of currency for consumers to carry out less obviously related kinds of transactions with themselves and with each other. In a sense, consumers have 'hijacked' brands for their own purposes. But all the ways in which brands can be used derive from the basic promise of certainty, and I will therefore argue that we are talking about one coherent, if complex, phenomenon. Brands as a badge, and brands as personality, are aspects of the same thing.

At its simplest, a brand is a recognisable and trustworthy badge of origin, and also a promise of performance.

## A Badge of Origin

All histories of marketing or advertising refer to the Bass Red Triangle, registered as the first trademark in England in 1876 and, I am glad to say, still going strong. It will serve as a good example of branding at its simplest – as a guarantee of authenticity.

This is something we rather take for granted, but it is of fundamental importance in underpinning the mechanisms of branding. When we buy a jar of Hellmann's Mayonnaise, we can be fairly sure it is a jar of

Hellmann's Mayonnaise. Rigorous legislation in this country prevents forgery or 'passing off'. When this was less true than today, many packaging designs were as elaborate as banknotes, to discourage forgery and emphasise authenticity ('None genuine without this signature'). Once this confidence is breached, the symbols and hence the satisfaction of a brand lose their potency. (How am I to recognise a real Lacoste sports shirt nowadays?)

Many of the higher-value satisfactions of brands depend crucially on this belief in authenticity. This point will be particularly stressed in the section that follows later, on 'transformation'. In the meantime, just consider this: A fake Rolex watch may fool everyone else, but it won't fool you.

## The Promise of Performance

The other reason that we believe in brands is that, overwhelmingly, they keep their promises. If every bottle of Heinz Tomato Ketchup tasted different from the last, the brand would have no meaning. If consumers are prepared to forgive the exceptional bad experience from a trusted brand, this is because they know it is exceptional. On a familiar product the brand name offers a replicable degree, and kind, of customer satisfaction.

The product itself need not remain, literally, unchanged. Certain products, such as newspapers, change constantly by their very nature. Most successful brands continually improve or update their products to remain competitive, or to meet changed market requirements. But if the product does not reliably live up to the promise, the brand, however strong its history, eventually loses its force. Coca-Cola, one of the world's best-loved brands, provoked howls of betrayal with its ill-judged reformulation of 'New Coke'. Even in a market where we tend to think of 'image' transcending product reality, the poor quality of Jaguar cars which were built in the early 1970s did great damage to the marque's reputation, which was repaired with difficulty. Even a gradual decline in product performance can have the same effect, as when Cadbury's reduced the thickness of their Dairy Milk chocolate bar by imperceptible stages, until it was competitively vulnerable to the launch of Rowntree's Yorkie.

At best, a strong brand may provide a time-lag between the product becoming uncompetitive, and consumer rejection of it. In the early 1970s Cadbury's Smash users remained loyal to the brand, despite the launch of a technically superior product from Wondermash. This provided a breathing space for Cadbury's in which to match the new formulation: but it is unlikely that it would have gone on for ever. Sooner or later, failure to deliver renders a brand meaningless.

The extent to which product delivery ultimately underlies the strength of brands is often, I suspect, forgotten by those who subscribe to the myth of 'the brand in the sky'. But sooner or later, product realities will rewrite reputations, however powerful they are. How many years will it be before the aspirational luxury car becomes a Toyota or a Honda, rather than a Mercedes or a BMW? I suspect not many: and if you doubt it, look at the motorcycle market (or cameras, or stereos, etc.).

At this stage the benefits to the consumer are clear. The brand offers a strong promise of both authenticity and replicability. Indeed without these, consumer decision-making would become a lottery and, probably, a nightmare.

But the promise is more than an aid to decision-making. A promise actually creates value in its own right, by enhancing the experience of owning or using the product.

## The Value of Reassurance

Consider the satisfactions of owning a motor car. Many of these are tangible experiences: the comfort of the seats; the pleasure of driving it; its added comforts, such as air conditioning or a stereo; its beauty to the eye; its speed and performance, for those who like that sort of thing.

But there are other requirements from a car which are less tangible. It is important, for example, that the car won't break down. The fact that it hasn't done so in the past is real; the expectation that it won't do so in the future is hypothetical. The degree of reassurance I personally feel as to whether the car will break down, when starting my journey, makes a major difference to my satisfaction as a user of the car. Branding can make a major difference to that reassurance. What the brand name does is translate a very hypothetical, negative kind of product superiority, into a real and immediate experience. I set out confident, relaxed, able to enjoy the trip. The value that I place on this feeling is part of the value that I may be prepared to pay for the brand, over and above the value I perceive in the nuts and bolts of the visible car. (For years, Volkswagen advertising in the UK has been founded on the brand's reliability: as a result the marque commands a significant price premium over comparable cars in its class.)

This is one example, but it is generally applicable to many other and less obvious situations. The reassurance I derive from the brand name (of performance, of authenticity) actually enhances the value I derive from the use of the product, over and above the physical evidence of my senses. While buying, cooking or serving my preferred brand of baked beans, I derive a heightened pleasure of anticipation long before I taste them. If serving drinks to guests, I am confident that a certain brand will be enjoyed by them, which puts me at my ease. If wearing clothes bearing the label of a famous designer, I feel more confident that they will look good under all circumstances – even if I lack confidence in my own judgement of style. In every case the added value consists in the fact that I can relax and enjoy the experience, confident that the brand promises that all problems are taken care of.

## Transformation of Experience

What we have discovered here is that the subjective experience of using a brand can be different from the subjective experience of using an identical product without the brand reassurance. At one level, you could say this is just a matter of paying for peace of mind – not that we should underestimate this. But there's more to it. There is evidence that beliefs about the brand can actually affect perceptions of the physical product characteristics.

The simplest example is of the blind vs. branded product test. It can very commonly be shown that consumers tasting two food or drink brands comparatively may express a clear preference for one over the other (often the one with the greater market share), while the same product test conducted 'blind' shows no clear preference. Branding, in short, transforms the actual experience of using the product — and thereby adds to its value.

One of the most striking demonstrations of the real value to the consumer of the brand experience is found in the analgesics market, as reported by Cooper and Branthwaite in an article in The British Medical Journal.[1] Patients taking their own preferred brand of analgesic (as opposed to a chemically-identical own-label product) claimed faster relief from pain. Doctors recognise this as the placebo effect, and it demonstrates that certain symptoms respond to the ritual of taking medicine as much as to the physical substance. The blind vs. branded product test demonstrates that this principle is applicable in many other circumstances.

The idea of transformation is a very powerful one and reflects the way in which much advertising and branding works. In 1987 many people's imaginations were gripped by the story of the Nanking Cargo, a load of porcelain sunk for 200 years in the South China Sea. The items themselves are no different from much other porcelain already available: but the experience of owning or handling one of these bowls is rendered quite different by the knowledge of its extraordinary and romantic history. As a result such dishes sell for a considerable premium: the added value for which collectors will pay. The parallel with a commercial 'brand' is clear: both hinge on the authenticity of the goods.

It is commonly asserted that paying more 'for the name' is a foolish delusion on the part of the customer, and little more than a confidence trick on the part of the seller. Yet the benefit to the customer is a real enhancement of his experience of consumption, whether it consists in peace of mind or an imaginative experience.

To understand this we need to understand that the benefits sought by most consumers are subjective, and go a stage or two beyond the product's literal function. Charles Revlon used to say that others sold cosmetics, he sold hope. Parallel benefits can be imagined for any other type of product. People who buy toothpaste actually want confidence and security — that their teeth won't fall out, that their breath won't smell. People who buy tennis rackets or golf balls are buying the belief that they can win. A mother buying detergent is buying a way of presenting and showing affection for her family. Children selecting breakfast cereals are choosing fun, and so on. What is really on sale is an abstraction – and in all these cases, it will come from the brand, rather than the product. (Frequently, as the blind vs. branded tests show, the benefits are projected back on to the product itself.)

## Differentiation and 'Brand Personality'

So the transformation that takes place is not merely an intensification of the experience, but an import of ideas which translate the simple function of the product into a relevant emotional metaphor. It is in this way that brand differentiation, and the idea of a brand 'personality', are created. If Persil is about 'caring', it evokes at one time both the perceived effect of the powder on the clothes (gentle and effective) and also the kind of emotions a mother may have about her family while washing their clothes (contrary to what cynics may think, such emotions are not entirely an adman's myth). In this way the experience of washing with Persil is qualitatively different from using, say, Ariel, and satisfies a different (perhaps a complementary) set of emotional needs from the process. Washing clothes is not after all an act which has to take place in the way in which we do it; it is part of a social context of relationships both within the family, and between the family and the world outside, and this creates needs beyond the merely functional.

In further work done by Cooper into the analgesics market, the enhanced effectiveness of certain brands on individuals can be related to the specific characteristics of how the brand was perceived to work. These were expressed through a role-playing exercise in which, for example, one brand behaved as soothing the pain away gently, the other as a powerful force attacking it.

It is when we enter this realm of differentiation that the metaphor of brand personality becomes extremely valuable. But it all develops naturally from the idea of consistency and familiarity. In dealing with people, 'personality' describes the ways in which we anticipate an individual will behave in particular circumstances. Of course, no one is totally predictable: but on the whole, they are predictable enough for human relationships to depend largely on this construct. Thus, we create our friends, our acquaintances, and our enemies. The same is true of brands.

Consumers, as Stephen King[2] pointed out, can easily be encouraged to talk about brands in terms of human analogy – a technique still widely used, both qualitatively and quantitatively. What this really means is that consumers feel different relationships to different brands, depending on the type of subjective needs which the brands do or don't satisfy. Sometimes different brands appeal to different personality types; sometimes they fulfil complementary needs for the same person. In this way, functionally similar products can remain competitive on grounds other than simple price.

To sum up our argument so far: a brand is fundamentally a promise, rendered credible by law and by experience. At one level this simply makes the decision process easier; at a higher level it can actually add to consumers' beneficial experience of a product, thus creating a value for which people may be prepared to pay.

The way in which the experience is transformed can be very particular to the brand, thus creating differentiation between similar products and the metaphor of personality.

## Social Dimension

So far, we have (deliberately) talked as if the individual consumer and the brand manufacturer were the only two parties involved in this process. This has made the story simpler, but it is of course never true. Everything we have described so far has an added social dimension. An attitude towards a certain behaviour (following Fishbein)[3] is not simply determined by my own beliefs or experiences, but also by what I imagine other (relevant) people might think of the same thing. Our discussion of the satisfactions of owning a motorcar was noticeably incomplete, because this element was left out. It may be helpful to take up this example again, in order to explore the various ways in which our decisions and perceptions can be affected by what we think other people think.

First there is a need for reassurance. Few people, in most situations, are prepared to trust their own judgement totally in isolation, without some reference to what others in the same situation believe (those few probably have a tendency to become either millionaires or bankrupts). In a complex and high-investment decision such as choosing a car, buyers characteristically make this need overt by soliciting advice in the office or pub, and by buying car magazines. At the end of the day they will often find their choice assisted by the thought that the huge numbers of people like themselves buying Fords or Vauxhalls can't be wrong. In many markets this feeling of safety in numbers contributes to the reputation of the brand leader, and is not uncommonly exploited in advertising ('a million housewives every day', etc.).

But this is not in itself the most important way in which others become involved in my purchase decisions. Patterns of consumption are not just driven by functional benefits – they are social statements which continually define or redefine our relationship with others, our position in society. This is true in all kinds of human society, by no means only those in which brands exist. Anthropologists (such as Mary Douglas[4]) have shown how in certain tribal cultures the ownership, production, giving and consumption of certain types of food define social relationships. I have basic functional needs (to eat, to keep warm), but what and how I eat, and what I wear are partly conditioned by what society deems appropriate (to my power, status, life-stage) and partly by what kind of role I wish to assume for myself.

In the case of a car purchase, this creates strong pressures which may conflict with each other, and indeed with some of the functional criteria for a choice. All this would still hold true independent of brands: but brands are one of the key ways of defining and codifying the world, and so become an important part of the language in which these social statements are expressed. Because brands are authenticated, they become particularly robust currency for social exchange. Patterns of relative affluence, of peer group endorsement, of conformity or non-conformity, create strong social meaning for BMW vs. Mercedes, Volkswagen vs. Peugeot, etc.

The social power of brands can be at its most overt in communal rituals of consumption such as beer drinking. Heavy drinkers of lager tend to be young working-class males, for whom the evening's 'session' is a highly-structured event with strong pressure to conform. In the context a brand of lager needs to be accepted by the group before it is OK to order it – Hofmeister, as an unknown brand, was unacceptable until George the Bear (an aspirational, surrogate group leader sharing in the group's sense of humour) positioned it.

It might also be important for the young lager drinker to be wearing the right clothes. Clothes are one of the most obvious social signs of conformity or non-conformity with a particular group, a phenomenon which of course exists separately from brands. In some contexts it might be a sufficient symbol to wear jeans; in others it might be necessary to wear a certain brand of jeans, particularly now that jeans are acceptable among a wide range of social groups and situations. Branding adds an extra level of clarity and complexity to the social language of clothes. Obvious parallels exist in many other markets: cigarettes, watches, shoes, and also household durables. (Why does your fridge have its name on the front?)

It is important to stress that the outer-directed value of a brand (as a badge to others) and the inner-directed value of the brand (as transformation of the user's experience) are not distinct from each other. They continually overlap, interact, and in some cases may even be different ways of looking at the same thing. Most designer labels, after all, are inside the clothes, not outside. A tie says 'Pierre Balmain' or 'Yves Saint-Laurent' on the back, not the front. Realistically, most people will never see it or know what endorsement it carries. But because you feel you know what they would think of it if they did. You have the same (inner-directed) confidence or sense of style that comes from the name. The satisfaction of owning a particular make of car and knowing that it is socially regarded as a symbol of a certain kind of success can exist without reference to any other people actually being involved – 'it will remind you that your life has not been totally without success', as a famous ad for Jaguar once put it. Is this inner-directed or outer-directed? And does it matter? The social dimension is so pervasive in branding that it is hard to separate it out, and probably a fruitless exercise to do so.

If I had to venture a one-line definition of branding, perhaps to sum up what may have seemed like an over-complex analysis, it would be to do with 'the intangible values created by a badge of reassurance'. The intangible values may be simple (peace of mind, structuring choice) or increasingly complex (gaining the approval or approbation of others, or actually defining the experience of the product itself). In the majority of cases – possibly in all cases – the satisfactions of branding are potentially a combination of these, in varying proportions. Some recent authors[5] have suggested that brands can be classified into those which are simple, non-emotional badges of product quality, and those which offer rich emotional or symbolic values. This must have some validity in so far as some brand choices involve an important rational component related to product characteristics (e.g. garden tools), while others are more obviously concerned with differentiating essentially similar products (say, cigarettes). But it seems to me simplistic in that it ignores the intangible, often indeed emotional benefits which branding confers on superficially 'functional' product choices – and also the fact that emotional or socially symbolic brand values are generally based on some genuine (if perhaps historic) product qualities.

An example may illustrate the first of these points. You might consider paint to be a very functional product, where the brand name simply stands for a particular chemical composition, and qualities of covering power, durability, etc. Yet when people paint they do far more, usually, than simply cover their walls. First, they derive a powerful sense of transformation and renewal from the decorating process: brand values of a less tangible sort, 'freshness', 'naturalness' become potentially important. Second, if they apply the paint themselves (the most usual procedure) there is a strong sense of pride and achievement in 'doing the job properly' – and part of this is the choice of the 'right' brand of paint. To be seen as 'the one experts use' can be a powerful discriminator. This is, of course, underpinned by consistent product quality: but nuances of covering power or durability (which is a promise for the future anyway) are in themselves of secondary importance. By consistently making use of ideas like these in advertising, Dulux has for many years dominated the UK paint market. It may remind us that even in apparently very functional markets (washing-up liquid, kitchen towels, bathroom cleaners, etc) product performance is still a very subjective matter.

Even in industrial purchasing decisions, which we might imagine to be completely 'rational', difficult or complex choices are likely to be referred to beliefs about the suppliers' reputation – or quite likely influenced by the perceptions of other relevant managers. 'No one ever got fired for buying IBM' ran a famous slogan. The mechanics of branding are essentially the same here as anywhere.

Branding begins by satisfying a basic human need for control and reassurance. Because it offers consistency in an otherwise uncertain world, the brand then has the potential to become a tool for dividing up the world, and a medium of social exchange. In offering reassurance and in creating rituals of consumption, branding always creates value to the consumer beyond the merely functional.

# References

1. Branthwaite, A and Cooper, P (1981) 'Analgesic effects of branding in treatment of headaches', *British Medical Journal*, 282.

2. King, S (1970), 'What is a brand?', JWT.

3. For a description of Fishbein's expectancy value model, see Tuck, M (1976) How Do We Choose?, Methuen, ch 6.

4. Douglas, M (1982) *In The Active Voice*, Routledge and Kegan Paul.

5. De Chernatony, L and McWilliam, G (1989) 'Representational brands and functional brands: the strategic implications of the difference', Admap, March.

Selections from:

# Testing to Destruction:
## A Critical Look at the Issues of Research in Advertising

# By Alan Hedges

*Alan Hedges is the author of the legendary "Testing to Destruction," one of the most important writings on advertising research. His research career began as a Mass Observation trainee. He was a director of Interscan and became Research and Marketing Director of S.H.Benson, where he pioneered early experiments in video-taped group discussions. He then became a consultant dealing with a wider range of business, social, and research problems.*

## Some Broad Conclusions

It is not possible to make a realistic test of the effectiveness of a commercial in a laboratory situation in advance of real-life exposure.

Until this simple but uncomfortable truth is grasped, much advertising research will go on being sterile and unproductive.

The most important contribution that research can make to increasing the selling effectiveness of advertising is at the planning stage before anyone has even begun to think about particular advertising ideas.

Research can heighten our understanding of the market and of the consumer so that we can better define the job that advertising has to do and the climate in which it has to operate. If this is done properly it not only guides and stimulates the creative process but also provides a much better basis for eventual decisions about the likely worth of a campaign.

Once work starts on specific advertising ideas the role of research is to provide feedback from the consumer enabling the creators and managers of advertising to learn about the properties of different ideas and approaches.

Feedback helps us to choose and modify ideas at an early stage, and what we learn from this campaign development process helps provide a basis for eventual management decisions about the advertising. Research at this stage should be done early on, before ideas and attitudes harden and while there is still time, freedom, and money to benefit properly from what has been learned. Research should be rich and stimulating, and should aim at increasing understanding.

**Once the campaign is running, research can help to show how far objectives are being met and to redefine the objectives for the future.**

This can be a very valuable function which eventually leads back into the planning phase for the next campaign. On the other hand, it rarely gives a clear picture of the effects of advertising in isolation since these are usually difficult (or impossible) to disentangle from the effects of other selling efforts, or indeed from the general flux of the market place.

# On Qualities and Quantities

## Hedges' Observations on Focus Groups

Unstructured interviewing using group discussions or individual interviews in depth is one of the most useful tools available for coming to an understanding of the consumer and of his likely reactions to your advertising, at any stage. It has a directness and immediacy which most other kinds of research tend to lack. It is possible to get a degree of participation and interest from creative people and from advertising management, which is again difficult to inspire with less direct research forms. It is not (or does not need to be) the slave of anyone's prejudices or preconceptions. It is, in other words, apt on occasions to produce unexpected findings. It is capable of dealing with richer and more illuminating material than is generally possible with structured questionnaire research. Finally, it is attractively quick and inexpensive to carry out, so that discussion projects can often be reported before anyone has had time to forget what they are supposed to find out.

With such a catalogue of virtues need we look further? Indeed we must, because qualitative research also has problems and limitations.

The most important of these are:

1. Samples are inevitably small (if costs are not to escalate prohibitively). A typical project might involve forty or fifty people and a very large one still less than a hundred. There is some risk that responses will be atypical.

2. Numerical estimates cannot be made. Information tends to be of the "some think this, others think that" kind and we cannot put numbers to the different viewpoints. This is partly due to the small samples involved and partly to the unsystematic nature of the information collected.

3. Although the accessibility of qualitative data and ease of participation by non-research people are important advantages, they are not without dangers as well. It is easy to jump to conclusions from hearing one or two people state a particular view, even if it is very untypical (indeed in a sense the more unusual the view the more likely it is to seem 'interesting').

4. Furthermore, the very speed, cheapness and simplicity of "running a few groups" is likely to make their use seductively appealing, even where some other form of research is really required. Companies who have been bitten through carrying out vast and complicated survey projects, which they have then been unable to make any real practical use of, are easily tempted to go to the other extreme and devote their research budgets to streams of individually inexpensive group discussion projects, which can be commissioned with few qualms and little thought; each of which have small but direct and immediate payoffs, but which do not collectively provide a proper planning framework because they cannot be assessed into a single coherent set of organisable data.

Some of these problems (like the last two) can be simply avoided by proper management of the research programme. The problems of quantification and sample size matter more in some situations than others, and again they can largely be avoided by choosing the right tool for the right job. Where numerical estimates are genuinely required one should either:

1. not use qualitative research at all, or

2. if there is some other reason for using qualitative techniques, make sure that these are accompanied or followed up by proper quantification.

It is, however, easy to succumb to the lure of large numbers and feel that precise measurements need to be made where in reality they are either unnecessary or impossible to procure. In fact there is a positive danger in insisting on quantified evidence about matters that by nature cannot be properly quantified.

Attempts to pre-test advertising quantitatively are good examples of this. It is easy to see why an advertiser spending large sums of money on his advertising should look for reassurance that his money will be wisely spent before he actually spends it. What he would really like to have is some simple way of measuring advertising effectiveness which he could apply to each new advertisement before it appeared. Since he may have to justify or explain his decision to his colleagues or superiors, he wants numbers (which have a kind of hard and unarguable feel about them), however meaningless they may be, and he wants them simple and unambiguous.

The advertising researcher tells him that such measurements cannot really be made, and that any measurements he *does* make will bear an unknown and probably very tenuous relationship to the problem of effectiveness.

Unfortunately many managers have opted to have *some* kind of measurement, however doubtful, rather than facing up to the undoubted challenge of accepting that advertising effectiveness is essentially not capable of being measured simply and directly in advance of marketplace exposure.

In general it is probably from qualitative research that we are likely to get the most stimulation, understanding and insight in the realms of advertisement research, although we must be continually on our guard against the problems of scale and subjectivity. We should never be content with just "running couple of groups".

This does not mean, however, that there is no place for quantitative research. There are often circumstances where no one can pin down fairly precisely what one needs to know about an advertisement, perhaps because it has already been researched in ways which highlight particular problems. If these are capable of being covered in a questionnaire format it may well be worth getting the reactions of a larger audience in numerical form.

Suppose, for example, there are worries as to whether a press ad which seems generally to perform well will in fact register its brand name clearly enough in people's minds. This is a type of problem which group discussions are entirely unfitted to consider. Then again we may want to know what proportion of viewers will be able to grasp the sequence of usage instructions in a demonstration commercial after one viewing, and we may want to look separately at the responses of people who have never used products of this type before. Or we might be worried that people had not understood a particular sequence. These again are probably best treated by quantitative research.

Before we decide whether to use quantitative or qualitative methods in a particular situation we should ask ourselves very clearly what we are trying to achieve by the research and then choose the best technique for the purpose, conscious of the severe limitations of all our tools in this field. Above all we must avoid the assumption that the mere fact of getting some numbers constitutes an objective assessment of the quality and effectiveness of the ad.

## Impact in Advertising

In one limited sense it is of course self-evident that advertising needs 'impact'. That is to say one wants advertising to affect the situation in favourable ways, and not to disappear without altering anything. But this is like saying that advertising does not work unless it works.

People often use the word impact in a different and more specific way, however, usually to refer to the conscious perception and recall of advertising messages.

Does an ad need to be 'noticed' in order to work? Clearly it must be 'seen' (or at the very least 'glimpsed') in order to have any effect – unless of course we rely on advertising being passed on by word-of-mouth.

But whether or not an ad is seen depends on media planning and buying rather than on creative content, providing that we refer only to its having been physically exposed to the gaze.

Creative content can of course affect whether or not the ad is 'noticed' or 'remembered' by those who have 'seen it'. It is noticing and remembering which tends to reflect in recall studies.

Now it sounds as if it might be common sense to say that only ads which are consciously noticed (and probably remembered) are likely to work, but unfortunately there is no evidence to prove that this is true. Nor does it in fact seem quite so inevitable if you examine the question a bit more closely.

The assumption rests on the belief that advertising communicates at the conscious and rational level, and that anything which is not the subject of conscious attention will not be taken in. Consumers are like children learning from a teacher; if they don't pay attention the lesson won't sink in. I won't deny that *some* advertising works at this level; or that some part of many ads does so. But that is certainly not all there is to it (it is not all there is to education either for that matter, but that is beside the point).

I have pointed out several times in the course of this book that human beings can pick up a good deal of information from a large number of signals exposed in rapid sequence and for a very short time. Anyone who has been on a rapid reading course is amazed how easily he can take in and remember quite a long sentence flashed on a screen for such a short exposure that he can hardly see it. A wealth of impression can be derived from a very quick glance at a picture, since visual and pictorial symbols give up their meaning very readily.

I have also pointed out that there is far more advertising than anyone can reasonably be expected to attend to, and that interest is likely to be fairly low for most product fields.

This provides the advertiser with a dilemma. Does he work on the assumption that his main task is to get conscious attention, to do which he has to outpace the majority of other ads on the market (particularly if he is not in a high-interest field)? Or does he recognise that most of the time his ad will get only skimmed or inattentively viewed, and design it so that it communicates even at that level?

Both courses have their dangers, and the right one must depend on the nature of the market and advertising message. Some important types of message are almost impossible to put over *except* to an attentive audience.

However, the natural bias is in favour of conscious and attentive communication, because it is easier to think about and to measure (although even there it is not actually as easy to measure as it looks). There is something worrying about spending your money on advertising which you do not particularly expect people to notice and study.

Nevertheless, in today's crowded media we see many ads performing extraordinary contortions in order to get noticed. In many cases the quest for superficial impact has come to dominate the essential message content. If an ad has to work so hard to get itself noticed, how hard can it work in delivering its message? Is there not a danger that the attention-getting device actually *becomes* the message?

So perhaps advertisers should concentrate harder on getting advertising which communicates rapidly at a low level of attention rather than striving to get noticed at all costs. The sort of things which may enable an ad to communicate rapidly are:

- communication through pictures rather than words
- brevity in verbal messages
- attention to the total gestalt and not merely the detailed parts
- clear use of logos, symbols and other coded signals
- continuity of theme

Perhaps sometimes our advertising research should examine the impressions created by fleeting or inattentive exposures rather than (as is generally the case at present) by prolonged exposures or focused attention. This is not easy, however, since one single exposure of this kind taken in isolation is not likely to have much discernible effect at all (and I have argued that this would also be the case in the real-life situation). 'Massive dose' exposure, on the other hand, is unrealistic, even if attention is focused away from the ads (by burying them, for example, in a programme of other matter).

In many ways the clinical psychiatrist and the student of the psychology of the abnormal have an easier time of it than advertising researchers do. They are at least dealing with matters which are important to their subjects; whereas it is the transience and triviality of the consumer's relationship with advertising which makes it difficult to study. As soon as you hold it up to look at it you are removing it from its essential context.

However, the fact that it is *difficult* to measure or study inattentive communication must not blind us to the fact that this is where the real action is in most cases; or to the fact that the kind of reactions we get in our group discussions or cinema tests are a good long way away from it.

## Some Points about Communication

One might define communication as the transmission of information from one entity to another. Many books could be (and indeed have been) written about it. I simply want to pick out some points which seem important for advertising but which are sometimes overlooked.

A particular communication may or may not be intended by the person transmitting it (in the case of human communications which is what interests us here). For example, two women meet. One is very expensively dressed, is proud of her clothes, and refers frequently to them in conversation. She intends that the other woman should be impressed with her taste, her wealth and her appearance. The other woman, on the contrary, goes away thinking that she has been talking to an ostentatious snob whose clothes she personally would not want to be seen dead in.

This is not a case of miscommunication in the sense that the second woman did not hear or understand what the first was saying; nor indeed that she disbelieved what she heard. But she was receiving lots of messages from the way her companion looked and spoke which (taken perhaps into conjunction with her preconceptions about the woman) overrode the intended communication.

This anecdote also brings out the point that communications are not only often unintended, but they are also not necessarily explicit. There are many ways of conveying meaning other than by saying something straightforwardly or in words or pictures. When you talk to someone the tone of your voice, your gestures, your facial expressions, your eye movements, the phrases and cadence of your speech will all convey meanings at least as potent as your actual words; and your choice of words may sometimes convey a good deal more than their purely semantic content. These non-verbal and non-explicit communications may of course be intentional or unintentional; poets and artists convey broad and powerful messages deliberately through largely indirect means.

If we want to convey facts, detailed arguments and logical propositions we need to express them directly through verbal or pictorial means. If we want to convey feelings and emotions we need to work very largely through indirect communications.

Communication can take place at very low levels of consciousness, and everyone is continuously receiving a vast number of communications from his environment, both from other people and from things.

People can receive and process vast masses of signals at any one moment. It would take several pages of words to give even a brief outline of a small number of the more important communications received and acted on by the driver of a car approaching a busy junction, even within a few seconds. In fact, quite clearly, people can take in a vast amount of information, screen out what is irrelevant for the purpose at hand, and process the remainder as a basis for action in a very short space of time indeed. But very little of this information needs to be *consciously* received or handled.

If the driver had to work out *ab initio* what each signal meant and what he should do about it, he would quickly become paralysed with information overload and consequent indecision. This is incidentally one of the main problems facing people first learning to drive when coming into heavy traffic. They have not learnt to recognise broad patterns of signals and to habituate their responses to them.

These brief notes on the communication process are meant to suggest that:

(a) Unintended communications can sometimes be louder than intended communications, and implicit ones stronger than explicit.

(b) People are capable of receiving vast numbers of signals which can be handled at a low level of consciousness. It is at this level that much advertising communication necessarily has to work.

## Advertising as Wallpaper

I have cautioned at several places in this book against considering advertising *in vacuo* without relating it closely to the marketplace context. Advertising is part of a general background to product purchase, and consumers will rarely have occasion to separate it from the background as a whole.

Traditionally we have tended to think of an advertisement as something whose properties and powers are intrinsic to itself and capable of being studied quite in isolation.

In reality, the way an advertisement is perceived and the kind of influence it has will depend intimately on a whole host of other factors external to the advertising itself.

Take a typical housewife and her relations with (say) the floor polish market. Let us trace her contacts with this market through an imaginary week, not forgetting that this is just one tiny thread among thousands, which I am drawing out and magnifying for purposes of illustration. The housewife herself would certainly not have it in sharp focus.

Let us suppose that this market (for simplicity) contains only three brands. Let us imagine they are called Lewis's, Whistle, and Glo. The new product, Glo, is our brand.

The lady starts the week with an inherited bundle of impressions of floor cleaning and of the three brands. She has some Lewis's in her cupboard. She has also used Whistle on odd occasions, but she has never tried Glo. Her impressions which are vague and hazy in the main, are a compound of her own experience, odd remarks from neighbours, past advertising seen or half seen, the look of the products and their packages, a fact or two from a *Which?* report she once started to read, some bits of lore learnt at her mother's knee, the names of brands, the reputations of their makers, and who knows what else.

Monday is her regular floor cleaning day. She gets out the Lewis's and sets to work. She sees the pack. She doesn't really look at it, it is so familiar, but perhaps just the way it looks reinforces a tiny particle of an impression. She doesn't read the words on the pack (maybe she did years ago, when she first bought it, perhaps not even then), but perhaps she half notices an odd word, and another flake of meaning joins the mixture in her mind.

Even after all these years of using Lewis's she enjoys the smell of it, it reminds her of the way her mother's floor used to smell. She thinks about her childhood home; polishing the while. She hardly notices how long it takes her to get a really good shine to the floor. After all, Lewis's gets you good results, but you have to be prepared to work at it. Another image crystallises a fraction.

She puts the polish away, noticing that the pot is nearly empty, and making a mental note to get some more.

At lunchtime, flicking through a women's mag, her gaze wanders over an ad for Whistle for a few seconds. She doesn't think about it, but somewhere her mind ticks up the impression that she has heard a lot about Whistle recently. A bit further on in the mag, there is an article about labour-saving types of flooring. She wonders for a moment whether all this polishing is really worth it, when you come down to it. A tiny curl of displeasure winds around the Lewis's she has been using.

Later that afternoon she goes shopping. On the way she passes one of our new Glo posters. She doesn't even glance at it, although later in the week she will notice the Glo on the supermarket shelf and wonder for a split second where she saw it before. The poster shows a beautiful, highly polished wooden floor, and a pack of Glo.

In the supermarket she checks off her shopping fairly methodically, although she forgets she is running out of floor polish. She even passes the polish shelves without the penny dropping. There is a good long facing of Whistle in that eye-catching new pack. If you asked her leaving the shop she wouldn't remember seeing it, but that is the second time already today that it has flashed in front of her eyes.

There is that familiar old Lewis's pack on the shelves too. She doesn't look at that either — why would she? But every time she catches sight of it, it reinforces that familiar old image. It looks so old-fashioned, but so good. Satisfying, somehow.

There are some of our Glo packs there too, although not many — the trade promotion hasn't really got off the ground yet. But we've done a good job with the pack — even at a glance you feel that here is a modern brand which will really get results good enough for the fussiest. But the lady doesn't look. She is worrying about the meat and keeping an eye on the time for meeting the kids from school.

That night, watching the television, she sees two of our ten-second launch commercials for Glo. When the first one comes on she is trying to shoo the children off to bed. Second time round she's still laughing at the show she's just seen. If you rang her that evening and asked her what ads she had seen she wouldn't mention Glo, that's for sure. But by the end of the evening her latent interest in the brand is a little higher than it would have been that morning. She has no occasion to think about it yet, but when she does she will find that she has a few small and elusive impressions tucked away.

In the morning she opens the hall cupboard to get out her dustpan and her eyes slide over that familiar old Lewis's pack. On the way to the shops she passes the Glo poster again. In the housewares store she visits for some clothes pegs there are big stacks of Whistle right inside the door, and some kind of competition. She doesn't look at them.

In the afternoon she goes to her sister's for a cup of tea. Leafing through a magazine she passes the Whistle ad again. She recognises the pack in the ad... where has she seen that recently? And stops for a couple of seconds to look at it. Mmmm, might be worth trying, looks a bit easier, like a sort of spray. But she passes on without reading the copy. Her sister comes in with the tea. Later she notices a can of Whistle on her sister's windowsill. She picks it up and looks at it. She glances at the instructions on the pack. It *does* sound easy to use. She puts it down and turns to look at the new snaps of her sister's children.

On the front of the bus that takes her home is an ad which tells the world that Whistle is the cheapest floor polish on the market. She doesn't notice it, but a faint impression slithers into her mind.

The bus passes a store with a big stack of that attractive Whistle pack in the window. It goes past a Glo poster. She doesn't look at either, not more than a passing glance, anyway.

That evening she sees a commercial for Glo again, and one for Whistle. The Lewis's pack is still there when she opens the cupboard.

In the morning she remembers she needs polish. When she arrives at the store (passing but not noticing the Glo poster), she goes in due course to the polish shelves, where she reaches instinctively for the Lewis's. Her eyes pass the Whistle display, and slide back to it. She picks up a Whistle pack, reflectively, and looks at the instructions again. She looks at the Lewis's pack, indecisive. No doubt about it, that's the one for results. You can't beat the old stuff really. But this does look a bit easier – and probably cheaper. Her mind runs over the article on labour-saving floors. She looks at the price. It is heavily cut. She shrugs and drops it into her basket. Her brow furrows. Can she *really* afford the steak she was plan-ning? Mustn't forget mother's birthday card...

At home she unloads her purchases. She doesn't remember having passed the Glo poster again on the way home. She holds the Whistle in her hands for a second as she puts it in the cupboard. She looks at the Lewis's pack. She shakes her head. There's really no substitute for the good old stuff. This new stuff just doesn't *look* like proper polish.

She begins to feel a little sorry she bought the Whistle. She pulls out the Hoover and forgets all about polishing floors. Catching sight of the magazine she was looking at on Monday, she wonders for an instant as the memory darts through her mind if she could persuade her husband to lay out for some floor coverings that don't need polishing. Still, the wood looks nicer really. She compares her home with her sister's, which is a bit plastic. She hoovers on.

The week goes by. She passes heedlessly the Glo poster a dozen times. She flicks past press ads for all three brands. When she notices a Whistle ad she stops to look at it, remembering that she has a can waiting in the cupboard. She reads the copy idly, reading of the low price, the miracle ingredients, the special high-gloss finish and the ease of use. She frowns absently. Not like a real polish. Still, she could do with saving a bit of time. She passes on. She sees at least half a dozen commercials for the various brands. She half notices the Whistle ad and nods agreement at the mention of cheapness. She doesn't give it a second thought. Every time she opens her cupboard she sees the Whistle and Lewis's packs, but she has lost interest in them — although seeing them half a dozen times gradually reinforces the polarisation in her mind. She sees other displays around.

On Monday she opens the cupboard to get the polish out. For a microsecond she wonders whether to finish the Lewis's first, but she is a bit curious to see whether that Whistle is as easy as they say it is. She glances at the half-remembered instructions and misapplies the polish. It's easy to put on, bit hard to get off. She looks at the instructions again, and corrects the procedure. Well, it **is** quite easy. It polishes all right… but it's not the same really. There's not the same sort of feeling about it. She probably won't buy it again.

Her mother calls while she is finishing the polishing. Her eyebrows rise at the sight of the Whistle. Their brief conversation confirms the housewife's tentative resolution to go back to good old Lewis's. After all, that's what polishing's really about, isn't it?

That afternoon she goes to the shops again, once more passing the Glo poster without a glance. In the supermarket she is walking past the polish shelves when she notices the display of Glo, slightly bigger than last week. She doesn't stop – she has a lot to get, and she won't need any more polish for a month or so yet. Her brief flicker of interest in new polishes has died. Well, more or less died anyway. As her eye lights on the Glo the thought crosses her mind that she has heard good reports of it. With that one you really *would* get a finish you could be proud of. Now, where did I see those tomatoes?

She has this vague feeling about Glo now (which strengthens a tiny bit as she passes the Glo poster on the way home, and gives it a quick sideways glance as she wonders whether the last shop short-changed her). It comes partly from the look of the pack, which has a kind of traditional polishy feel about it; and partly from that beautiful shiny floor she keeps passing on the Glo poster without apparent recognition; and maybe even partly from the brand name, who knows. The lady herself certainly doesn't – and wouldn't care much if she did. After all, it's only polish.

Maybe if this seed of an idea germinates and is properly nourished she will buy Glo next time round – or the time after that. Maybe she will just go back to good old Lewis's (she knows where she is with that one). It all depends what happens next week – and the week after that – as the same processes go on and on.

Even this long account has had to be concentrated and dramatised, and the real-life processes are probably even more diffuse and casual than those depicted, for many markets at least. Advertising is certainly less prominent than I have made it sound.

What I have been trying to make clear in this fictitious account is how interdependent our advertising is with the advertising of our competitors, and with the nature of the products, the packs, promotions, names, past experience, hearsay, editorial matter directly or indirectly related to the product field, and so on.

In my example the stimulus which really opened the lady's mind to the idea of a new polish was an article about labour-saving flooring, nothing directly to do with polish at all.

Then again her reception of our messages about Glo might very well have been quite differently interpreted if it had not been for her recent flirtation with Whistle, and her rejection of an important part of the Whistle copy platform (the bit about getting good results).

I hope the foregoing passage also makes it clear what I mean about advertising having its effect gradually, and largely at lower levels of consciousness. It would be very difficult to put one's finger on the precise point at which our housewife really decided to give Whistle a try, or the precise influence which tipped her into doing it.

Finally it should show just how difficult it is to separate the influences of advertising, promotions, distribution, packaging, naming, public relations, product formulation, and so on; and conversely, just how important it is to see advertising as just one manifestation of the product which needs to work in harmony with all its other manifestations in order to be truly effective.

---

This is just some of the provocative thinking in Hedges's piece.

We recommend that you read it in its entirety. Though no longer in print, the complete text of this important document is available free of charge at: www.apg.org.uk/publications/books/testing-to-destruction-intro.cfm

# Section III: Tools

You've read throughout this book that "understanding the consumer" is the defining responsibility of the account planner.

So, how does one achieve real empathy with consumers, see the world from their point of view, and experience the product or service as they would?

In this section, we learn about the tools planners use in achieving these goals from practitioners who spend their lives searching out the keen insights that drive great advertising and marketing programs.

# A Review of Qualitative Methods

## By Wendy Gordon

*Wendy Gordon is a co-founder of Acacia Avenue, a brand research and strategy consultancy specializing in qualitative and quantitative methodologies. In 1998, she co-founded the strategic brand consultancy, The Fourth Room and before this co-founded The Research Business International (TRBI). Wendy is a Fellow of the Market Research Society, a visiting professor at Birmingham Business School and has been honoured by The Women's Advertising Club of London as one of its "Women of Achievement." She is the author of* Goodthinking – A Guide to Qualitative Research, *from which this chapter was excerpted.*

ALMOST A DECADE HAS PASSED since I wrote the first words of *Goodthinking* – enough time to revisit this chapter with another ten years of qualitative research experience under my belt.

On reading it again, I was surprised how much is valid today. That qualitative research is ultimately about Insight rather than descriptive data or information has indeed become the *crie de coeur* of research buyers and practitioners world wide. In 2007, several conferences chose Insight as the key theme – what it is, how you get it, and what you do with it when you have found it. Insight is now the Holy Grail and, as a result, it is a stick with which to beat each other, or a carrot held out as a promise.

Back in 1997 a debate was beginning to emerge about the limitations of the 'focus group' compared to what were then called 'alternative' approaches such as ethnography, semiotics, observation or interactive methodologies. I used the analogy of the adversarial relationship between scientific conventional medicine and 'alternative' therapies to describe the fact that many of these qualitative methods were considered gimmicks practised by researchers who did not adhere to the principles of objectivity and sampling that have become the acceptable protocol for qualitative research.

The analogy still holds true in 2007. Just as cranial osteopathy, homeopathy, nutritional therapy, and Chinese herbs (now termed 'complementary') have been accepted by an ever-widening group of believers alongside conventional medicine, so have qualitative methods (such as ethnography, semiotics, discourse analysis, interactive workshops, citizen juries, online forums, and blog trawling) become accepted as complementary qualitative methods.

However, to put the record straight, while there are more believers in this style of thinking today, there are still relatively few client or advertising agency doers of it. The focus group is the default method for qualitative research, especially so when it comes to communications development and evaluation research.

This short introduction is not the place to explore the reasons why, but to say that a sure result of digging in the same hole is that you get the same dirt. The challenge – whether you are a practising researcher or planner – is not only to understand complementary approaches but also to sell in methods outside of focus groups credibly to research buyers and end users. Without being able to do this, people will fall back on tried and tested methods.

# Introduction

There has been a growing trend over the last five years among both buyers and practitioners of qualitative research to search for more innovative and creative methodologies to crack complex marketing or business problems. There are two reasons for this. First, the disillusionment with conventional qualitative group discussions and depth interviews has led to a search for new ways to reveal insight. Second, there is a mistaken belief that new methods have more power to 'delve beneath the skin of the consumer', 'reveal the true needs and drivers of consumer behaviour', or 'reach the truth'.

It is probably true that a new method of interviewing the target group or the relevant application of a new projective technique might provide a different perspective, one that may enrich the picture obtained through the conventional methods. Innovation in itself, however, brings the practitioner and end user no closer to the truth – because it would seem that there is no single truth to be found! Truth is a relative concept and the best we can achieve as researchers is a multi-faceted view of the problem from which we make the best interpretation.

This chapter reviews the qualitative methodologies that are in use today and offers criteria of evaluation so that the most relevant combination can be chosen for the problem at hand.

# The Debate

There has been a growing debate among qualitative practitioners about the limitations of the 'focus group' (as it has come to be known) and the individual interview compared to ethnographic, observational or interactive methodologies. For some strange reason, these latter approaches have been called 'alternative' – rather the way aromatherapy and acupuncture are called 'alternative medicine' – and yet they are based on the sound academic principles of scientific research. The term 'alternative' has brought with it an underlying suspicion in some quarters that these methodologies are simply marketing tools and 'gimmicks' for research agency promotion rather than the result of a genuine need to find more robust, relevant and insightful means of understanding the complexities of human behaviour.

Participant observation and ethnography, where the researcher enters the consumer's world, reflect our need to understand the cultural context surrounding purchase and consumption, the experiential dimension of brands, and the importance of symbolic meaning to the post-modern consumer.

Experiencing context is the critical step... a participating experience with its myriad of details creates and recreates authenticity and coherence in the world being studied[1].

In contrast, focus groups, which import respondents to the researcher's world, have their roots in the experimental, laboratory-based, traditions of social psychology and the group dynamics work of the psychotherapists[2].

These two orientations are neither right nor wrong — they simply produce different perspectives. The psychological or psychotherapeutic model tends to be wary of surface responses and consumer explanations of the reason-why underlying behaviour; hence the extensive use of projective questioning and techniques to aid interpretation. The sociological and anthropological models accept the face validity of people's behaviour and their explanations of it and use the contextual frame of culture to develop an interpretation.

## Methodology: What Are the Choices?

There are four types of qualitative methodology:

- **the group interview**
- **the individual interview**
- **observational methods**
- **interactive workshops.**

The depth-versus-breadth argument is generally cited to justify choice of a group versus an individual approach. Individual interviews are believed to provide more detailed information of the attitudes and behaviour of the individual, while group discussions are claimed to provide breadth in terms of the range of behaviours and attitudes between individuals attending the group.

## The Group Interview

There are many different variants of the group interview but the group discussion or focus group is the most commonly used method around the world. This consists of seven to nine people in the UK and ten to twelve in the US, who have been recruited according to a pre-determined set of criteria such as age, gender, life stage, social class, and product, service or brand usership. Conventional group discussions last under two hours in length. At the most simplistic level, each group discussion has a moderator (or facilitator) whose role it is to create an environment in which participants feel safe enough to share their attitudes, behaviour, thoughts, and feelings with a number of strangers. Moderators are trained to:

- guide the discussion over a number of topic areas that are of interest and relevance to the paying client

- recognise important points of view and encourage the group to explore and expand on these

- deal with group dynamic processes effectively

- internalise the research objectives of the study so that he or she can listen carefully and, at times, play back his or her understanding to the group to check meaning and interpretation

- use forms of questioning, research material, stimuli, tasks and exercises with discrimination to enable the members of the group to articulate thoughts and feelings that they may not be used to accessing or expressing.

The most common reasons for adopting a group approach are:

- a less intimidating environment than the individual interview[3] since most human beings welcome 'safety in numbers' when confronted with an unusual event, together with an atmosphere that generates feelings of anticipation, excitement, and energy

- a way of encouraging people to build on each others' views, expressing similar or opposing experiences, attitudes, thoughts, and feelings within clearly defined parameters

- a method that highlights the range of behaviours, attitudes and points of view between people within a relatively short period; a time-efficient way of obtaining consumer feedback, suited to time-poor executives

- 'live' research which can be observed through a one-way mirror or video relay system, by members of the client organisation so that they can experience customer response, consumer vocabulary, attitudes, accounts of behaviour, perceptions of the market, and reactions, first-hand

- a window into the cultural and social experiences of the group

- a 'laboratory' in which the responses of the group to a wide range of different stimuli (advertising, packaging, products, brands, brochures, below-the-line material) can be explored.

The argument against using the group interview approach alone may involve any or several of the following reasons:

- people have different levels of knowledge and understanding – 'expert' participants will intimidate those with less experience, making an unbalanced group, e.g., financial confidence and sophistication, home decorating and DIY capabilities, gourmet cooking, etc.

- social norms and the need to conform to an ideal which is socially or politically correct will predominate, such as teaching children road safety, bottle versus breast feeding, parental discipline, eating healthy food, and racial attitudes

- detailed behaviour and attitudinal histories are required, e.g. tracing the pattern of car ownership, sequential processes of finding a mortgage for a new home, deciding which holiday to go on this year compared with previous years, exactly how a product is used, etc.

- intimate subject matter (sexual behaviour, sanitary protection, body odour, constipation), or personal financial situations (wealth management, insurance, pensions), where disclosure is potentially embarrassing in front of strangers or observers

- difficult-to-recruit respondents such as highly paid senior management, farmers, pre-selected names from company listings, minority brand users, the homeless, people who travel a great deal

- complex political and social issues such as 'the meaning of motherhood today', 'gay parenthood', 'surrogacy', 'the portrayal of men in the media', 'work and the next millennium'

- matters of fashion and taste where personal preferences are likely to be extremely varied, e.g. music, decor, fashion.

Variations in the group interview method – such as the mini-group, friendship group, extended group, 'conflict' group, reconvened group and sensitivity panel – have all been developed to overcome the perceived limitations of the basic format.

The *mini-group* consists of four to six people and usually lasts for a shorter length of time. It may overcome problems of embarrassment, expertise differences, and recruitment difficulties.

*Friendship groups* are usually recommended for children and teenagers where problems of shyness can be overcome by recruiting a group of friends or pairs of friends. Often this approach means that a greater number of groups needs to be conducted; the mini-group format is a solution.

The *extended group* (or 'extended creativity group') may last as long as four hours or even longer and allows sufficient time for respondents to participate in tasks and exercises such as words and pictures, psycho-drama, brand mapping, exploring advertising both inside and outside the category of interest, brand personality exercises, and so on. This method can overcome problems of embarrassment or political correctness since greater attention can be paid to forming the group and creating a safe environment for disclosure. It also allows for a wide range of research objectives and stimuli.

The *conflict group* is designed to highlight the differences between people and to use this 'clash' to understand the core issue or to explore with the group if and how these differences can be resolved or negotiated. The moderator thus makes it explicit in the forming phase of the group that people have been recruited with very different viewpoints and agendas and that the task for the group is to explore the nature of these differences. For example, a group could be constructed with people who buy and passionately support British brands (e.g., cars, appliances, and airlines) versus those who actively prefer European, Japanese, or other non-British brands in order to understand the nature of 'Britishness'.

Moderating skills need to be finely honed in order for this kind of group to be productive, since the group can become stuck, locked in conflict and hostility, to the detriment of the research process.

The *reconvened group* is one of the most useful and under-used variations of the group interview. A group is recruited for two sessions separated by one week. The first session covers some of the key topics, usually the more straightforward ones. During the interim week the group is asked to conduct a number of exercises. These are designed to sensitise the members of the group to certain aspects of their own or other members of their families' or friends' behaviour and to come back to the group with a mini-analysis of their observations. For example, the members of the group might be asked to visit two different retail environments and make observations about the display of goods, the behaviour of the shop assistants, the behaviour of other people in the store and details of the environment. A group might be asked to stop doing something that they take for granted like drinking tea, cleaning the toilet, driving the car. This kind of behavioural change highlights vividly the key drivers of attitude and behaviour.

At the reconvened session, it is noticeable how much more involved people are with the subject and the aims of the research. They are more willing to disclose and share 'heartfelt' thoughts and feelings and thus many of the topics become easy to discuss.

The *sensitivity panel* is a psychodynamic, group-interview process first described by Bill Schlackman in 1984[4]. A number of people are invited to attend a series of group discussions exploring various subjects over a period of time. During these sessions, they are 'taught' how to access hidden thoughts and feelings – those that might be repressed for one reason or another or have become highly defended. They learn such techniques as free association, analogy generation, 'gestalt dialogue', and stream of awareness, and require almost no preparation to engage in a new subject. The fact that the group members come to know each other facilitates an atmosphere of rapport, and this intimacy enables 'sharing' to take place, since the trust level between them is high. This kind of approach is valuable if the moderator has the appropriate experiential training and theoretical understanding of psychoanalytical theory and group psychology.

Sensitivity panels are not the same things as qualitative panels. The latter is a sample of people, usually customers of an organisation (such as a bank or a credit-card company), who have been recruited to a panel and have agreed to attend a group discussion or to conduct an interview, when asked. Bank or credit-card behaviour of each individual is well documented and thus groups or interviews can be conducted with people whose behaviour is fact, not fiction. Panel members can be interviewed once or several times. Panels do decline over a period of time and thus they constantly need to be 'topped up' with new members.

There may be even more variations than those discussed above. The underlying principle is the same: each variant has evolved in response to a particular limitation of the basic group discussion or 'focus group'. None are the magic answer to greater truthfulness. In combination, they provide a more colourful picture of the behaviour and attitudes of a target group.

## The Individual Interview

The individual interview has had a chequered history in contemporary qualitative market research. In the early days of motivational research it was the primary 'deep digging tool' and still is, according to Chrissie Burns[5] who, like many experienced qualitative researchers, believes that this methodology has an important complementary role to play alongside group interview methods.

For the purposes of definition, the individual interview is a conversation conducted between a trained qualitative researcher or depth interviewer and a 'respondent' selected according to agreed criteria (age, life stage, gender, social class, marital status, usership profile, etc.). It can last anywhere between half an hour and two or more hours, depending on the nature of the enquiry.

Generally, the standard 'depth' interview is an hour in length and is conducted in the home of the recruiter, in the respondent's own home or place of work, in an agreed venue (pub, club, retail environment), or in a research facility. The place influences the nature of the interview in the same way that the venue effects the nature of the group discussion.

Over the past two decades, use of the individual 'depth' interview has declined as the popularity of the 'focus group' has risen. This decline is due to a number of reasons:

- the nature of the information obtained in a 'one-on-one' interview is believed to be similar to that elicited in a group discussion when, in practice, it is very different

- the lack of entertainment value for the observers of a 'depth interview' compared to a group discussion is often an underlying reason for a preference for the latter

- a mistaken belief that it is easier to interview one person alone rather than a group of eight to ten people; hence depth interviews are considered a suitable training ground for young and inexperienced researchers to test their wings; this can lead to naïve research recommendations based on reportage rather than interpretation

- buyers often balking at the relative costs of depth interviews compared to group discussions, as they do not place enough value on a senior practitioner conducting them, nor appreciate the complexity and the chameleon-like qualities that are needed.

One of the fundamental problems is that individual interviews are usually advocated *instead* of group discussions – in other words the two methodologies are seen to be in opposition rather than having the potential to enrich and complement one another.

In the UK particularly, practitioners prefer to recommend group discussions rather than depth interviews for the simple reason that, in terms of time and energy, they are more profitable.

Generally speaking, the individual interview is considered appropriate for sensitive subject matter such as redundancy, medical problems, relationship difficulties, or intimate hygiene products, where it is important to understand in some detail how the individual's attitudes and behaviour evolved over time. Today, in the West, it is relatively easy to encourage a group of people to talk about AIDS or sanitary protection, but this is not the case in all cultures. The findings of the experiment in methodology discussed later in this chapter suggest that the nature of the information and understanding is different, depending on whether it was approached through the vehicle of a group interview or an individual interview.

The individual interview is also useful for product categories, brands and services where overclaiming or underclaiming is likely to occur. This happens in many product categories, even those that appear to be straightforward, like the use of spices in cooking. Women will often overclaim on creativity and experimentalism in preparing food just as people over or underclaim about the amount of wine or whisky they drink.

While the same dynamic occurs in the individual interview, it is easier for a well-trained moderator to detect it and to work out how to enable the individual to show his or her 'private face'[5].

Individual interviews can help reconstruct the process of decision making. For example, the step-by-step process of choosing a telecom supplier including the influence of advertising, direct mail, point of sale, word of mouth, advice of family and friends, and so on can best be tackled through a one-to-one approach. A historical reconstruction and review of key events in the process is difficult to achieve in the group interview. There is no time to elicit the necessary level of detail for each member of the group, and contamination by the views of other members of the group, who tend to make value judgments as the individual is speaking, interferes with the flow.

Sometimes it is relevant to try to find out whether a particular point of view or behavioural trait is idiosyncratic or common. By conducting 20–30 individual interviews it is relatively easy to come to a conclusion about this. If this sample supports the findings of previous group discussions, the combination of the two approaches is robust enough to eliminate a follow-up quantitative exercise (provided the objective is to understand proportions rather than to obtain percentages).

Communication issues connected with press advertising or brochures, magazine readership behaviour, participation in product promotions and response to promotion mechanics (e.g. 10% extra versus BOGOF – Buy One Get One Free), or any other instance where the relationship between the stimulus and the individual is uniquely individual, benefit from this kind of interview[5]. Researching communication in a group is a frustrating experience – the brightest individual 'gets it quickly' and articulates it for the group. The moderator never knows how many other members of the group would have absorbed the same message or expressed it in the same way.

Behaviour such as cleaning the car, cooking a curry, taking photographs on a day out, drinking behaviour in a club, or watching television as a family cannot be tackled through the conventional focus group – members reconstruct a 'memory amalgam' of behaviour rather than the real behaviour. Here, the individual interview needs to take place in the real context, not in a research venue, office, or front room.

Difficult-to-interview respondents are best interviewed individually, perhaps because of geographical dispersion (farmers, people who buy from catalogues, lists of customers), status (managing director, CEO, head of finance, IT and telecoms directors, journalists, opinion formers, etc.), expertise and knowledge, and low penetration purchasing.

Individual interviews can also be used as a pre-quantification exercise in order to ensure that a questionnaire designed for a survey reflects consumer or customer vocabulary or that the list of attitude statements or behavioural variations that are to be included in 'closed questions' represent the key parameters of the market.

There are variations on the basic interview format: mini-depth interviews, semi-structured interviews, pair interviews, and family interviews, as follows.

*Mini-depth interviews* are short — between 20 minutes and half an hour — and are used to explore a very focused issue such as the communication effectiveness of an advertisement or some other stimulus (pack design, brochure, promotion, visual, icon, logo), or the presence or otherwise of a comprehension problem. In a short time, someone can be shown an advertisement (or any stimulus) several times and responses explored in an open and flexible way.

Mini-depths are also used alongside conventional survey research, particularly central location pre-tests, to provide 'flesh to the bones' of quantitative survey data. Sometimes, a respondent who has already completed the main questionnaire can be re-interviewed by a qualitative researcher in order to understand the responses in more depth or a 'fresh sample' can be recruited to complement the main survey.

*Semi-structured interviews* are usually conducted by trained quantitative field interviewers using an open-ended questionnaire. The interviewer is trained on probing techniques and rapport skills but is required to ask the question exactly as it is written and not deviate with follow-up questions of his or her own. This kind of interview is used extensively in business-to-business research as well as medical, agricultural, and pharmaceutical research where large numbers of interviews are required.

Semi-structured interviews can provide a useful 'booster' sample for conventional individual or group interviews especially where there are many cells in the sample.

*Pair interviews* are self-explanatory. A pair of respondents — best friends, spouses, co-habitees, employees, mother and daughter (or some other family combination), or users of the same brand are interviewed simultaneously. These interviews are useful for gaining insight into the dynamics of purchase decision making that often occur between family members or friends, or can help to create a less intimidating environment for the interview than a one-on-one, and are therefore frequently used as the interviewing format for children and teenagers.

*Family interviews* are similar to pair interviews except that the whole family is interviewed either separately, in pairs, or all together (sometimes in all three ways). Understanding the dynamics of a family relationship around food, watching television, leisure activities, or parental discipline is not easy. Any one spokesman for the family (mother, father, or one of the children) has a particular perspective, which may or may not be shared by the others. The 'push-me, pull-you' dynamics of parent and child can best be explored using this interview format.

The AQRP runs a training course each year called 'An Introduction to the Principles and Practice of Qualitative Research' in which one of the modules is the 'depth interview'. The notes from this course make useful reading for those who have not conducted many depth interviews. Written by Joanna Chrzanowska, the module covers:

- the importance of planning the interview beforehand and ensuring that it has an introduction, a warm-up, open-ended questions to find the unexpected, a topic outline, and stimuli to generate response

- learning the relevant skill set such as: personal presentation; clarity of communication; dealing with someone of a different age, sex, social class, or background; listening skills; creating trust; drawing someone out; non-verbal awareness; dealing with dominating, arrogant, passive, withdrawn, or uninterested interviewees; making assumptions too quickly; and generalising – to name but a few.

Chrissie Burns[5] adds yet more: knowing when to challenge; the manner of executing challenge; what to challenge and how to become aware of one's own role in reinforcing game playing; performing well within the safety net; and 'withholding'.

- Know thyself – what are you bringing to the interview? What personal baggage? How quickly do you judge people by their appearance? How tolerant are you of those less or more intelligent than yourself? Self-awareness is crucial – prejudice is often highlighted in the individual interview dynamics.

- The importance of the introduction – people do not know what to expect when they agree to be interviewed. They may try to please, believe there is a correct answer, or respond as they would to an authoritarian parent, a dismissive schoolteacher, an indulgent friend, or a flirtatious stranger. There are no cues from other members of the group and certainly no benchmarks as to the level of sharing expected. In a depth interview, just as in a group discussion, it is essential to give the respondent the reason for the interview, confidentiality reassurances, some personal information about yourself, indications of the kind of conversation you wish to have, and a time limit.

- Non-verbal communication is very powerful in a one-to-one, particularly body language, pacing, mirroring, time and space language.

- Understanding the psychosocial dynamics of human relationships is essential to good interviewing. There are different roles people play in an individual interview – all of which are worth thinking about in terms of how to interact with someone who has taken on a particular way of being. There are those who are 'over-talkative', 'withdrawn or passive', 'emotional', 'cut-off', 'know-it-all', 'a complainer', or 'self-deprecating' for example. All of these are symptoms of past baggage, responses to anxiety at being the focus of attention, finding the subject difficult to talk about, or a manifestation of the games people play.

## Observational Methods

There are two types of observation: 'simple observation' and 'participant observation'. In approaches using simple observation, the observer functions impartially, almost as a machine, recording details of individual behaviour. However, no human being is a machine and therefore at some level, unconsciously, selective perception takes place.

Nowadays, video recorders are used to record the behaviour of individuals in public places like airports, shopping centres and retail store environments. Places where people consume products and services are suited to observation: restaurants, bars, theme parks, holiday venues, tourist attractions, hotel lobbies, and garage forecourts.

Much new work is being conducted at 'the moment of truth', that is, the moment when someone selects a product from the shelf. Several advertising agencies in London have set up specialist units to conduct observation studies for clients. BMP DDB Needham is currently engaged in an innovative commercial observation exercise that involves members of its specialist unit – Culture Lab – living with a selected number of British families for two weeks at a time.

In the early 1980s, the BBC conducted a famous experiment on the television-watching habits of the nation. A video camera was installed in the television itself, which filmed the viewer(s) as they watched the pro-grammes. Viewer reactions could be linked to the programme watched[6]. Of course, the 'subjects' had given permission but it was clear from the footage that, over a period of weeks, they forgot about the existence of the camera. One of the key findings was that people rarely watch televi-sion with absolute concentration: they talk, eat, sew, read, walk in and out and interact with the announcers and advertisements. There was much footage that could not be shown!

The primary emphasis of this type of observation is recording what human beings do, not what they say they do. There is a great deal to be learned from this type of work for this reason alone.

The following extract is from an article by Malcolm Gladwell origi-nally published in *The New Yorker* magazine on 4 November, 1996.

> *... when potential shoppers enter a store, it's going to take them 10 or 15 paces to adjust to the light and refocus and gear down from walking to shopping speed. [Paco] Underhill calls that area inside the door the Decompression Zone, and the thing he tells clients over and over again is never, ever put anything of value in that zone – not shopping baskets or tie racks or big promotional displays – because no one is going to see them ... Underhill believes that... customer interaction with any product in the Decompression Zone will increase at least 30% once it's moved to the back edge of the zone and even more if it's moved*

*to the right... one of the fundamental rules of how humans shop is that upon entering a store the shopper invariably and reflexively turns to the right...*

The recommendations that stem from pure observational research can be enormously helpful provided there is a large enough database. Underhill's observations go back 20 years and therefore are based on a sufficiently robust sample of observations.

The main disadvantage of simple observation is that we can find out *how* people behave in a particular context or situation but not *why*.

Observation supplemented by interviews, studies of records, or conversations with other experts is called participant observation. This is defined as a process of research that 'looks at social phenomena from the inside as well as from the outside' (*The Dictionary of Sociology*). Participant observation is based on rigorous methods developed for cultural studies and involves establishing a rapport in a way that helps to watch, record, and understand behaviour. Importantly, researchers need to learn to distance themselves from their own cultural or social 'baggage' and at the same time be aware that their very presence is altering the behaviour taking place.

How many observations make a robust sample? There is no absolute answer but a few suggestions are:

- enough to represent the target market that is being observed
- enough to represent the process or segments of the process (e.g. arriving at an airport, stages of the embarkation process)
- enough to represent changes in behaviour over time (e.g. different times of the day or week)
- enough to represent different cultural perspectives (international studies).

There are two main ways of setting up this kind of methodology. The first is to re-recruit an individual or group and enroll them in the process. For example, a qualitative researcher is given permission to accompany the individual(s) through the process under investigation – a teenage nightclub, a mother-daughter shopping spree, a friendship group 'hanging about the city on a Saturday', a woman shopping for groceries at the supermarket, and so on. The researcher observes and asks questions at different points in time in order to understand what the individual might be thinking or feeling at that moment or why an event is taking place.

The second way is to obtain permission from the retail outlet and observe people over a period of time. The researcher selects a range of behaviours to explore and asks questions for clarification: 'I noticed that you took quite a time to order your meal and then asked the waitress to come back a few times, could you tell me what was going on?' Or 'I noticed that you picked up a number of packs and seemed to be reading the backs before choosing which one to put in your trolley. Can you tell me what was running through your mind?'

Observation is far more difficult than it appears. The researcher first needs to be familiar with the environment and types of behaviour, then he or she needs to notice patterns of behaviour, particularly the most frequent ones, and then to validate the importance of these through talking to the people involved.

The information can be recorded by audio-tape, written notes or video. It is then captured for later analysis and can be edited for illustration to the client or used as stimulus in further research (perhaps using a group interview method).

Participant observation, variously called 'Being There' (a term used by The Research Business *International*) or 'Accompanied Trips' (*AQRP Handbook*, e.g. accompanied shopping, drinking, eating, cooking) is becoming an increasingly widely used qualitative methodology with the following applications.

- *Process stories* – visiting a showroom for a new car demonstration, taking the car on a test drive, being 'sold' the car by the salesman. Travelling to Paris on Eurostar from the time of departure at London Waterloo to arrival at Gare du Nord (buying a ticket, arriving at the station, boarding the train, the journey, buying a snack, and so on).

- *Extended relationships* – with a brand, product or service over time, such as following the photographic endeavours of a new camera owner over a period of six months including buying film, collecting the prints, showing the photographs to people, storage, and many other associated activities.

- *Brand context* – and all the cues in the environment that communicate messages and influence choice of brand or product, e.g. male toiletries, storage of brands in the home, 'alcopop' usage in a pub.

- *'Moment of truth' and the point-of-sale influences* – when someone purchases or experiences a product or service, a number of factors have an important role in the choice: merchandising, point of sale, promotions, and advertising (so do spaces and places). The interior design and layout of environments such as shopping centres, record stores, book shops, and urban spaces all play a part in choice, although the influence is often subliminal.

There are many issues to be resolved in this relatively new application of qualitative methods for commercial market research:

- training qualitative researchers in film technology

- confidentiality issues such as the ethics of filming people without their initial permission

- the nature of video 'data' and how they should be analysed and presented to clients so that their limitations are well understood.

In January 1999, AQRP and BMP DDB Needham arranged a forum on ethnographic and observation methods, which was attended by a small number of practitioners and academics currently involved or interested in these qualitative methods. The purpose of the forum was to explore the range of approaches currently in use and to make explicit the theoretical and professional issues involved.

## Interactive Workshops

These take many shapes and forms. The basic premise is that all human beings can be a problem-solving resource if given enough time and the right environment.

Interactive workshops came about as a development of 'extended creativity groups' that encourage respondents to engage with a complex problem and use techniques to enable the group to 'work' through problems because the issues and parameters have been made clear. Most importantly, they came about through a change of attitude whereby researchers came to realise that, by treating people as 'laboratory subjects from which to extract information and responses', the contribution of customers and consumers was undervalued. People can be willing problem solvers, especially those who have relevant experience to contribute.

Usually, a workshop consists of both consumers, people from the company sponsoring the project, and representatives of its agencies, such as R&D, the advertising agency, the design company, market researchers, and any other professionals who may have an area of expertise to offer.

The session takes place in a facility large enough to hold 'break-out' sub-groups so that combinations of the large group can work at the same, or on different, tasks or problems. Workshops often last a whole day or may be broken up into two sessions, one with consumers in the evening – observed by the team, followed by a brainstorming workshop with the wider team the next day.

This methodology requires that the facilitator is well trained in brain-storming techniques and that he or she also has the skill to handle large groups, since the numbers can reach 20 people or more. Interactive workshops are helpful for:

- new product development programmes
- brand problems (such as deciding whether or not a dormant or old-fashioned brand can be revitalised)
- exploring the consumer-company interface
- understanding the issues involved in internal employee-management relationships.

The output of these workshops is usually a vast number of flipcharts or Post-it® notes. One of the roles of the facilitator is to record the progress of the workshop and to provide a summary for the team to revisit as the project develops.

## A Comparative Methodology Experiment

In 1997, The Research Business *International* sponsored an experiment to compare the nature of the similarities and differences in qualitative 'information' derived from three methodologies[2]. These were conventional group discussions of two hours duration, accompanied shopping preceded by in-home individual interviews and participant observation using video and 'field notes' conducted in home at two different points in time. In the latter case, the respondent was asked not to clean the toilet for as long as possible in order to heighten awareness of the key issues!

The subject was toilet-cleaning attitudes and behaviour, chosen because it is an intimate and personal topic which would stress test the different methodologies. The research objectives were extensive:

> ... *to understand consumer behaviour and attitudes to cleaning the toilet, the role of the family, the products used, the purchase cycle and context, the imagery of the main brand players, indications of possible brand partners and idea generation for new products.*

Not surprisingly, each methodology has its strengths and weaknesses. The experiment proved the value of mixed methodologies in providing richness of information, depth of understanding and unique insights, the three elements required of qualitative research.

The ethnographic method (participant observation)[7] was based on videoing the process of toilet cleaning combined with respondent explanations to the researcher while engaged in the process. Video was also used to record the individual interview that took place before and after the toilet cleaning exercise which covered the other topics of relevance.

This methodology brought the consumer alive for the client and convincingly demonstrated real people, in real toilets, using real products, and expressing thoughts and feelings closely connected to the task itself. The respondents played an active part in the research, offering insights of their own. In this sense the participant became 'lay researcher' or 'co-researcher' rather than 'respondent'.

The very act of 'behaving' (i.e., cleaning the toilet) releases personal insights and explanations that do not occur out of context. Through the enactment of behaviour, the individual is able to access thoughts and emotions that are not accessible via other research methods. However, it is important to acknowledge that the behaviour is not 'real' since the observer changes the behaviour in some subtle way that is impossible to assess. Good rapport may lead the researcher to discuss the degree to which the individual might be behaving differently for the camera.

The other strength of this approach lies in understanding the in-home repertoire of brands and products used for bathroom and toilet cleaning. The co-existence of own-label and brands allow a comparative discussion of their differences and similarities in terms of usage, perceptions, storage and display.

The group discussion method, not surprisingly, did generate insights into the process of cleaning a toilet; that is, what people actually do. The researcher had to rely on reconstructed memories of behaviour expressed through 'the dense veil of interpretation' – the individual's own projection of how she wanted to be 'seen' by others, as well as the researcher's interpretations of 'the consumer' or 'consumer behaviour, attitudes, and emotions'.

The main strength of the group discussion methodology lies in the arena of the emotions, which could be placed in the broad social, cultural and psychological values of the target market. Here the use of projective techniques, such as thought-bubble completion and personification exercises, brought into the open the ways in which human beings attach human motivations to inanimate objects.

*The very fact that women were released from the real context of home and toilet allowed participants to share with each other and bring to the surface feelings that had remained hidden before ... A group discussion that has moved beyond the realm of politeness into a space where there is a willingness to expose, reveal and divulge personal feelings without fear of embarrassment becomes a powerful vehicle through which to gain insight into the dynamics driving the category. This is clearly rich territory sympathetic to marketing and advertising objectives such as understanding the core motivations on which brand positionings and propositions can be built[2].*

The intimacy of the subject matter did not deter the group. Once they had formed and normed, the members of the group became voyeuristically involved in the intimacy of their own behaviour. A side issue was that the group so enjoyed this process of disclosure that they hijacked the agenda and refused to cooperate with what they perceived to be more boring areas of enquiry, i.e brands, packaging.

Psychodynamic group discussions, conducted by a researcher highly skilled in the use of projective and enabling techniques, is able in the space of two hours to offer insight into the psychological, social, and cultural meanings that underpin human behaviour and actions. It should perhaps be made clear that, from this experiment, two hours was insufficient time to cover all the research objectives, and, therefore, extended group discussions would have been the preferred choice of group interview variant.

*The accompanied shopping interviews,* where the researcher accompanied the respondent to two different retail environments after having conducted a brief interview in the home, provided an insight into the brand-consumer interface that neither of the other methodologies could accomplish.

*The accompanied shopping method allows researchers to understand real people in real shops at the real brand-consumer interface defined by the chosen retail environment. The cues within the shopping environment serve as stimuli through which the researcher can understand how an individual makes sense of the overwhelming amount of products, brands and information in-store[2].*

This method offers a specialised but restricted opportunity to understand how brands operate in the complex competitive environments in which they have to search for competitive advantage.

Again, it is important to emphasise that accompanied shopping (or accompanied trips of any kind) does not demonstrate true behaviour. The respondent acts as co-researcher and through the real-life environment is able to explain how he or she decodes and interprets point of sale, merchandising, packaging, promotion and environmental cues.

The experiment also revealed differences in rapport between the three methodologies. Briefly, the rapport between the researcher and participant was strongest in the ethnographic approach and most superficial in the accompanied shopping method, which was strongly context-bound and rational. The nature of the rapport in the group interview is created between the members of the group, including the moderator, rather than between any one member and the moderator — evidence of the nature of 'the group psyche'.

## Mixed Methodologies: A Real Option

This review has demonstrated that qualitative researchers are in the fortunate position of having a large toolbox from which to select the most effective combination of tools for the job.

Combinations of methodologies add richness of insight and robustness, within the boundaries of the majority of project budgets. When combining methodologies, the whole is more than the sum of its parts, and therefore it is not necessary that each approach consist of a 'stand-alone' sample. Each element of the combined method does not 'have to replicate the sample design for the whole study'.

There are many ways of combining methodologies in addition to that described in the experiment:

- people can be interviewed individually or in pairs before attending a group discussion

- groups can be conducted in situ such as in a retail shop, a place of work, a restaurant, hotel, or leisure club

- participants in research can be set a task prior to the interview or group discussion in order to heighten awareness of the subject to be covered.

It is possible to offset the disadvantages of a 'pure' methodology by incorporating some of the benefits of another approach. A group discussion held in an office at a supermarket, which includes a trip around a section is not meant to replicate the real purchase occasion, but does bring to light some of the group responses to the look and feel of the store environment. It jogs people's memories about their behaviour, which is not possible in an off-site group venue.

If the budget does not allow for in-home or in-store individual interviews, then unaccompanied shopping is an option. Here the recruited respondent is asked to visit a number of stores before the group discussion to observe the fixtures of interest. People are prepared to conduct a great deal of work provided they are given an understanding of the importance of the task. Cupboard, freezer, larder, bathroom, garage, and storeroom 'audits' are all ways to understand real-life contexts for brands and products.

The biggest obstacle to the use of combined methodologies, particularly observation and individual interviews, is research practitioner/company profitability. For small companies of qualitative researchers or single-handed practitioners it is far more profitable to conduct eight standard groups (two per night) than to conduct five extended groups, or even to combine two extended groups with six accompanied shops and ten individual interviews.

In addition, the smaller research companies tend not to have invested in training and experimentation, and therefore lack the skills and resources necessary to conduct participant observation sessions using video. This is more complex than simply wielding the camera reasonably competently; it involves rigour in editing, integrity in acknowledging the presence of the camera and researcher, and authority in presenting the findings to the client.

It is therefore incumbent of users of qualitative research to find out which suppliers have the resources, expertise, and experience to provide mixed methodology solutions to contemporary problems. Many researchers argue for conventional groups because this is more profitable and easier, not because it is right — a sad observation.

It is also incumbent on all qualitative researchers to provide more extensive training in methods other than the group interview. The alternative methodologies, particularly participant observation and individual interviews, should not be used as initiation rites for untrained young practitioners. Each requires its own particular training 'module' to ensure that it delivers against expectations.

## References

1.  M. Denny, 'Inspiring Details: The Role of Ethnography in a Kaleidoscope Age', ESOMAR Congress, Paris, 1995.

2.  R. Pike and W. Gordon, 'Carry on round the "U" bend: an experimental comparison of three qualitative methodologies', ESOMAR Congress, Edinburgh, 1997.

3.  W. Gordon and S. Robson, 'Respondent Through the Looking Glass: Towards a Better Understanding of the Qualitative Interviewing Process', MRS Conference, 1982.

4.  W. Schlackman, 'A Discussion of the Use of Sensitivity Panels in Market Research', MRS Annual Conference Proceedings, 1984.

5.  C. Burns, 'Individual Interviews' in S. Robson and A. Foster, *Qualitative Research in Action*, Edward Arnold, 1989.

6.  R. Wynberg and M. Synnivig, 'Watching You, Watching Us, Watching You', MRS Conference, 1986.

7.  H. Marianpolski, 'Ethnography as a Market Research Tool' in P. Sampson (ed.). Qualitative Research Through a Looking Glass, ESOMAR, 1998.

## Further Reading

W. Gordon and R. Langmaid, Qualitative Market Research: A Practitioner's and Buyer's Guide, Gower, 1988.

AQRP Directory and Handbook of Qualitative Research.

C. A. Restall and R. Auton, 'From Passivity to Interaction? The Future of Qualitative Research', 49th ESOMAR Congress, Changing Business Dynamics: The Challenge to Marketing Research, Sep. 1996.

Annual Study of the Market Research Industry, ESOMAR, 1997.

# When/How/What

## By Alice Kendrick

*This piece was written by Alice Kendrick, Professor of Advertising at Southern Methodist University. You may recall that we dedicated this book to her. Alice believes that life, whether of the personal or the marketing communications variety, is one big series of questions. She teaches the value of making informed decisions and the tools and processes necessary to generate needed information. She is also the co-author of* Successful Advertising Research Methods, *has published more than two dozen refereed research articles, and acts as a research consultant to agencies and clients including Texas Instruments and The Richards Group. She received her Ph.D. in communications from the University of Tennessee, and her B.A. and M.A. in journalism from LSU. She has served as Chair of the Academic Division of the American Advertising Federation. She has a way cool new book out on the State Department's advertising project in the Muslim world, titled* Advertising's War on Terrorism.

THIS PIECE WAS ORIGINALLY WRITTEN to be part of an introductory book on advertising. Its function is to be a summary of the basics for advertising research – which includes planning.

## The Need for Evaluation

Today, advertising and marketing have to evaluate every step of the way – you can't wait till it's over to see how you're doing. Sometimes the process is, as marketing guru Tom Peters described it, *"Ready. Fire. Aim."*

And sometimes, as Jack Haskins, former Ad Research Director for Ford Motor Co., would say, *"Post-campaign research is like a 'post-mortem' inquiry – it's really too late to do anything for the victim."*

Hopefully, your projects will have happier results.

To help achieve those results, we'll see how account planners have found ways of doing just that, and we'll see how various research tools and approaches are improving the development of advertising, media, and other parts of the marketing process.

## Time Is Money

To make things even more interesting, choices must be made and challenges met under extreme time pressures. For many marketers, waiting can be an expensive proposition.

We want good information and we want it fast.

## Here's what we'll cover

1. **When to Gather.** We'll identify key "apertures" or opportunities where research can play a valuable role.

2. **How to Gather.** We'll introduce you to various available research tools.

3. **What to Gather.** We'll discuss the types of information that need to be gathered and how to prepare a Research Plan.

4. **Challenges for the Future.** Computers now put out incredible amounts of data. Learning how to get useful information out of this data is a critical skill for tomorrow's marketers and advertisers.

So, let's get going.

## A Practical Definition of Research

A practical definition of research is simple: *"systematic gathering of information to answer a question or solve a problem."* Conducting research can be as simple as looking up a word in a dictionary (hey, that's systematic).

- It could involve observing consumers as they use a product.

- It could be engaging in a quantitative demographic analysis of government census information as you plan a campaign.

- It could be testing a number of concepts or copy approaches for your new campaign.

- It could be conducting a post-campaign telephone survey of consumers to determine their usage of and attitudes toward your brand and its advertising.

As you can see, that one definition covers a lot of activities.

## Insurance, Information, Insight, and Inspiration

One way of viewing research is as "insurance" – insurance against making the wrong decision. The primary way we do this is to get very specific kinds of information that help us know more about the decisions we must make.

Throughout, we've talked about the importance of informed decision making. Research can, and does, help reduce the many uncertainties that surround something as complicated as the planning of an integrated campaign. But it's not just avoiding negatives. Good research can give you true insight into the problem you're trying to solve.

We'll take a look at how The Richards Group does it for Motel 6.

Finally, when you do get it right, you have a better chance of finding the vision and inspiration that can result in a big win.

And it's a lot more fun to keep score when we're winning!

# 1. When to Gather

The stereotypical view of advertising research held by many is that of scorekeeping after a commercial or a campaign is up and running in the marketplace.

Sort of like the Nielsen overnight ratings – or the day after the Super Bowl – the next day you get a number, a score. Well there's much more to the research puzzle than post-campaign analysis.

## Four Ways to Get Smarter

We always want to get smarter, but here are the four critical research stages in the advertising development process.

**A. Planning Research.** The information needed for upfront planning is critical. It may include last year's "scorekeeping", but more importantly it involves a substantial amount of additional new work and new thinking.

**B. Developmental Research.** Research can help develop thinking, strategies, insights, and advertising. With the introduction of the

British account-planning approach, it has become an even more active partner in the development process.

**C. Implementation Research.** With the increasing cost of television production and media, insurance can be a smart investment.

Here, we can test the implementation of the strategy we developed — usually tests of ad concepts.

Sometimes there is a complete market test.

**D. Measuring Results.** Finally, when we've done our best in the marketplace, we need to see how we've done.

It's time to see what the score was. Maybe we won big, maybe we lost, or, more likely, it was somewhere in between.

We'll use that information to make next year even better.

Now, let's take the four "whens" one by one.

# A. Planning Research

This is also known as Background Research. Planning research, or background research, is critical to understanding the environment in which your next ad campaign will compete.

Essential to this environmental evaluation is a document generically referred to as the **situation analysis,** or marketing situation analysis – the compilation of material from a variety of sources gives us a firm idea of "what is" with respect to the marketplace and our product.

## Brand Analysis Checklists

The brand-analysis checklists below are useful starting points for gathering and then developing background on your brand.

**Checklist I** focuses on getting started on your brand or product category.

**Checklist II** focuses on collecting additional marketing and advertising information.

# Brand-Analysis Checklist I

This is a good way to get started collecting information on a brand:

## I. Company:

- Location
- Organization and major activities; subsidiaries
- History
- Financial data
- Annual report
- Key personnel/managers
- Recent news from database sources, newspapers, etc.

## II. Category:

- Category definition
- Size of category in units, dollars, etc.
- Category history and growth
- Category growth projections
- Distribution channels/methods of distribution
- Major manufacturers/players
- Seasonal factors
- Regional factors
- Other factors relevant to category
- Legal considerations
- Major trade publications/trade organizations in category
- Legal considerations

## III. Products within Category:

- Share of category by product form
- Product-form description (size, flavor, model, etc.)
- New product introductions
- Benefits and appeals of new products
- New packages, innovations, etc.
- Recent news about/affecting product category

# Brand-Analysis Checklist II

This is the second part of the brand-analysis checklist, focusing on the collection of marketing and advertising information for a brand.

## Brand Analysis:

- Top brands by dollar or unit sales
- Growth trends of top brands
- Category share nationally and by region
- Pricing trends
- Recent news about/affecting brand

## Consumer Profile:

- Demographics of users
- Frequency of purchase/usage
- Place of purchase
- Heavy-user profile
- Awareness and attitudes toward brand
- Decision-maker vs. purchaser
- Normal purchase cycle
- Brand loyalty/switching

## Advertising Messages:

- Creative strategies of top brands
- Specific promises, appeals, claims, special effects
- Examples of past and current executions

## Media:

- Category and brand spending
- Seasonality (by quarter)
- Regionality (spot buying)
- Major media employed by top brands
- Spending patterns: flighting, continuous, etc.
- Spending compared with market share

## Promotion:

- Promotions used in category

- Major brand promotion types and examples
- Success rates of promotions

**Other Pertinent Information:**

- Personal interviews
- Other information sources

# Electronic Resources

You can gain access to much of the information you need for producing your situation analysis through electronic resources such as online databases or via the Internet.

Typically, the information you'll use will come from a combination of printed sources available in places such as libraries or company archives, customized research reports available through research vendors, competitive information gathered from the Web, and periodical articles and industry reports from online databases available primarily through public or university libraries. Examples are *LexisNexis* and *Infotrac.*

## Different Kinds of Information

Campaign planning requires several different kinds of information:

- **Competitive activity**
- **Market share data**
- **Current examples of advertising in the category**
- **Advertising expenditures**
- **Marketplace trends**
- **Demographic data**

The list goes on. Ultimately, this information must be organized into a coherent report.

## Brand-Analysis Checklist

An example of how to organize planning information is included in those Brand-Analysis Checklists on the previous pages. They include a series of topics for which secondary and primary research can supply information. Taken together, this information forms the backdrop for the upcoming ad campaign.

# The Web: A Word of Warning

Internet websites contain widely varied content produced by a wide array of individuals and organizations – some more credible than others.

Always be careful to check the original source of the information you are quoting in your research. Is it simply someone's opinion, or is it the result of objective empirical research, etc.? Many websites contain highly filtered information that reflects the point of view of their publisher – take this fact into consideration when evaluating the information therein.

The planning process involves getting a lot of specific information about your brand and your category. This is often the first kind of research you do.

**Remember, Secondary Comes First.**
It begins with secondary research.

# B. Developmental Research

A fundamental shift in thinking about the ability of research to contribute to better and more effective advertising came in the late 1980s and 1990s with the introduction of the account-planning discipline in US agencies.

This British approach to planning an advertising campaign placed research emphasis squarely on the *development* of the creative and media strategies.

The underlying belief is that the gathering of information from consumers will lead to insights. These insights will then lead to more relevant advertising concepts. This will lead to more effective messages, which will increase the chances that the advertising will accomplish its objectives as determined by post-campaign (evaluative) tests. You get the point.

## Developing Strategies as Well as Ads

Developmental research ultimately contributes to the formulation of the creative strategy, usually taking the form of a creative brief. The major types of research activities that can be useful at the developmental stage are:

- Focus groups
- One-on-one interviews

• Observation, etc.

These will be discussed later in this section.

## Briefs and Planners

A creative brief reflects the consumer insights determined through the developmental research and employs them as the basis for a creative strategy, which then acts as the blueprint for the creative executions to follow.

Account planners are responsible for making sure that all ads produced by the creative department are "on strategy."

Sometimes it takes a lot of thinking and work on the front end to get it right.

# C. Implementation Research

The third "aperture" for conducting research gives us the opportunity to gather reaction from consumers through more focus groups or by way of field experiments to one or more creative or media strategies.

## Two Basic Forms

Implementation research is likely to take two basic forms:

1. **Concepts or ads are pre-tested:** consumers are allowed to react to ad concepts or rough executions to determine which is most likely to have the greatest impact in the marketplace.

2. **Test markets or "pilot tests"** are set up to compare the effectiveness of the creative message, the media strategy, or both.

## Pre-Testing with Concept Ads

Here are some ads for the somewhat well-known "Got Milk?" campaign. Above, is a brand collage from a "Got Milk?" focus group. Below, is an award-winning ad in the series.

In this case, a brand collage exercise in the pre-testing stage revealed a strong advertising idea.

## Test Markets

Due to faster competitive responses and the increased cost of in-market tests, we don't see test markets as often as we used to. But they can still be important and yield important and surprising results.

Here's an example for Campbell's Soup.

The "Soup Is Good Food" campaign was put into test market by Campbell's. There were no quick dramatic results, but the campaign remained in test market for over a year.

Slowly, it became clear that the new approach was generating increased sales and improved attitudes.

Based on the test market results, "Soup is Good Food" became the national campaign for a number of years.

*[Read the whole story in "The Care and Feeding of Ideas" by Bill Backer, founder of Backer & Spielvogel, the agency that created the campaign.—Ed.]*

# D. Measuring Results

The final opportunity for gathering information regarding the advertising campaign is after the advertising is up and running in the marketplace.

Periodic measures of effectiveness can be taken during the course of the campaign, or an after-campaign measure of effectiveness can be taken.

## Types of Post-Campaign Research

Some of the most common ways marketers evaluate the results of their ad campaigns are:

- Standardized copytesting
- Attitude, awareness, and usage (AAU) studies
- Dollar sales or volumetric analyses

## Standardized Copytesting

Determining whether ads are on strategy is one of the most important activities in the creation of a successful campaign. Measuring the communications impact of an ad is known as **copytesting.**

Here is an argument for the importance of copytesting from *Advertising Works II* (published by the Institute of Canadian Advertising).

*"Copy is usually a more important decision than media or budget.*

*"Up-front decisions on advertising and promotion roles and objectives, market strategy, and positioning are all synergistic with effective copy generation.*

*"Top management should organize the advertising and promotion areas so that they can spend more on generating and testing highly varying creative program alternatives.*

*"Management should encourage variability in creative output by not overly constraining the creative teams and using creative teams that are most likely to have different creative approaches."*

With all the possible variables, consistency of measurement and evaluation can become quite important. If you've ever weighed yourself at home, then weighed in at the doctor's office and been told you're five pounds heavier, you can appreciate the value of consistent instrumentation and measurement.

Two scales, side by side, may not yield the same result. Just as our doctor might advise you to keep using the same scale to more accurately gauge your gains and losses, so advertisers often choose to stick with a particular type of measure to judge the effectiveness of their advertising over time.

## Copytesting Services

Examples of major national standardized copytesting firms are Starch INRA Hooper, Gallup & Robinson, Readex, and McCollum Spielman. Each has its own way of assigning a numeric score to an ad based on its ability to be noticed, understood, and liked. For Starch, the measures of "noted" (those who remember seeing the ad in the magazine), "associated" (those who can associate the brand name with the ad), and "read most" (those who claim to have read most of the ad's copy) are used.

**Ad A.** "Colgate Plus was designed by a team of scientists to accurately fit the shape of the human mouth…"

**Ad B.** "The Colgate Plus toothbrush has a unique design that works like a dental tool to fight bacterial plaque at home…"

**Example 22** from *Which Ad Pulled Best?* Want to find out which ad worked the best? Guess you'll have to buy the book!

Colgate-Palmolive used the standardized copytesting services of Gallup & Robinson to test print ads in major national magazines over a period of years.

Above are two examples for Colgate Plus toothbrushes from a great little book *Which Ad Pulled Best?* Can you guess which ad pulled best? That's the point.

You really do need some evidence from consumers to measure the relative strength of different appeals: fits the shape of your mouth or works like a dental tool at home.

## AAU Studies

Periodic assessments of how a brand and its advertising are being perceived in the marketplace are useful in establishing brand presence, competitive noise, and market share.

An example of such a study is commonly called an **Awareness, Attitude, and Usage survey (AAU),** and is conducted among a random sample of consumers, usually by telephone interview. On the next page is an example of the results of an AAU study for Amdro fire ant killer. It shows the "un-aided awareness" of leading brands through three waves.

**These were the questions asked in the Amdro AAU study:**

"Now, thinking about fire ant control products, which one brand of fire ant control product first comes to mind?"

"What other brands of fire ant control products can you think of? What others?"

"For which brands of fire ant control products have you seen or heard advertising in the past two to three months? What others?"

**Base = Total Respondents**
    **Wave I: n = 525 | Wave II: n = 525 | Wave III: n = 526**

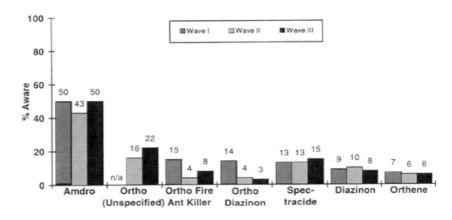

UNAIDED AWARENESS OF LEADING BRANDS

*Proprietary Research. American Cyanamid*

The result of this research is that "Amdro continues to dominate un-aided awareness of fire ant pesticide brands, with half of the respondents mentioning it on an un-aided basis."

This research also monitors the competition. "Ortho also has high un-aided awareness, with more than one-third of the respondents mentioning the brand name by itself or a specific Ortho product."

## Sales or Volumetric Analyses

All clients "keep score" by way of periodic sales reports, which can take the form of retail sales figures, warehouse removal data, or orders placed to a central facility.

Although advertising is rarely the only factor in sales success (or failure), it is common for advertisers to look at how advertising expenditures and sales figures correlate.

## Test Marketing

Test markets are an important way to see how products and advertising messages perform in the marketplace.

The speed of competitive response has made this tougher.

Today, competitors can "read" a test market quickly, and, by the time the test is over, a competitive response or product improvement has been prepared. Still, they can be very valuable as they provide a "real world" measurement of market response.

The Campbell's Soup example cited earlier is a good example.

# 2. How to Gather

Earlier we discussed the importance of using secondary research to form the situation analysis. This section will focus on primary research — that which we produce ourselves by employing one or more research designs or data-gathering methods.

## Qualitative and Quantitative

Two basic types of primary research are available.

**Qualitative research,** which typically is conducted in a relatively short period of time among relatively small, non-random samples.

**Quantitative research,** which is typically conducted using large and preferably randomly selected samples.

## Qualitative Approaches

Here are some interesting ways research people have developed to discover consumer thinking about products and brands.

Since people don't usually go around thinking about these things, these techniques help them focus or uncover their feelings and attitudes. In fact, the first technique we'll discuss is called the focus group.

## Focus Groups

Focus group research remains one of the most commonly used qualitative data-gathering methods.

Though definitions may vary slightly, a basic focus group consists of a group of 8 to 12 carefully chosen members of the target audience who are convened for an interview/discussion of up to two hours led by a moderator who follows a discussion agenda.

Often these group sessions are conducted in focus group research facilities whose interview rooms can be viewed by client or agency personnel through a one-way mirror.

Here's an example of an Amdro Fire Ant Killer Focus Group Agenda:

In this case, there were seven segments:

1. The Self-Treatment Process

2. Category Evaluation/Brand Awareness

3. Brand Evaluations

4. Advertising Awareness

5. Purchase Decision Process/Influencers/Retail Environment

6. Packaging

7. An Amdro :30 TV commercial

Here it is in more detail:

### 1. The Self-Treatment Process
- What is it like to have fire ants on your lawn?
- What are the challenges/issues you face in treating for fire ants?
- How did your experience with fire ants last year compare with previous years?

### 2. Category Evaluation/Brand Awareness
- What are the product choices for treating fire ants? Types: liquid, bait (probe for level of understanding of bait vs. contact), powder, granules, etc.

- Which brands have you used? (probe for loyalty)
- Overall, are fire ant treatments effective?
- How do you define effectiveness?
- How long does it take to treat fire ants? Are some products faster/more effective?
- What are the major brands of fire ant treatments?

3. **Brand Evaluations**
   - Probe for images of Spectracide, Amdro, Ortho Fire Ant Killer, GreenLight, Orthene

     a. present board featuring each brand name
     b. first words that come to mind for each
     c. brand collages (as time permits)

   - Does the cost of fire ant products affect your purchase decision?
   - Which are the most expensive? Least expensive?
   - Which are the best value?

4. **Advertising Awareness**
   - Have you heard/seen any ads in the past year for _____?
   - Describe advertising heard/seen
   - What was the major message the ad was trying to communicate?

5. **Purchase Decision Process/Influencers/Retail Environment**
   - How/when do you go about purchasing fire ant treatments (when problem occurs, beforehand, etc.)?
   - How/when do you typically decide which brand to buy (beforehand, in store, etc.)?
   - Where do you purchase fire ant treatments?
   - Describe the "fire ant section" of the store (shelves, displays, etc.).
   - Do you consult with store clerks for information? Are they knowledgeable?
   - Are there other sources you consult? Probe for influencers/sources of information.

6. **Packaging**
   - Participants examine current category packages.
   - Which type of package do you like the best? Why?
   - Could packaging be improved? How? (Note: Participants may resume brand discussion upon encountering packages.)

7. **Amdro :30 TV commercial**
   - What is the main message this TV commercial is trying to communicate?
   - What do you like or dislike about this commercial?
   - Is this message relevant to you?

Proprietary Research © American Cyanamid

---

A focus group can be quite versatile — in addition to discussing a product, participants can also view existing or prospective advertising, sample new or existing products, or engage in a number of projective techniques discussed in the section below.

## One-on-One Interviews

In situations where it is either difficult to convene a focus group or when the topic might not be one easily handled in a group setting, a researcher might opt to conduct one-on-one interviews (sometimes called depth interviews) with selected members of the target audience.

Upper-management personnel or doctors or other busy professionals are often interviewed one-on-one at their convenience, though obviously it is more time-consuming to hold a large number of individual interview sessions than a small number of group interviews.

Another instance where one-on-one interviews might be recommended would be when the subject might be considered personal or sensitive; e.g., financial planning for retirement.

## Observation

Working for Chupa Chups USA, manufacturer of Pop Rocks, Crazy Dips, and other candy brands, Southern Methodist University ad research students observed dozens of nine- to eleven-year-old children as they made candy purchases in mass merchandise outlets and convenience stores.

## Four Eating Styles

Later, they observed the children as they consumed the candy.

Four eating styles were observed. A number of ways of opening the Pop Rocks package were also observed. Below, you can see how this was turned into a very engaging presentation.

This sort of information can be very helpful as you're working to find advertising and product approaches that appeal to your target. And, as a planner, you soon learn that engaging and entertaining presentations seem to help the client and creative team make a better connection with the insights that you are presenting.

## Projective Techniques for Qualitative Interviews

While a direct line of questioning is useful for gathering certain types of information from consumers (e.g., "What was the last brand of jeans you purchased for yourself?"), sometimes the real brand insights are gleaned from less direct, more creative responses to projective lines of questioning.

Projective techniques allow an interview participant to express brand attitudes indirectly through pictures or words or picture/word combinations.

Examples of projective techniques are:

• **Brand collages**

• **Storytelling**

• **Word association**

• **Drawing**

Let's take a look at these interesting approaches.

## Brand Collage

**What's cool?** This collage tells a story – from a 10-year-old's point of view.

Few exercises hold as great a potential for zeroing in on the often subtle differences among brands than the brand collage.

Respondents are provided with hundreds of assorted images clipped from magazines and are asked to choose and mount on a blank sheet of paper those which *"best represent your idea of Brand X."* At the end of the collage exercise, participants are encouraged to explain why they chose the images they did.

In evaluating and interpreting collages, the researcher looks for themes and trends across responses.

## Storytelling

It may sound silly to ask a focus group respondent to write a story about a pair of Reebok basketball shoes visiting the grocery store – *"What time of day did the shoes go food shopping? What conveyance did they arrive in? Which brands did they buy?"* – but it's actually a highly calculated and disarming way of communicating the nuances of brand image and personality using grocery aisles as the responsorial canvas.

If similar grocery shopping stories were produced by consumers for Nike, Adidas, or other brands of athletic shoes, imagine the opportunity for comparison of brand images.

## Word Association

One of the most instructive methods of getting to the bottom-line evaluation (i.e., *"Tell me what you really think?"*) of a product, service, person, or advertisement is to give a consumer a one-word opportunity to size up the entity in question.

One useful way to structure the word association exercise is to ask the consumer to write or say out loud the *first* word that comes to mind after being presented with the brand name, product, or ad.

In marketing communications, first impressions may mean the difference between consumer acceptance or rejection, so the importance of "first-word" associations should not be underestimated.

If "confusing" is the first word used to describe a new ad or strategy statement, the advertiser needs to rethink how to effectively communicate the brand message.

## Drawing

Qualitative research presents a situation in which the expression "a picture is worth a thousand words" most definitely applies.

Allowing participants to express ideas about products or brands through paper-and-pencil illustrations often prompts a quality of response that might not have occurred with direct questioning. Illustrating is particularly useful when interviewing young children who are not yet adept at verbalizing experiences.

# Quantitative Approaches

Quantitative techniques are designed to produce results and information in which you can have a high degree of confidence. Part of this is due to the larger numbers (quantities) of respondents. The other factor is the design of the research.

## Surveys

A sample survey involves measuring a part of a population (called a *sample*) in order to estimate the characteristics of the entire group (as opposed to a *census*, which involves measuring each member of the population).

This enables a researcher to obtain information about products, consumers, and markets by measuring a relatively small percentage of the overall group. Sample surveys are referred to frequently in the advertising industry for information about audience sizes, product usage, and total market size. There are a number of syndicated research reports. There are three, in particular, you should become familiar with.

## Nielsen, MRI, and SMRB

The Nielsen ratings, which are intended to represent the national audience for network programs, are based on a sample of only a few thousand television households.

Nielsens are the current standard for television audience measurement. They also produce other important marketing research related to product sales.

Mediamark Research, Inc. (MRI) and Simmons Market Research Bureau (SMRB) provide this information through annual surveys of 20,000 randomly selected households.

## Samples: Random versus Non-random

In order to ensure the projectability of findings from a sample to the larger population, a randomly selected sample should be used and a sufficient number of responses should be collected.

Randomness ensures that each member of a population has an equal chance of being selected for inclusion in the sample – that no bias is employed in choosing who will be interviewed or measured.

An example of a population could be women age 25 to 49 who have ordered children's clothing through specific mail-order catalogs.

An example of a sample would be 500 such women, randomly chosen from a list of the children's clothing catalog databases.

Professional survey research firms can advise an advertiser about types and sizes of samples and the acceptable resultant degree of sample error.

## Questionnaire Design

Once the sample specifications are decided upon, a questionnaire can be used to measure the desired characteristics of the group.

A questionnaire is an instrument of measurement and, as such, consists of individual items designed to measure specific variables (e.g., awareness of particular brands of children's clothing).

Writing items for a questionnaire begins with formulating question objectives, such as *"to measure brand awareness of cellular telephone services."*

After specifying the objective for the question or questions, then an appropriate questionnaire item can be created.

The section titled "What to Gather" gives examples of specific questions used in advertising surveys.

## Advertising Surveys on the Internet

The Internet has made possible almost instantaneous concept and copytesting possibilities for advertisers. Through pre-screened Internet panels, target-audience consumers are invited to view advertising or advertising concepts over the Internet and then answer a series of questions online.

An advertiser can receive topline results of the Internet survey that same day. Here's an example of types of Internet advertising survey research from Decision Analyst, Inc.

### Internet Questionnaire: from Decision Analyst, Inc.

Types of studies available include:

- Advertising tracking studies
- Awareness, trial, and usage studies (ATUs)
- Conceptor™ new product concept testing
- CopyTest® for radio
- CopyTest® for print ads
- CopyTest® for TV storyboards
- CopyCheck® for early-stage creative
- Customer satisfaction monitoring

- Employee satisfaction tracking
- Package graphics testing
- Optima™ product testing
- Market segmentation studies
- New product concept testing
- Promotion concept testing
- Brand name evaluation
- Strategic positioning studies

# Experiments

When the research question asks about cause and effect (e.g., *"Does twice as much advertising result in twice as many sales?"*), experimental design is needed.

An experiment is a highly choreographed research study in which the effects of one or more independent variables (such as ad spending levels) are measured by noting changes in one or more dependent variables (such as ad awareness, brand attitude, or – sometimes – sales).

## Example: Got Milk? A Focus Group Experiment

As the Got Milk campaign was being developed, the account planners at Goodby Silverstein tried an experimental approach. Traditional focus groups were not generating insights: milk was milk and there was nothing new or exciting.

So, they asked focus group participants to go without milk for two weeks before coming in for the focus group. This was the beginning of what became known as "the deprivation strategy." When the focus group participants arrived after having gone without milk for two weeks, the results were both exciting and insightful. Clearly, there were times when milk was a "must."

This insight was the basis for the entire campaign. Here's how Jeff Goodby, Co-Chairman of Goodby Silverstein & Partners, described the insight-gathering process.

*"If we had started with the idea of milk as a glass of milk you drink alone, we would have ended up addressing the health benefits or the nostalgia of milk. Exactly as had been done in previous campaigns. Exactly wrong.*

*"We looked for the truth about milk.*

*"We asked people to go without milk for two weeks. 'Sure, no problem,' they said. They came back, and told us how hard it was.*

*"What else goes with cereal?*

*"What are you going to do with a fresh-baked chocolate chip cookie?*

*"We arrived at the truth: Milk is never just milk. It is always _____ and milk.*

*"Milk is accompaniment. After that, everything fell into place."*

That's the agency point of view. A little later in this chapter, we'll let you hear from the client: Jeff Manning, Executive Director of the California Milk Processor Board, the industry group for whom Goodby Silverstein originally developed *Got Milk?*

Now it is being used by milk producers nationwide.

And it all started with an experiment.

## Controlled Environments or the Real World

Some experiments take place in controlled environments such as laboratories. For example, that's the proper environment to determine whether certain layout formats achieve the desired eye movement around the page using an "eye camera."

These types of research studies are rather expensive and, not surprisingly, they are fairly rare. They may involve the use of a mechanical measurement device, such as an eye camera, which tracks and records eye movement around a page.

Many experiments in advertising and marketing communication are conducted in the real world, so the effects of independent variables can be gauged under actual marketplace conditions. Such field experiments are expensive, and sometimes they can be quite time consuming, but their results can be very instructive and strategically useful.

### Example: Price Promotion versus Promotional Products

One such field experiment was conducted for the purpose of determining whether price promotion (using discounts) or imprinted promotional products (aka "specialty advertising") would result in greater consumer loyalty to a dry cleaning establishment.

Using a field experiment design involving two treatment groups and one control group, researchers monitored the number of dry cleaner visits and the dollar amount of each visit for nine consecutive months.

The results were almost counterintuitive to what one might expect in the heavily price-promotion oriented dry cleaning business.

The experimental group that periodically received imprinted promotional items (such as sewing kits, stress relievers, and notepads) visited as frequently or more frequently than did the experimental group which received periodic discounts, and it spent as much or more per month than the discount group.

Both the promotional product group and the discount group demonstrated more loyalty (in both sales and visits) than the control group, who received only a letter thanking them for being a customer.

The control group fared far worse than either the promotional products or the discount group.

Results convinced the management of the dry cleaning business to initiate customer retention programs, several of which involved the distribution of promotional products.

## The Importance of Good Information

A lot of time and trouble goes into designing, executing, and then measuring the results of an experiment like this.

But, if you were running a dry cleaning business, or any kind of business, and wanted to know how you could improve it, this kind of information is tremendously valuable.

Sometimes, the only way to really get at how people view a familiar product is to take it away. And, sometimes, the only way to get information like this is to roll up your sleeves, pull out your wallet, and get it done.

# 3. What to Gather

Variables that can be measured in the course of conducting advertising research range from simple awareness of a brand or an ad to actual purchase, and all steps in between. Much advertising research is involved with determining what, if any, communication impact an advertisement might have had.

## Such measures include:

- Brand awareness
- Ad awareness
- Brand knowledge/information
- Ad knowledge/information
- Attitude toward the brand
- Attitude toward the ad
- Purchase conviction/intention
- Actual purchase/sales.

## Example: Nike Research

Here's the kind of work that Nike does on an ongoing basis to stay in touch with their target. (From an interview with Marc Patrick of Nike.)

*"We conduct a qualitative study on the youth, fitness runners, and hardcore runners to understand what motivates them to run, what their perception of Nike is versus our competitors, and how inspiring they view our advertising for a sport that is typically not embraced as well as other sports, like basketball, for example.*

*"At Nike, we consistently track consumer trends and behavior in major markets to stay relevant with our advertising.*

*"While we remain the number one brand in our industry, we always stay abreast of our competitors' advertising activity within each sports category."*

That's an excellent example of staying in touch with your market.

While the planning process tends to focus on qualitative insight-generating techniques, as you can see, sometimes you have to take a thermometer and measure the temperature of your marketplace. That's what these measurements can do for you.

Let's take a look at them and, in general, how they're generated.

## Ad/Brand Awareness

Here's an example of how this measure is achieved.

**Question Objective:** Measure awareness of TV advertising for high-tech companies.

**Recall Question:** *"Please list the names of the technology company or companies you remember having seen advertised on television during the past week."*

**Recognition Question:** *"Which of the following technology companies do you remember seeing television advertising for during the past week?"*

___Microsoft

___IBM

___Apple

___America Online

___Dell

___other (please specify: _____ )

## Ad/Brand Knowledge/Information

Here's an example of how this measure is achieved.

**Question Objective:** Measure perceptions of price promotion for long-distance phone services. *"Which of the following long-distance telephone services is currently offering 10-cent per minute long-distance telephone calls?"*

___Southwestern Bell

___Sprint

___MCI

___Excel

___Other (please specify: _____ )

## Brand Attitude

**Question Objective:** To determine which flavor of a new ice cream is preferred in a taste test. *"Which flavor of ice cream did you enjoy the most overall?"*

___Banana Nut Crunch

____Mocha Roca Munch

____Chocolate Bungee Marshmallow

____Caramel Peanut Topple

____Cherry Almond Avalanche

## Conviction/Purchase Intent

**Question Objective:** To determine purchase intent at the current retail price. *"How likely would you be to buy the flavor you enjoyed the most if it were available at your local grocery for $4.59 per pint?"*

____I would definitely buy it

____I would probably buy it

____I'm not sure whether I would buy it

____I would probably not buy it

____I would definitely not buy it

## Other Measures

Various measures are available, and sometimes multiple measures are appropriate:

- **Awareness:** such as AAU studies of category, brand, and brand advertising
- **Knowledge:** of category, brand, and brand advertising
- **Attitude:** toward category, brand, and brand advertising
- **Conviction:** a surrogate for behavior
- **Behavior/Sales:** Did the cash register ring? When agency TLP ran their Mountain Dew beeper promotion, the results could be measured with actual sales and usage of the beeper.

# A Case Study: Hallmark

Now we'd like to show you how it works when it all works together. The first example we're going to show you was done by students just like you.

It was done by the 1998 winners of the American Advertising Federation National Student Advertising Competition (AAF/NSAC) – George Washington University (GWU).

The client was Hallmark Cards, and the faculty adviser was Dr. Lynda Maddox. Let's take a look at how they put it together.

## Background

Hallmark, one of the most beloved brands in the US, challenged the 250 AAF university chapters to devise an integrated marketing campaign designed to increase brand insistence, not simply brand preference, for its line of greeting cards.

More than 150 schools accepted Hallmark's challenge, and the national winner was GWU, whose student ad agency developed a strategy they called "successful convenience" to move consumers to insist on Hallmark products.

The GWU team designed a detailed research plan, beginning with secondary research. Let's take a look at what they did.

## Marketing Decisions: Major Competitors

### American Greetings.

American Greetings charges for most of its cards, usually in value packs, $14.95 for 20 electronic cards, $9.95 for 10 e-cards, and $1.95 for animated greetings.

- Ranked second in US greeting card market, with 30% share
- First with mass distribution in retail outlets, drugstores, supermarkets, and large retail stores
- Trying to catch up to Hallmark in reaching changing lifestyles and demographics through "The All New American Way"
- Trading on the New York Stock Exchange as of February, 1998
- Partnering with America Online as exclusive provider of e-mail greetings to its 10 million members
- Hallmark's biggest threat

### Gibson Greetings

- Ranked a distant third, with 15% of market share
- Desires to be the leading discount brand
- Distribution 50,000 independent supermarkets, drugstores, and mass merchants

- Allied with Greet Street, which sells 10 greetings for $10 online
- Markets electronic greetings, known as "E-Greetings"
- Caters mostly to price-sensitive shoppers, but also captures convenience-oriented shoppers

### Indirect Competition
- Growth of e-mail
- Greeting card software for personal computers
- Telephone use increasing, with calls less expensive than sending cards. But a greeting card is something tangible. It can be saved.
- Flower companies, such as 1-800-Flowers or FTD

The competitors, however, are not in the same price range as Hallmark.

## Primary Research

### Objectives
- To learn about card buyers decision process
- To assess current levels of brand insistence and loyalty
- To better understand consumer attitudes regarding Hallmark

### Research Tactics
Based on those objectives, the student agency developed a research proposal that used the following research tools:

- Focus Groups
- In-depth Interviews
- Surveys
- Retailer Interviews

Based on this information, they developed a unique and insightful marketing strategy. Their key phrase: "successful convenience."

Here is how that part of the proposal looked.

## Research Proposal: Successful Convenience

Research confirmed that consumers believe Hallmark offers the highest-quality greeting cards. They believe Hallmark has the best quality paper and design, the largest selection, and most importantly, the best writing in the business. In short, they prefer Hallmark.

So why doesn't this result unconditionally in brand insistence?

*The answer lies in the consumer's need for convenience.*

When respondents were asked why they bought from a particular store, 65% cited convenience. Insistence for Hallmark is often thwarted by the consumer's perception of convenience. This often translates to picking up a greeting card when buying a loaf of bread or a carton of milk. It may also mean buying from the closest store.

## Consumer Dissatisfaction

The research shows, however, that a large percentage of card shoppers become dissatisfied at the convenience store, because they cannot find the perfect card. They have a strong need to find the right card and describe stressfully running from store to store to find the perfect card.

In the end, they confess, this hunt-and-peck buying process actually takes so much time that it becomes inconvenient.

*So what really defines convenience?*

The research shows that consumers are beginning to rethink the meaning of convenience. Just as many shoppers today are looking for value, instead of merely low price, our research suggests that many of these same consumers are redefining convenience. If consumers can find the perfect card on the first try, they have "successful convenience."

Our research strongly shows that consumers prefer Hallmark due to its superior level of quality. They want Hallmark. If they believe that by insisting on Hallmark they can actually save time, they will become more loyal insisters. In fact, our research shows that consumers have a greater propensity to seek out and insist on Hallmark when buying for special occasions and people.

## Good Information/Good Results

Based on this thinking, GWU was able to develop some excellent advertising aimed at developing more "loyal insisters."

The GWU campaign illustrates the importance of employing appropriate research methods to answer questions critical to campaign decision making, especially those decisions which require a thorough understanding of consumer motivation.

## Professionals at Work

The GWU work was very professional. Just because you don't have a string of letters after your name doesn't mean you can't do very good, very useful research. And, armed with the information this research provides you, much can be accomplished.

Let's look at one more example. Here, we've put in another creative brief from The Richards Group. And, then, we show you the ad that resulted.

---

### Learjet Creative Brief

Warning: People don't like ads. People don't trust ads. People don't remember ads. How do we make sure this one will be different? *[Source: The Richards Group]*

**Why are we advertising?**

To create excitement about the Learjet 60 as a cost-effective solution to prospects' need for a trans-continental jet and to reinforce Learjet's high performance mystique.

**Who are we talking to?**

High-level corporate executives, corporate fleet managers, and chief pilots who need a corporate jet with trans-continental capability. Learjet buyers are motivated by emotion, but must justify their decision to peers and constituents in rational, financial terms.

**What do they currently think?**

*"I'd love to own a Learjet and get that kind of high performance. But you pay a price: either in dollars, in range, or in comfort. I think they have a transcon jet now, but it's probably just a longer version of their old 55."*

**What would we like them to think?**

*"Learjet does have a jet that will fly my longer missions, and it's not just a stretched version of the 55. And it's cheaper to fly than any transcontinental Hawker, Falcon, or Citation 10."*

---

> **What is the single most persuasive idea we can convey?**
> Learjet performance in a cost-effective transcontinental jet.
>
> **Why should they believe it?**
> - Transcontinental range (2,750 nautical miles) is the highest of jets with comparable performance.
> - Seats up to eight, stand-up room for passengers, stand-up private lavatory.
> - Learjet allure.
>
> **Any creative guidelines?**
> - Call to action: "Call Ted Farid, VP Sales & Marketing."
> - Consider a new themeline.

**How to Save Money on Your Long Distance Calls.**

This ad looks absolutely gorgeous in four colors. And it integrates everything we understand about the product, the target, and the task from the creative brief.

Along the top of the ad, small well-crafted icons deliver key selling points (range, stand-up cabin, and economical fuel consumption), while allowing plenty of room to show the beauty of the plane.

It sells hard. But with the right tone for the target. Good advertising like this doesn't just happen.

## From Information to Inspiration

In general, getting good advertising and good marketing means you have to add one more "I" to your information – Inspiration. From data to information to insight to inspiration.

The visions that helped create important new brands were often based on just a few bits of information.

Pattern recognition helps visionaries see a picture of the future – and it can help us see new opportunities and new ways to connect with consumers.

## The Importance of Insight

Insight into the consumer and the product category is one of the ways effective advertising gets produced.

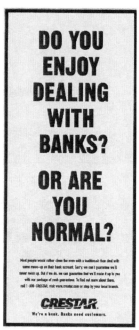

Above to the right, an insight into how people feel about banks leverages a campaign with a theme line that's easy to understand – and one that might make us believe we'll be treated better at this bank.

*"We're a bank. Banks need customers."*

Below that, a bit of humorous and human insight into the purchase decision for a piece of jewelry.

## A 10 Point Planning Process

Here's a simple way to start planning how to get there. [*Source: Successful Advertising Research Methods by Jack Haskins and Alice Kendrick. NTC Books, 1993*]

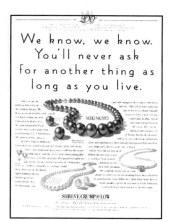

1. Become aware of an advertising problem.
2. Define and clarify the problem.
3. Secondary research: review existing knowledge.
4. Primary research: define one specific problem.
5. Prepare a detailed research plan.

6. Implement the research plan and gather data.
7. Process the data.
8. Interpret the data.
9. Communicate the results.
10. Apply the results to solve the advertising problem.

## Tools for Success

When you face adversity, you want all the help you can get. And you need all the information you can get. That's what this chapter has been about – getting the information you need to solve today's problems and have tomorrow's visions.

There's a lot of opportunity for you to do both in The Business of Brands. And, as long as we're talking about adversity, let's mention a few other challenges you may run into along the way.

# 4. Challenges for the Future

Usually, we evaluate what we're asked to evaluate. And sometimes, you have a little more latitude – sometimes you can actually pick what you want to evaluate. Here are some things we think you should evaluate as you deal with information in tomorrow's marketplace.

- **Data overload**

- **Innumeracy**

- **Low-quality qualitative information**

- **Information cost**

## The Blur of Diversity

Alvin Toffler observed that once, in a mass market economy, it was "one size fits all." Today, in our diverse economy and diverse society, information is also diverse – you can find an example of almost everything. This diversity of opportunity is a wonderful thing, but for marketers concerned with accumulating good-sized audiences and markets, it can make finding the right answer even more daunting.

As marketers, we'll all have to deal with this. It's all the more reason you have to be very clear-headed about the information you're going after

— even though there's a lot of information lying around, it might not be the right information.

Let's look at some other challenges you may face.

## Data Overload

When there were only three networks, it wasn't that tough to know what was on TV every night. With over a hundred, it's impossible. Today, we often have to deal with too much data — without a channel changer in sight.

In business, where we have to turn that data into useful and actionable information, that can be a real problem. The good news is there are a lot of jobs out there for someone good at turning all of those numbers into something useful.

The bad news is there sure are a lot of numbers out there. And, sad to say, there are a lot of people who aren't as good at working with those numbers as you might hope.

UPC scanning data, survey data, and all those other bits of information we can generate in our information-rich environment means we'll all have to get real good at knowing how to manage all of that data — and edit it into the information we need.

## Innumeracy

Innumeracy is like illiteracy, only with numbers. When we're "GAF" (Good at Figures), numbers on a spreadsheet mean something. We can extract what we need to know.

When we're not GAF, it's a blur. And, for a lot of people out there, that's what it is — a blur. Don't let one of those innumerate ones be you.

That said, becoming GAF isn't all that easy. Because data overload means we often get a lot of numbers — but not exactly the numbers we need. We have to know how to work with those numbers — and to recognize what's useful and what isn't.

Work to make sure you don't grow up innumerate. One way is to become familiar and comfortable with good numbers. By that we mean the kinds of worked-out data that are clear and useful.

Learn to read a *Nielsen* study. And one from *IRI.*

Look at readership scores.

Get a feel for how good information looks and feels.

Then start to get involved in generating your own information. The AAF/NSAC is a great place to start.

Design a survey for a class project. See what you discover. You'll find that 100 opinions on a survey will really open your eyes about how others view the world.

And the fact that you helped create that information… well, you just might like the way that makes you feel.

## Low Quality Qualitative Information

Everybody has an opinion. And, you can probably find at least one example that "proves" almost anything. Should we drive more slowly? You can show where someone driving too slowly caused an accident.

Should we wear seat belts? You can probably find an example where, under some circumstances, it was a problem. Still, we shouldn't speed and we should wear our seat belts.

Focus groups are one place where it's very common for marketers and advertisers to have "information accidents." A loudly held opinion can sway a room full of people who don't care that much. A distracted moderator can let things get off track.

An important executive watching the focus group may only be capable of hearing what he or she wants to hear. That lady on the end agrees with you – she's smart, represents the consumer, and proves that you've got the answer, even though it's only one opinion.

And, no surprise, you might not like that other person at the other end of the table who didn't much like your ad – and you manage to tune out what he or she is saying.

Getting qualitative information, while it is fun and stimulating, can also be imprecise and contradictory. Be careful. Don't have an accident. Don't just go out to prove your bias by finding a few agreeable folks in a mall. Remember, we often learn more from the people who disagree with us a bit. Listen. Buckle up and figure it out.

The real gift of qualitative research is when it can open our eyes and help us see the world in a whole new way.

## The Cost of Information

Good information can be expensive – in money and time. And, since the payoff is sometimes distant or uncertain, and resources are always a little tight, it's an easy expense to cut.

This is another challenge – and it's one you might be able to meet early in your career.

First, good information doesn't have to be expensive. Digging into secondary sources might get you just the help you need. Can't afford a focus group? Talk to some customers.

One-on-one interviews, done by someone who really cares (you) and who isn't afraid of a little hard work (you again), can really get a project rolling. And it's just amazing that, when a little bit of good information gets everyone feeling a little bit smarter, you can often find the money to get a little more. Because, after all, who doesn't want to feel smarter?

## Keep Doing It

Nike, one of today's smart companies, has an ongoing commitment to staying in touch with their customers – and staying ahead of their competition.

The same commitment to winning that old runners (like Nike founder Phil Knight) or young runners (like Marc Patrick) bring to their job is a big part of what it takes to win in the marketplace. Evaluation, like athletic training, is what smart companies do.

Scorekeeping is OK. Winning is better.

# Summary

In this piece, we covered ways that the systematic gathering of information can help answer questions and solve problems.

- The key "apertures" or opportunities where research can play a valuable role.
- Various research tools available to answer those questions and solve those problems.
- The types of information that need to be gathered.
- We showed you how this information can be the key ingredient in inspiring better marketing and advertising.
- Finally, some answers may not be advertising at all. As you look at the inherent advantages of your brand, information and inspiration might lead to exciting new territory.

We began by defining research as, *"the systematic gathering of information to answer a question or solve a problem."*

Now let's finish with a few more ways to develop those skills.

# Things to Do:

Here are some ways to get some exercise on these topics:

## 1. Questionnaire Questions

Write four questionnaire objectives for a survey research project whose purpose is to determine what is considered "cool" among undergraduate students at your university.

After you've written the objectives, write 10 (total) questions, which correspond to the four objectives.

## 2. Four Research Stages

Using the brand of your choice, discuss possible research efforts at each of the four research stages or apertures:

- Planning Research
- Developmental Research
- Implementation Research
- Measuring Results

## 3. Internet Information Search

Using search engines on the Web, locate, summarize, and analyze five information sources about a product or product category.

In your analysis, be sure to ask, *"How current is this information?"* and, *"What is the original source of the information?"*

Does the information appear to be credible/believable?

## 4. Brand Collage Exercise

Clip up to 300 images and words from magazines. Ask five people to choose and tape down any three of those clippings which they believe illustrate what a specific brand, television show, etc., is like. Ask participants to explain why they chose the images they did.

**Bonus:** Choose a campus program or philanthropy as your "brand" and diplomatically share the results with the program administrator. You'll be surprised at the undivided attention you will get for your research efforts.

# Concepts & Vocabulary:

**Account planning** – System of planning advertising. Relies heavily on qualitative consumer research and representing the consumer at all stages of ad development; originated in London in the 1960s.

**Apertures** – Term borrowed from photography to refer to opportunities or "openings" for results of research to be applied to the development of effective advertising messages.

**AAU (Awareness Attitude Usage)** – Survey of consumers to determine knowledge and use of brands and brand advertising in a category of products or services; also called tracking studies.

**Brand collage** – Qualitative research exercise. Focus group participants select and arrange images cut from magazines to represent their impressions of a specific brand.

**Copy testing** – Consumer evaluation of rough or finished advertising; can be conducted in focus groups or in large-scale surveys.

**Creative brief** – Agency document which contains advertising strategy, specifically the reason for advertising, the target market, consumer perceptions, and how advertising can change them.

**Demographic data** – Quantitative information describing age, income, education, marital status, employment, etc., of target audience.

**Developmental research** – Information gathering among consumers to determine appropriate advertising strategy; takes place before advertising is created.

**Experiment** – Highly structured research method which involves determining the effects of a stimulus (independent variable) on the behavior of a particular sample (dependent variable); can be conducted in a research laboratory or under marketplace conditions (field experiment).

**Feedback** – Responses of a target audience to marketing communications messages; used by advertisers to gauge effectiveness of advertising and to take steps to make it more effective.

**Focus group** – Gathering of up to 12 members of a target market for a discussion of a brand and its advertising. Led by moderator who follows agenda of questions/topics. Usually lasts two hours.

**Innumeracy** – Numerical form of illiteracy; can't use numbers.

**Lexis/Nexis** – A proprietary database, available by subscription, which includes periodical articles and press releases about new product news, marketing developments, and market share.

**One-on-one interviews** (also called monadic or depth interviews) – An in-depth data-gathering method which requires that an interviewer question one participant at a time; specified in situations where the topic being discussed is considered sensitive to the participant or where convening a focus group is not possible.

**Pattern recognition** – Ability to see the whole picture based on just a few points of information.

**Primary research** – Gathering and analysis of original information from a sample or population (see secondary research).

**Projectability** – The ability to generalize or extrapolate findings from a relatively small study or survey to a larger group or population; random sample surveys have the highest projectability.

**Qualitative research** – Systematic information-gathering activities which do not involve the assignment of numbers to results (see quantitative research); includes focus group interviews, one-on-one interviews, observation, and other techniques.

**Quantitative research** – Systematic information-gathering activities which result in analysis of numerical data collected from a sample; includes sample surveys, experiments, analysis of sales data, etc.

**Questionnaire** – Instrument of measurement used in a survey research effort; contains items (questions) which result from a list of objectives arranged in a way easily understood by a respondent.

**Randomness** – The principle that each member of a specified population or group had an equal chance of being selected for inclusion in a sample to be studied.

**Research** – The systematic gathering of information to answer questions and solve problems.

**Sample** – A subset of a population or large group designated for measurement; samples can be selected randomly or nonrandomly.

**Secondary research** – Gathering and analysis of information which is available in published form, i.e., printed or online sources.

**Situation analysis** – Written evaluation of marketplace factors affecting a specific brand and its category competitors; this document is used as a basis for marketing and advertising strategy.

**Storytelling** – Qualitative research technique. Participants create a fictional scenario involving a specific brand in order to provide insight into brand personality (e.g., Describe what would happen if L'Oréal and Suave shampoos went on a double date with two brands of beer—please specify which brands of beer would be involved).

**Survey** – Systematic measurement of a subset of a population for the purpose of projecting the results to the entire population.

**Word association** – Interview technique. Participants are asked to write or say words or phrases which come to mind when a specific brand name is mentioned; used to obtain insight into brand personality and status.

# Seven Exercises
## Techniques and Tools To Help You Become a Better Planner

## By Alice Kendrick

*Professor, Temerlin Advertising Institute,*
*Southern Methodist University*

*This piece is adapted and expanded from Alice's original work in*
*Chapter 11 of* Advertising & the Business of Brands.

## Introduction

I USED TO PLAY A BIT OF TENNIS.* I even coached it some.**

That's when I learned that helping others learn is really a lot different than working on your own game. With that in mind, I've been working on the kind of exercises that can help you develop the right kind of "inner game" for planning – both the right mind set for understanding consumers and the necessary basic skills – listening, observing, analyzing, and presenting – that you need to "win" in the competitive marketing world.

These are the training exercises that have, so far, made the cut.

We use them in our classes at SMU at the Temerlin Advertising Institute, and with our AAF/NSAC teams. We've developed some of them during our summer classwork in London, where we really concentrate on the planning mindset.

Incidentally, studying a slightly different culture can be a great way for you to develop the necessary mindset. All too often, we carry around quite a few unspoken cultural assumptions that can really get in the way of our observing things clearly.

When we go live in another world – such as London – it's easier to see that even though we may all speak the same language, we can live in very different worlds.

So these seven exercises are designed to help you learn to see the different worlds that are all around us with a new perspective. They'll help teach you how to analyze and synthesize information in such a way as to develop useful insights.

Finally, some of these exercises will show you ways to present your findings to other people (who also aren't exactly like you) and help them internalize the insights and perspectives that you've discovered so that they can use those new perspectives to develop more effective communication.

## A Quick Summary

Sometimes it's best to "tell 'em what you're going to tell 'em." This helps everyone get ready for the information you're going to present. With that in mind, here's a quick summary of the exercises and the skills they'll help you develop.

**1. Ethnography: Estate Sale Investigator (ESI).** You're going to do some detective work. This will develop your observational and synthesis skills. Your deliverable for this project will be a list of 'hunches,' complete with supporting evidence, such as photographs.

**2. Target Consumer Presentation: "We've Got You Covered."** This is a two-part project. First, you have to 'walk a mile in another's shoes' via observation, participant-observation and depth interviews.

Then, you concept a new magazine for that type of consumer.

The deliverable for this project will be a **Magazine Cover** – a mock-up of a new magazine, complete with title, visuals, teaser headlines, and even an explanatory table of contents designed to reflect consumer insights. This will help you with both the groundwork you need to do and then the creative work you'll need to do to put together an effective presentation.

**3. Dear Diary, The Reality Check is in the Mail.** This exercise will help you come to grips with the always surprising reality that what people say they do is different from what they actually do.

In this case, that person is you – and the deliverable will be a diary and a photographic record of some of your actual purchase behavior. It will also teach you about one of the tools we use to track behavior – the diary.

**4. The DOG Book (<u>D</u>aily <u>O</u>bservational <u>Gee</u>Whiz).** This disarmingly simple assignment can be completed simply by writing down (or drawing, or cutting out and pasting) an interesting daily observation – either in your regular day planner, or one you dedicate to these daily observations. This is affectionately known as "The DOG Book."

We first did this in London, but you don't really have to fly to London to get started. The purpose is to help you develop the skill of looking at the world with fresh eyes, to investigate why some things are the way they are, to describe phenomena that are taken for granted but not always articulated, and to seek to learn various way of referring to rituals, practices and products.

The deliverable will be one you'll want to keep – a compilation of your daily observations and any accompanying explanations of what you observed.

**5. The R.I.P. Rap (The Brand Eulogy).** This is an exercise in virtual and/or actual deprivation of an existing product, service, or brand. The skill you'll develop is an improved ability to generate a new perspective on a topic that might seem ordinary.

It's also a fun way to exercise your presentation skills. In this exercise, students must ask themselves and those they interview and observe how they would feel and what they would do if a particular brand or product decided to 'retire,' died (i.e. RIP = Rest in Peace), or was otherwise not available.

The deliverable will be an obituary/memoir/eulogy which you will have to deliver. The script for this piece, by way of key quotes, facts and examples, will communicate insights gleaned from your research in a dramatic and entertaining way. The in-class part of this exercise can be a lot of fun.

**6. People Who Aren't Like Me (And What I Learned from Them).** This is more like an agency assignment in the real world, where you have to go learn about something with which you have no personal experience.

**7. Easy as ABC: Apertures, Behaviors, and Clues.** How do consumers go about determining what 'normal' behavior is regarding product use, and anything else. What's the best way to reach them? What are the behaviors associated with this product? And what are the clues and cues that help you generate useful insights? This will require that you do a lot of observing and questioning.

If you're doing this in a class, your instructor will set out the ground rules for your particular situation. If you're learning on your own (congratulations on your initiative), we hope that these instructions and guidelines will help you get it done.

Ready? Let's get started.

## Exercise 1: Ethnography: ESI
## You Become an Estate Sale Investigator

You're going to do some Estate Sale Investigation. This is a great way to get started as an investigator. Estate Sales are full of clues. You're going to want to focus on observational and synthesis skills. Your clues will be the people and things you'll find at an estate sale. Naturally, this involves visiting an estate sale — so the first thing you'll have to do is find one. They're usually listed in the local newspaper. If you can't find an estate sale listing, a single-household garage sale or yard sale will do. Try to find a big one so you have more 'data' to sift through.

**Insight Investigation.** What you want to discover is insights about the people whose belongings you must study without benefit of an interview. Eavesdropping is allowed.

**Your ESI Report.** The deliverable for this project is a list of 'hunches,' complete with supporting evidence and photographs. This will develop your observational and synthesis skills. Remember, eavesdropping is allowed.

## Exercise 2: "We've Got You Covered"
## Your Magazine Cover Assignment

The final product of this consumer research assignment is a mocked up magazine cover complete with magazine title, cover story and "art" (suggested visuals would be fine, especially if your art direction skills aren't completely honed), and additional teaser headlines on the cover indicating other stories inside.

Every element of your mock-up magazine cover must indicate your understanding of and familiarity with the target audience.

In addition to the cover, you should attach a rationale – about one-page typed – with a few sentences explaining each editorial decision (each cover element).

To gather your information and insights for your new magazine, you need to conduct personal interviews (with the help of a discussion guide) with at least five members of a particular target market. Examples might be high school juniors/seniors deciding where to attend college, students who eat on the campus cafeteria meal plan, customers of a local ice cream shop, members of a yoga or exercise class, etc.

You also need to attach the discussion guide.

Review what you have learned carefully, then distill your information into "stories" or topics that reflect the activities, interests, motivations, information needs, desires, fears of your target market. Now you're ready to become a consumer insight publisher.

First, you need to name your magazine (go ahead and use those creative juices, but remember that everything you do must be dictated by your learnings, and not clever plays on words).

Take your list of learnings/insights and start to write headlines or blurbs for each.

This list and your notes will also help you put together your rationale.

Consider alternatives for your cover photograph/art.

What would draw your target audience in?

Finally, in the address label part of the cover, write a creative fictitious address, that is also on strategy for your publication (Example: A.B. Student, 18 Crossroads Lane, Upwardly Mobile, NY).

Your presentation will have:

1. **Your magazine cover**

2. **Your rationale**

3. Your discussion guide

4. **Anything else you think might help you "sell" your magazine concept.** For example, a short report on your discussions with learnings and insights.

# Exercise 3: Dear Diary, The Reality Check is in the Mail

First, you need to predict what, where, and how you will spend money in the upcoming week and, then, document your actual out-of-pocket spending via diary and photos of what you actually purchased.

This assignment is designed to demonstrate the differences between reported behavior and conviction, and actual behavior. It also serves as an opportunity to introduce you to the use of a diary as a method of information gathering.

The deliverable for this project will be a photo-essay or your week as a consumer – and a quantitative analysis (using charts and graphs) of a spending-week-in-the-life-of you. You can be creative in your visual presentation, but your numerical/quantitative presentation will have to be clear and rigorous. And don't forget the insights.

## Step One: Get a Diary

Any notebook will do – after all, you just have to keep track for a week.

## Step Two: Make Your Predictions

It's OK to use your calendar. Predict how much you'll spend each day – newspaper, coffee, magazine, movie. (By the way, if your prediction is 100% "on the money," we probably won't believe you.)

## Step Three: Keep Track of Your Spending Every Day

Sometimes it helps to make a note of your cash at the beginning of the day and leave a place to clip or staple all receipts.

## Step Four: List and Compare

Do some number crunching. Any surprises? Try to build some interesting statistics – Media vs. Latte expenditures by day, etc.

## Step Five: Add Insights and Build Your Presentation

What did you discover? How do diaries work? What are the strengths? What are the problems? How will you present your financial report? What have we learned about you as a financial animal?

# Exercise Four: "The DOG Book"
# Daily Observational GeeWhiz = DOG

Among other things, account planners take on the role of professional observer/sleuth/purveyor of insight. Sometimes that simply means being a bit more observant than you normally are, and possibly trying to understand something you've never really given a lot of thought to or just taken for granted.

Every day for a period of one week, you will demonstrate your observational and information-gathering skills by producing a Daily Observational GeeWhiz (DOG).

At the end of the week, compile your DOGs into a brief report.

Here are some examples of DOGs.

• **"Process DOG"**: how things work; explain "it" for us as if we know nothing about "it." How does a commercial dry cleaner actually clean your clothes without using water? How do highly trafficked grocery stores that are open 24 hours manage to clean and wax their floors?

• **DOG Decoder**: what things mean, expressions you've heard. What words do sixth-graders use for "cool"? What words do 60-year-olds use for "cool"? Visit a local printing or paper company. Ask for some samples. What words are used to describe the various types of paper?

• **Name that DOG**: Account planners strive to succinctly and creatively communicate their consumer learnings to a host of others in the agency — creatives, media planners, and account executives.

By assigning an original name/label on a consumer experience or phenomenon, you can demonstrate that you understand an experience and/or phenomenon, as well as the fact that you can communicate it creatively by way of a unique expression or combination of words.

**An Example:** One student who studied in London and had to navigate busy "tube" (train) stops each day used "The Treadmill Tube Walk" to describe her inclination to continue to walk quickly even once she climbed the steps from the train and emerged on the street. She likened the experience to the feeling you get when you first step off of a treadmill. It is easy to see how she had to thoroughly understand the challenges of tube transportation to create an expression that uniquely captured the experience.

Done well, this exercise will help put "new eyes" in your head – and you'll start seeing things with a fresh new perspective.

## Exercise Five: The R.I.P. Rap
## You Deliver a Brand Eulogy.

This is an exercise in virtual and/or actual deprivation of an existing product, service, or brand. Students must ask themselves, and those they interview and observe, how they would feel and what they would do if a particular brand or product decided to 'retire,' died (i.e. R.I.P., Rest in Peace), or was otherwise not available.

The deliverable is an obituary/memoir/eulogy script which, by way of key quotes, facts and examples, communicates insights gleaned from your research. Be prepared to deliver your eulogy in person to your 'brand team congregation.' Dress appropriately.

## Exercise Six: People Who Aren't Like Me
## I'm not myself. And what I learned from it.

The purpose of this Qualitative Research Assignment is to allow you to study behavior, motivations, language, and issues associated with product usage or behavior that you do not engage in yourself. It represents an opportunity for you to immerse yourself in something you have no personal experience with.

The assignment involves interviewing and observing people who qualify as your participants, analyzing the information you gather, and communicating your findings. Keep in mind that this isn't a large-scale sample survey, so you're looking for insights, trends, motivations, processes, consumer "rituals," consumer language for the product/category, and so forth.

## Suggested Activities

**I. Determine the desired product usage/behavior you wish to study** (such as playing computer games if you do not play, coloring one's hair if you don't, shaving one's face if you don't, etc.). Please note: cigarette smoking is *NOT* a good choice here (trust me), nor are other true addictions.

Depending on how extensive this assignment is for your particular class, your instructor may wish for you to conduct secondary research in the library before beginning your participant selection and interviews.

**2. Determine how you will connect with your group.** Since you will only be required to interview a small number of people, consider ways you might refine a set of screening questions to obtain a more homogeneous group of subjects.

For instance, try not to mix heavy users (professional skydivers) with light users (jumped out of a plane once on a bet). Go with one or the other.

**3. Write a series of screening questions** to qualify your potential participants based on the criteria established in #1 and #2 above.

**4. Recruit your participants and arrange visits/interviews with them**, as well as observation of others. You need to find a balance between talking to people, observing their behavior and the behavior of others, and participating in the activity yourself (this is not required, so do so at your own risk!). I suggest 5 depth interviews of at least 30 minutes each and some additional observation, depending on your topic.

**5. Compose a discussion guide for your interviews.** Your guide should include sections addressing: detailed description of behavior/product usage (including use occasions), specific language associated with the behavior/product usage, motivations involved in using the product, history of involvement with the product, brand considerations, and issues associated with the product usage.

Often the use of a deprivation-type question is useful. It's also very helpful to use one or more projective techniques such as word association, storytelling, brand/activity collage, etc. to add texture and depth to your analysis.

**6. Conduct your interviews.** I suggest one-on-ones or dyads. Consider tape recording, photographing, videotaping or taking notes to facilitate your report-writing.

**7. Compile and analyze your "data."**

**8. Write your report** using a standard research report format such as the following:

> Title
>
> Study Objectives
>
> Method – how you selected participants, how you gathered information
>
> Findings – Main "learnings" and your INSIGHTS (you can follow the discussion guide outline for this section, which will be longer than other sections).
>
> Conclusions
>
> Suggestions for Future Research

- **Papers will range from 5-10 pages in length.**

- **Oral reports need not be dull and boring.** Successful reports in the past have included (if appropriate and tasteful) "dressing the part," videotape segments, audiotaped interviews, role-playing, collage analysis or other projective technique presentation, photos, movie clips, demonstrations, and the list goes on.

Use your imagination to communicate your insights as effectively as you can!

# Exercise Seven: Easy as ABC
# Apertures, Behaviors, and Clues

How do consumers go about determining what "normal" behavior is regarding product use, and anything else. What's the best way to reach them? What are the behaviors associated with this product? And what are the clues and cues that help you generate useful insights? This will require that you do a lot of observing and questioning.

**Apt Apertures:** The importance of the consumer aperture has been mentioned throughout this book. Find examples of just the right place-ment/timing for a marketing communications message (strategically placed outdoor boards, daypart timing for radio spots, etc.), and explain the specific consumer aperture that inspired the advertisement or pro-motion, and other possible tactics the marketing communicator might have considered.

**Behaviors:** As consumers, we often develop almost ritualistic behaviors with a product or service. Understanding them can be an important tool not only for future product design but also for a marketer to communicate knowingly with a target audience.

Animals move through certain 'adumbrations' as they act — a snake handler could fill you in on this, and you've probably witnessed your cat's behavior in the litterbox or your dog circling a favorite nap spot before coming in for a landing. Well, we humans can be creatures of habit, too.

Habits often kick in as we repeatedly integrate use of products into our lives. If you drink coffee or tea, think of your ritual and how it compares to the behavior of others at the coffee shop. Completing this assignment will require a lot of observation and some discussion as well.

**Clues and Cues:** Sales guru Chris Lytle discovered "triggering events" from his accountant. For example, moving into a new apartment or com-ing back to school is a triggering event that starts all sorts of additional behaviors.

Now, what are the clues and cues that can help us with what we're studying?

For example, does getting one thing mean you need something else?

If you make or buy dip, can the chips be far behind?

Sometimes very effective co-promotions are born of the realization that certain products and services are compatible or linked in some way — the idea of travel agents or even airlines linking you to bookseller websites or stores — unrelated as the activities are, many people read for pleasure when they're traveling, even on business.

To find clues, you need to become a bit of a detective — talk to an auto mechanic to discover clues about customer satisfaction for cars, talk to a sales clerk to find out what's hot among certain age groups in the retail environment, etc.

**The deliverable for this assignment** is a report and presentation, complete with some sort of demonstration — either involving video, still photography, or 'acting out' what you've observed.

Apertures, behaviors, and clues and cues related to how consumers relate to the product or service. You are also required to use the alphabet to fashion descriptive names for the phenomena you are studying to better facilitate understanding and memorability among the brand team (a.k.a your class) — for example, "Moment of Trash," a play on words about life's moments of truth apertures, might be used to describe the split-second tinge of guilt felt by some who don't recycle aluminum cans as they look one last time at the recyclable container and take aim for the garbage can.

## A Final Note: Learning Can be Fun

If some of these exercises seem like they'd be kind of cool to do, it's because they are. Discovering insights into others and ourselves is one of the most exciting aspects of learning, and it is one of the most critical jobs in marketing.

If you have time to do all these exercises in class, terrific. But if not, tuck them under your pillow (figuratively) and when you think your planning skills need a bit of healthy exercise, why not try one of them and see what happens.

After all, in tennis and in planning, good exercise and lots of practice makes you a better player. Good luck.

---

\* NOTE: Before she was Professor Alice Gagnard Kendrick, Alice Gagnard played tennis competitively in the State of Louisiana.

\*\* While at Marquette University, Prof. Kendrick was also coach of the Marquette Women's Tennis Team.

# Consumer Insight:
# Getting in Character

## By Lisa Fortini-Campbell, Ph.D.

*This article was written in 1998 by the influential consumer insight author and consultant, Lisa Fortini-Campbell. She is the author of the consumer insight classic,* Hitting the Sweet Spot, *from which this article is taken. As president of the Fortini-Campbell Company, she has developed consumer insight education programs for Ford, Kraft, Hewlett-Packard, Motorola, and others. She also teaches as an adjunct professor at Northwestern University's Kellogg School of Management.*

I'VE ALWAYS BEEN A GREAT FAN OF MOVIES and the theater. Some of my happiest memories are of hours spent watching fine actors in beautiful settings and wonderful costumes do their work. I've always enjoyed the pure entertainment value of these performances, but the older I get, the more fascinated I am by the way the performers create their magic.

By "magic" I don't mean the special effect *tours de force* that films have become today. Instead, I mean the seemingly simple power of human actors and actresses to take on other personas, speak with other voices, and feel other emotions whenever they step into their characters' shoes. And because they can feel those lives, I can too. Actors and actresses can *persuade* me. They make me believe their characters are so real that at times I've laughed out loud and other times I've found tears streaming down my face at nothing more than an image on a screen. Sometimes, I even have become so thoroughly engrossed in a performance, that when I came out of the theater, it was my *own* life that seemed unreal and I needed an hour or so to reorient myself. This is the magic that film and stage can spin so well, even without the sensory boost of IMAX, surround sound, or virtual reality helmets.

We tend to take this magic for granted, but isn't it really quite amazing? I've always wanted to know how actors cast their spells. How do they persuade us that they are actually someone else, and make us feel more for them in our short two-hour acquaintance than we might for the real person behind the character after a much longer time? How do they manage to evoke in us true emotion – admiration or contempt, affection or hatred?

And I'm especially amazed by actors who animate and inhabit their characters so well that the actors themselves are barely recognizable from one role to the next. Consider Ralph Fiennes, who has the range to be both the hateful German concentration camp commandant in *Schindler's List* and the enormously sympathetic romantic lead in *The English Patient*. Or, for those of you who are fans of older movies, think about the range Robert DeNiro has displayed playing Travis Bickle in *Taxi Driver* and then Jake LaMotta in *Raging Bull*. And if you want a real study in contrast, see Angela Lansbury's performance in *The Manchurian Candidate* and then watch her in the role she made famous in the TV series, *Murder, She Wrote*. The list could go on and on. Meryl Streep as a Danish countess in *Out of Africa* and a concentration camp survivor in *Sophie's Choice*. Daniel Day-Lewis as a paraplegic in *My Left Foot*, an American Brahmin in *The Age of Innocence*, a frontiersman in *The Last of the Mohicans*, and a courageous athlete in *The Boxer*.

I find these transformations remarkable enough from my seat in the audience, but they are even more thought-provoking to me in my professional role as a marketer. I think we can learn important lessons from the interesting similarities and differences between what we do to market products and what actors do to move an audience. Like film and stage, our business of marketing is one of *persuasion*. That fundamental similarity is why acting can teach us something useful.

There are differences between acting and marketing, of course, and understanding those will help us too. One obvious difference is that we marketers want to evoke the emotions of a target market as part of persuading them to buy a product or service, to vote for a candidate, to continue doing something or to start doing something else. For an actor, however, the emotional impact on the audience at a particular moment in time is the point itself. The actor creates and sells illusions while the marketer uses illusions to sell something else. The actor must seek insight into a *character* – not into the audience – to create a more perfect illusion; the marketer must seek insight into the *audience* to be more persuasive.

The actor strives to draw the audience in by making the illusion as real, or authentic, as possible. To achieve that, the actor seeks to understand the character so well that he knows what the character would think and do in a variety of circumstances. The actor gets "in character" by acquiring *insight* into the character. Ultimately, the actor must persuade someone to buy the illusion. A member of the audience must be willing to pay for the chance to engage with the character the actor portrays.

And it is with this that the similarities between acting and marketing begin. Marketers must bring the same level of authenticity to their understanding of their target consumers that actors bring to the portrayal of their characters. When we do that, our chances of persuading – and making a sale – increase dramatically. Researchers and account planners must embody this understanding as thoroughly as an actor does in order to help their colleagues in product development, marketing, and advertising infuse their own activities with what I call true "insight."

The tantalizing possibility is that because what both actors and marketers do is try to uncover "insight" – one into characters and the other into consumers – then what the actor does to gain insight into a character can actually help us gain better insights into the consumers we study. Those of you who strive for insight, whatever your specific jobs, know how hard it can be to find. Anything that makes that easier is welcome indeed, because we marketers can use all the help we can get! Indeed, I think our lack of insight causes us to fail to persuade consumers with our products and marketing programs far more often than the typical actor fails at his or her task, despite the disproportionate effort and resources we put into understanding consumers and into developing and testing marketing activities of all kinds. But, perhaps our job is harder than acting because we're not just trying to be entertaining or cathartic but to actually affect someone's behavior. If so, then we need to become even better at understanding consumers than actors are at understanding characters. That's a serious challenge indeed. We have a far distance to go to catch, let alone to surpass, the finest practitioners of the acting craft.

So how do we improve? First, let me be very specific about the root cause of our difficulties and failures: too often we are satisfied with only the most rudimentary and superficial understanding of the consumers with whom we are trying to communicate, and we act on that shallow understanding without bothering to delve any deeper. Our skills of consumer understanding are weak and flaccid. We think to know a little is to know enough. No self-respecting actor would ever fall into this trap of arrogance. To do so would risk a silly, superficial performance, cat-calls from the audience, and the opprobrium of every movie critic in the country. Get too many "thumbs down," single "stars," or "dog bones" and an actor might never show his face in Hollywood again.

I think our problems as marketers start with the way we describe our targets and how quickly and easily we leap from simple demographics to what we think is an insight. Target descriptions that refer to nothing more than general demographics and simple purchase-history statistics are trite, superficial, and far too common. And worse, we think we know a lot because we know the target consumer is a woman, 25-54, with a $40,000-plus income, and three-plus children, who buys one or more gallons of orange juice a week. And there we stop, rather than begin the really hard process of thinking. We go from describing targets, and perhaps identifying some equally superficial product or brand "motivation," to writing strategies and crafting marketing communications. Can you imagine what would happen if actors tried to work that way?

Imagine you're Dustin Hoffman and your director has told you to play an out-of-work actor who impersonates a woman to get a job on a soap opera. She's short, middle-aged, a fussy dresser, with a Southern accent. That's it. You're handed your lines and told to go to it! You couldn't, could you? Neither could Dustin Hoffman. Before he'd even attempt it, he'd want to know the answers to all kinds of questions. What motivates this character? Why is he unemployed? What made him think of trying cross-dressing? What are his aspirations? What are his vulnerabilities? Why? Why? Why? Without the answers, even the gifted Dustin Hoffman would have difficulty interpreting the part.

Even Marlon Brando couldn't do it if you told him to play a 60-ish head of an Italian Mafia family who's trying to keep all of the other Mafia families in town from taking over his territory. And neither could Meryl Streep if you told her to play a rich Danish countess who buys a coffee farm in Africa. They would all have to understand more — more detail, and particularly more motivation. So much so that the classic actor joke is always someone with a bit part and one line pestering the director with the question: "So what's my motivation?"

Of course, Hoffman, Brando, or Streep might be able to invent the details of a fictitious character — after all, why can't the actor do that as well as a writer? But a marketer is trying to understand someone who really does exist, someone we must represent insightfully, truthfully, and fairly. Our job is a little tougher than acting, but the principles are the same.

In both cases, everything hinges on understanding motivation. Motivation is central to insight. Insight is central to empathy, and empathy is central to the power to persuade. Actors may sometimes overdo this sort of analysis, but at least they do it. And to be fair, we marketers try to seek motivation, too. Usually, however, we seek it too narrowly. We look for it only in the behavior of the consumer with respect to the product or brand. We don't consider the consumer as a whole person. We rarely look at how or why behavior grows out of deeper motivations. What if actors did that?

Pretend you're Meryl Streep playing Karin Blixen (Isak Dinesen) in *Out of Africa*. Your coffee warehouse has burned down, your fields have flooded, you're out of money, and your lover has just died in a plane crash. You have to sell out and go home to Denmark. Now play the scene. Give the speech at your lover's funeral. Of course, this is an impossible test because most of you are replaying the scene from the movie. But consider what you might have done if you hadn't already seen Streep's performance and you didn't have the lines from the script. You'd have to understand the character well enough to say what Blixen/Dinesen would have said. Would it help to know that you're also saying good-bye to your farm, your loyal workers, your friends, your adopted country, to years of work, as well as to the beloved man snuffed out in an instant? Even more, you're saying good-bye to the last vestige of your own independence, knowing that you're moving backwards into dependence on your family in Denmark. And ultimately, you're reconciling yourself to the idea that you cannot control anything in your life – not land, not weather, not people, nor what happens to the ones you love the most. All you can do is be grateful you experienced them for a while. Now think about the speech of farewell she makes over Denys Finch-Hatton's grave thanking God for the gift of knowing this man, if only for a short time. "He was not ours, he was not mine."

The business world is littered with the bombs of "bad acting" which result from superficial or misguided understanding of consumers. Today, the technology industry is a good case in point. How many businesses in this bubbling industry of innovation have obtained financing and brought products to market based on laughable misunderstandings of consumers, courting market failure from moment to moment? One company in the nascent category of devices to hold and display text – so called "digital books" – is proceeding under the delusion that women want to use such a device to read romance novels. Oh really? Then there's the digital camera attached to the personal digital assistant than can send pictures of houses you might be interested in buying over the Internet to your spouse who is at work halfway across the city. Something I certainly do with regularity. Do you remember the old idea that we would buy home PCs so we could organize our recipes? Kitchens haven't been the same since! It is easy to pick on technology, but every industry suffers from the same problem. And, yes, some shows close in Connecticut before they ever open on Broadway because they're fairly misguided as well.

As these examples show, when we do such a poor job of getting into our consumer "character" and achieving the true insight and understanding that requires, and then we start our "performance" in the form of a product, an advertisement or some other marketing program, we're likely to fall short. Our performances ring hollow. Our consumer targets don't get it. Our work betrays the fact that we have neither understanding nor real empathy for them. They don't identify with the characters in our spots and they think our clever ads are bizarre or off-putting. Or they simply ignore what could not possibly be intended for them. Obviously, consumers are not persuaded by jarring, off-key messages. And when they aren't persuaded, they don't buy. And when they don't buy – although we may make a thousand excuses and even blame them for their stupidity – we fail.

On the other hand, successful marketing programs are characterized by the exact opposite – by the ability of the people behind them to achieve real empathy with their consumers – to think from their point-of-view, to experience the product or service as they would, and then to act on that knowledge to design every element of the consumer's experience, from marketing communications to the product to consumer service and support. I think of Intuit's "Follow Me Home" program that puts developers in close contact with consumers. The developers are able to observe and question real users so they come to understand them very well. And out of that understanding come small but powerful ideas like having "Congratulations!" blink on the screen to reinforce the relief and sense of accomplishment a consumer experiences when he balances his checkbook with the company's popular Quicken software. A small thing, yes, but one of the software's most loved features.

Similarly, 3Com's PalmPilot is a famous example of succeeding by giving consumers exactly what they want in a very simple way. The product lets users keep names, addresses, phone numbers, and appointments in their purse or shirt pocket, lets them synchronize data at the push of a button, and runs for a month on two AAA batteries. The product developers understood that many consumers – even technically sophisticated ones – wanted a simple way to do those few things well, rather than a complicated way to check e-mail and run spreadsheets and do word-processing. 3Com resisted adding features that only engineers would enjoy and gave consumers the simple functionality they wanted instead.

This attention to the consumer really pays off when it permeates a whole company. In discussing one of the biggest corporate success stories in the last several years, IBM Chairman Lou Gerstner was recently quoted in *The Economist* saying that while he brought no technology background to his job as chairman when he took over in 1992, he brought something far more valuable – the perspective of a consumer. Look at IBM now. Clearly, the ability to internalize a consumer's perspective is a critical factor for consumer delight, competitive differentiation, and business success.

So what can we marketers learn from actors about how to probe deeper so that we can get beyond the superficial and find the kind of insight into consumers that would let us absorb them as well as actors absorb their characters? What do they know that we can use? How can their techniques increase our skills?

Over the past two quarters, I've had the chance to meet a gifted professor in the Theater Department at Northwestern University and to watch him at work with his students. Over the last 25 years, Professor David Downs has had the task of coaching young people, from sophomores to seniors, in his acting classes. Ostensibly, he is helping them become world-class actors and actresses. But what he's really doing is helping each student learn how to empathize with a character he's been assigned to play – a person whose circumstances and experiences may bear no resemblance to his own – so that the student can convincingly *become* that person on the stage or screen. That skill is an actor's life blood. As a teacher, Professor Downs knows, just as we movie-goers know, that the audience will never be touched, moved or transported unless the actor can *become* the person in the script or screenplay.

The Professor's coaching works. I've watched him help an ordinary suburban undergraduate *become* quite a convincing Queen of the Nile, and a perfectly sweet, well-adjusted young man become the mad, tortured Prince of Denmark. I've watched him help students play characters 50 years older than themselves, and even play characters of a different race or gender. And while their skills are yet imperfect, something gradually illuminates their performances. They achieve empathy, and it is their empathy with another human being — fictional though he or she is — that persuades you and me.

As I've watched him, I've realized that Professor Downs teaches his students to practice exactly the same techniques we market researchers and account planners do, but somehow he gets a different and more powerful result. To prepare his actors, he encourages them to observe other people, interview them, and immerse themselves in the lives these characters might live, just like we try to do in countless ethnographies, focus groups, and in-depth interviews. Yet, while we marketers often achieve only a superficial understanding of the consumers we study, even after months of work and thousands of dollars, his students achieve a depth of understanding quickly and after relatively confined investigation.

There are two main reasons why this is true. The first, simply put, is this: the acting students are able to let go of their personal biases and prejudices about a character — to empty themselves out, so to speak — to allow room for another person's character to absorb them. I admire that skill. But maybe it's not as hard as we're given to think. Maybe Professor Downs' students are better at that than we are because they actually try to become their characters while we marketers often do the opposite. We hold the consumer at arm's length and that distance sometimes allows us to scrutinize her, to judge her, and, consciously or not, make her what we need her to be, rather than become what she needs us to be. A cardinal acting sin.

How often have you seen a marketer interpret consumer "characters" through the lens of the marketer's own needs, judgments, and corporate objectives? How often do we think the mainstream consumers who are our target are not "cool" enough, so we just make them "cooler" in our advertising briefs? How often do we portray the "aspirational" dimension of our consumer because the reality of the person just isn't interesting enough to keep our attention? How often do we define our consumer as someone whose needs just happen to fit exactly the benefits of the product we're charged to sell? How often do we turn a product or an ad into something *we* would like to see or buy, rather than something the *target* would like to see or buy? And, as a consequence, how often do our marketing efforts come off as obtuse, self-indulgent, or ridiculous to the very people they are intended to persuade? And how often do we come up empty-handed as a result?

In all honesty, we see some actors who make the same mistakes — even famous ones, perhaps especially famous ones. In my opinion, in *The Great Gatsby, Butch Cassidy and the Sundance Kid, Out of Africa,* and *The Horse Whisperer,* Robert Redford doesn't play four unique, viable characters; he just plays himself in four different costumes. Again, in my opinion, Al Pacino isn't playing anyone but himself these days, although he does that with gusto, and neither did Elizabeth Taylor in the latter part of her career. Maybe that's the difference between stars and actors. The actors — like Daniel Day-Lewis and Anthony Hopkins — create real people, while the stars just dress up in someone else's clothes. And I think the same distinction separates real marketers, who can find real insight into their consumers, from people who just work in marketing jobs. The best marketers are the ones who "become" their consumers. The mediocre ones would rather pretend their consumers are just like themselves.

The second reason that Professor Downs' young actors and actresses are so successful is that once they are able to let go of themselves, they fill themselves up with the results of their finely honed skills of observation of another person's life. A young man assigned to play a very old one might spend an afternoon where old people gather watching every detail of individual behavior. How do a man's hands move as he opens a newspaper? What about his back as he lifts up his grandchild? How does a woman rub her face when she's tired? Or climb the stairs or get out of a chair? What does each and every one of those movements reveal about the psychology and motivations of that person? Then they figure out how they can use what they've learned to create the truth of their character.

We marketers hardly ever do such things. To start with, we hardly ever get close enough to real people in real life settings to even try, contenting ourselves instead with eating nice food and playing with Nerf balls behind the glass of a one-way mirror in a focus group room while we pay someone else to ask our questions for us. Go into the room ourselves? Go into someone's home to watch him use our product? Go shopping while someone tries to buy what we sell? Ye Gods!! Then too, we're afraid of observations of individual people, as if we have to have sample sizes of a thousand to know anything for sure. But actors tell a deeper and more resonant truth because they don't hide behind giant sample sizes and statistical analyses. They go out on a limb. Here's a case in point: do you think Jerry Seinfeld is funny? Do you think he reveals a truth about your life? Do you see yourself or your friends or other people you know skewered with penetrating wit episode after episode? The ratings for this enormously popular show would say yes. Where do you think Jerry got those insights? I doubt he spent a million dollars with Yankelovich to help him figure them out.

Professor Down's students are more creative than we are with techniques that immerse them in other people's lives. A student who has to play a wheelchair-bound woman might rent a wheelchair for a day and make her way around Evanston without ever getting out of it. How does she manage herself? What kinds of difficulties does she encounter? How do other people look at her? Treat her? How does she start to feel about herself? Professional actors are famous for doing the same thing. To prepare for his role in *The Last of the Mohicans*, Daniel-Day Lewis lived "in character," including keeping a rifle at his side 24-hours-a-day for months until it became an extension of his body. Christopher Noth and Jerry Orbach, who play detectives on TV's *Law and Order*, spent days watching policemen work, riding in cop cars, witnessing arrests, attending trials. As a result, they've created work so powerful that they get an inordinate amount of fan mail from real policemen and women thanking them for the truth and honesty of their portrayals. "You really get it," they say, "you're one of us." These real keepers of law and order have even made these actors honorary members of a slew of policemen's fraternities. I'd say that's evidence of an acting success. And to prepare for their roles in *Saving Private Ryan*, all of the actors, including Tom Hanks, went through a real boot camp staged by a retired Marine colonel, crawling in mud, eating rations, sleeping in foxholes, firing rifles and being fired at, and being screamed at every day. How else can you begin to imagine what it must have been like to face the beaches and cliffs of Normandy?

On the other hand, how often do we marketers take advantage of similar opportunities that present themselves in the course of our work? If you're a childless woman who works on a baby product, have you ever borrowed an infant for a weekend just to understand what it's like? If you sell any variety of computer products, have you ever installed one yourself, tried to e-mail a photo to a friend, or made a greeting card? Any of the things we insist consumers ought to be able to do without a hitch? If we market to someone who makes a lot less money than we do, have we ever tried to live on *their* disposable income for a month? I'd bet if we did, our insights would sharpen right up.

And finally, Professor Downs' students work hard on developing one of their most important tools, their imaginations. In a variety of exercises, he encourages them to think like the character and act like the character, beyond the confines of the script. Maybe the character doesn't fall in love in the play, but how would she do it if she had to? Maybe the character doesn't lose his job in the screenplay, but what if he did? And what if there were no script? What if you had to take a character from fiction that hasn't yet become a movie, like Ada from the recent bestseller *On Cold Mountain*, and create a moment in her life? What would you say? What would you do? Imagination is a powerful way to test whether you really understand someone or not. Professor Downs helps his students learn how to put themselves to that most critical of tests. If you had to convincingly role-play your consumer without turning it into a comedy routine just to protect yourself from embarrassment, could you do it?

Once he has helped his students arrive at a profound empathy for their characters, Downs stresses how absolutely essential it is for them to "integrate" that understanding into every aspect of their performance. He works hard to prove to his students how the ultimate "truth" an actor tells must show up in his or her body and total behavior. He encourages his students to make a connection between the idea they have of the character in their heads, the words they speak for the character, and the messages they convey through the movement and attitude of their bodies. He uses the other students in his class to help the student actor on stage understand whether the character has really come to life by analyzing and commenting on every detail of the total performance. When was the last time your marketing department or sales force reviewed, analyzed and criticized your representation of a particular consumer? When have we ever let the consumer do it herself?

We human beings are extraordinarily sensitive to lies, particularly to the kind that manifest themselves in discrepancies between a person's body language and his or her verbal language – or between an actor's body language and speech. Professor Downs helps students understand how subtly, yet completely, any disconnection between oral and body language can undermine the credibility of the actor's portrayal and completely defeat the effort to touch or to move an audience. And so, to be ultimately convincing, the acting student must become hyper-conscious of the implications of every nuance of posture, gesture, vocal pitch, and movement across the stage.[1] The lesson for us as marketers is to become hyper-sensitive to the elements of our consumer's experience with our product that we would prefer to ignore because they are hard for us to control – the pricing, the distribution, the design, the service and support, the durability, etc.

Eventually, Professor Downs' students are able to move beyond the intellectual understanding of the characters they are playing, which comes from thinking about and memorizing the playwright's words, to the truth of a real person, which comes from considering and mastering every aspect of his being. And at that moment, they are able to act "naturally," without over-thinking, without over-analyzing. They have become another person. They just do it. Just so, when we have empathy and insight, we marketers can move easily beyond shallow demographics and sterile behavioral data to the truth of human motivation. And our performances will resonate too.

---

[1] For more on David Downs' techniques and methods, see his excellent short book, The Actor's Eye. But, to read it, you'd better know your Shakespeare, Shaw, Ibsen, and Chekov.

It makes me sad to think how seldom we internalize our consumers as well or represent them as truthfully as Professor Downs' young and inexperienced students internalize and portray their characters. Indeed, I've watched countless professional researchers and account planners present analyses of consumer targets they've studied at great expense for months at a time. They always perform creatively, with state-of-the-art multimedia flash, to catch the attention of the art directors, writers, product designers, or marketing program managers whom they hope to inspire with the power of their insight. And I've usually walked away from those presentations with a reasonably good understanding of key points of target consumers' psychologies, but with no feel for the *real people* behind the overheads. On the other hand, I've watched a 20-year-old woman, alone on a stage in a dingy practice theater with neither costume nor prop, play Lady Anne railing at heaven and at Richard III over the death of her beloved husband, and I've cried.

We can learn to do it better. We can do what actors do. We can empty ourselves of our biases and pre-conceptions so that we can fill ourselves back up. We can practice the same techniques we always have, but we can strive to get more out of them. We can observe deeper and better. We can ask more probing and penetrating questions. We can refuse to content ourselves with superficial answers. We can focus more on the details. We can use our imaginations. We can act on what we've learned. And we can do it ourselves. Not everything has to be mediated by a professional statistician or focus group moderator.

The next time you watch a great movie or play, don't just let yourself be entertained. Watch a master at work and learn.

# The Coolhunt
## Who decides what's cool?
## Certain kids in certain places – and only the coolhunters know who they are.

## By Malcolm Gladwell

*Malcolm Gladwell has been a staff writer with the* New Yorker *magazine since 1996. His 1999 profile of Ron Popeil won a National Magazine Award, and in 2005 he was named one of* Time Magazine's *100 Most Influential People of the Year. He is the author of two books,* The Tipping Point: How Little Things Make a Big Difference, *(2000) and* Blink: The Power of Thinking Without Thinking *(2005), both of which were number one* New York Times *bestsellers. This article first appeared in the* Annals of Style *section of the* New Yorker, *March 17, 1997.*

### 1.

Baysie Wightman met DeeDee Gordon, appropriately enough, on a cool-hunt. It was 1992. Baysie was a big shot for Converse, and DeeDee, who was barely twenty-one, was running a very cool boutique called Placid Planet, on Newbury Street in Boston. Baysie came in with a camera crew – one she often used when she was coolhunting – and said, "I've been watching your store, I've seen you, I've heard you know what's up," because it was Baysie's job at Converse to find people who knew what was up and she thought DeeDee was one of those people. DeeDee says that she responded with reserve – that "I was like, 'Whatever'" – but Baysie said that if DeeDee ever wanted to come and work at Converse she should just call, and nine months later DeeDee called. This was about the time the cool kids had decided they didn't want the hundred-and-twenty-five-dollar basketball sneaker with seventeen different kinds of high-technology materials and colors and air-cushioned heels anymore. They wanted simplicity and authenticity, and Baysie picked up on that.

She brought back the Converse One Star, which was a vulcanized, suède, low-top classic old-school sneaker from the nineteen-seventies, and, sure enough, the One Star quickly became the signature shoe of the retro era. Remember what Kurt Cobain was wearing in the famous picture of him lying dead on the ground after committing suicide? Black Converse One Stars. DeeDee's big score was calling the sandal craze. She had been out in Los Angeles and had kept seeing the white teen-age girls dressing up like cholos, Mexican gangsters, in tight white tank tops known as "wife beaters," with a bra strap hanging out, and long shorts and tube socks and shower sandals. DeeDee recalls, "I'm like, 'I'm telling you, Baysie, this is going to hit. There are just too many people wearing it. We have to make a shower sandal.'" So Baysie, DeeDee, and a designer came up with the idea of making a retro sneaker-sandal, cutting the back off the One Star and putting a thick outsole on it. It was huge, and, amazingly, it's still huge.

Today, Baysie works for Reebok as general-merchandise manager – part of the team trying to return Reebok to the position it enjoyed in the mid-nineteen-eighties as the country's hottest sneaker company. DeeDee works for an advertising agency in Del Mar called Lambesis, where she puts out a quarterly tip sheet called the *L Report* on what the cool kids in major American cities are thinking and doing and buying. Baysie and DeeDee are best friends. They talk on the phone all the time. They get together whenever Baysie is in L.A. (DeeDee: "It's, like, how many times can you drive past O. J. Simpson's house?"), and between them they can talk for hours about the art of the coolhunt. They're the Lewis and Clark of cool.

What they have is what everybody seems to want these days, which is a window on the world of the street. Once, when fashion trends were set by the big couture houses – when cool was trickle-down – that wasn't important. But sometime in the past few decades things got turned over, and fashion became trickle-up. It's now about chase and flight – designers and retailers and the mass consumer giving chase to the elusive prey of street cool – and the rise of coolhunting as a profession shows how serious the chase has become. The sneakers of Nike and Reebok used to come out yearly. Now a new style comes out every season. Apparel designers used to have an eighteen-month lead time between concept and sale. Now they're reducing that to a year, or even six months, in order to react faster to new ideas from the street. The paradox, of course, is that the better coolhunters become at bringing the mainstream close to the cutting edge, the more elusive the cutting edge becomes. This is the first rule of the cool: The quicker the chase, the quicker the flight. The act of discovering what's cool is what causes cool to move on, which explains the triumphant circularity of coolhunting: because we have coolhunters like DeeDee and Baysie, cool changes more quickly, and because cool changes more quickly, we need coolhunters like DeeDee and Baysie.

DeeDee is tall and glamorous, with short hair she has dyed so often that she claims to have forgotten her real color. She drives a yellow 1977 Trans Am with a burgundy stripe down the center and a 1973 Mercedes 450 SL, and lives in a spare, Japanese-style cabin in Laurel Canyon. She uses words like "rad" and "totally," and offers non-stop, deadpan pronouncements on pop culture, as in "It's all about Pee-wee Herman." She sounds at first like a teen, like the same teens who, at Lambesis, it is her job to follow. But teen speech — particularly girl-teen speech, with its fixation on reported speech ("so she goes," "and I'm like," "and he goes") and its stock vocabulary of accompanying grimaces and gestures — is about using language less to communicate than to fit in. DeeDee uses teen speech to set herself apart, and the result is, for lack of a better word, really cool. She doesn't do the teen thing of climbing half an octave at the end of every sentence. Instead, she drags out her vowels for emphasis, so that if she mildly disagreed with something I'd said she would say "Maalcolm" and if she strongly disagreed with what I'd said she would say "Maaalcolm."

Baysie is older, just past forty (although you would never guess that), and went to Exeter and Middlebury and had two grandfathers who went to Harvard (although you wouldn't guess that, either). She has curly brown hair and big green eyes and long legs and so much energy that it is hard to imagine her asleep, or resting, or even standing still for longer than thirty seconds. The hunt for cool is an obsession with her, and DeeDee is the same way. DeeDee used to sit on the corner of West Broadway and Prince in SoHo – back when SoHo was cool – and take pictures of everyone who walked by for an entire hour. Baysie can tell you precisely where she goes on her Reebok coolhunts to find the really cool alternative white kids ("I'd maybe go to Portland and hang out where the skateboarders hang out near that bridge") or which snowboarding mountain has cooler kids – Stratton, in Vermont, or Summit County, in Colorado. (Summit, definitely.) DeeDee can tell you on the basis of the *L Report's* research exactly how far Dallas is behind New York in coolness (from six to eight months). Baysie is convinced that Los Angeles is not happening right now: "In the early nineteen-nineties a lot more was coming from L.A. They had a big trend with the whole Melrose Avenue look – the stupid goatees, the shorter hair. It was cleaned-up aftergrunge. There were a lot of places you could go to buy vinyl records. It was a strong place to go for looks. Then it went back to being horrible." DeeDee is convinced that Japan is happening: "I linked onto this future-technology thing two years ago. Now look at it, it's huge. It's the whole resurgence of Nike – Nike being larger than life. I went to Japan and saw the kids just bailing the most technologically advanced Nikes with their little dresses and little outfits and I'm like, 'Whoa, this is trippy!' It's performance mixed with fashion. It's really superheavy." Baysie has a theory that Liverpool is cool right now because it's the birthplace of the whole "lad" look, which involves soccer blokes in the pubs going superdressy and wearing Dolce & Gabbana and Polo Sport and Reebok Classics on their feet. But when I asked DeeDee about that, she just rolled her eyes: "Sometimes Baysie goes off on these tangents. Man, I love that woman!"

I used to think that if I talked to Baysie and DeeDee long enough I could write a coolhunting manual, an encyclopedia of cool. But then I realized that the manual would have so many footnotes and caveats that it would be unreadable. Coolhunting is not about the articulation of a coherent philosophy of cool. It's just a collection of spontaneous observations and predictions that differ from one moment to the next and from one coolhunter to the next. Ask a coolhunter where the baggy-jeans look came from, for example, and you might get any number of answers: urban black kids mimicking the jailhouse look, skateboarders looking for room to move, snowboarders trying not to look like skiers, or, alternatively, all three at once, in some grand concordance.

Or take the question of exactly how Tommy Hilfiger — a forty-five-year-old white guy from Greenwich, Connecticut, doing all-American preppy clothes — came to be the designer of choice for urban black America. Some say it was all about the early and visible endorsement given Hilfiger by the hip-hop auteur Grand Puba, who wore a dark-green-and-blue Tommy jacket over a white Tommy T-shirt as he leaned on his black Lamborghini on the cover of the hugely influential "Grand Puba 2000" CD, and whose love for Hilfiger soon spread to other rappers. (Who could forget the rhymes of Mobb Deep? "Tommy was my nigga / And couldn't figure / How me and Hilfiger / used to move through with vigor.") Then I had lunch with one of Hilfiger's designers, a twenty-six-year-old named Ulrich (Ubi) Simpson, who has a Puerto Rican mother and a Dutch-Venezuelan father, plays lacrosse, snowboards, surfs the long board, goes to hip-hop concerts, listens to Jungle, Edith Piaf, opera, rap, and Metallica, and has working with him on his design team a twenty-seven-year-old black guy from Montclair with dreadlocks, a twenty-two-year-old Asian-American who lives on the Lower East Side, a twenty-five-year-old South Asian guy from Fiji, and a twenty-one-year-old white graffiti artist from Queens. That's when it occurred to me that maybe the reason Tommy Hilfiger can make white culture cool to black culture is that he has people working for him who are cool in both cultures simultaneously. Then again, maybe it was all Grand Puba. Who knows?

One day last month, Baysie took me on a coolhunt to the Bronx and Harlem, lugging a big black canvas bag with twenty-four different shoes that Reebok is about to bring out, and as we drove down Fordham Road, she had her head out the window like a little kid, checking out what everyone on the street was wearing. We went to Dr. Jay's, which is the cool place to buy sneakers in the Bronx, and Baysie crouched down on the floor and started pulling the shoes out of her bag one by one, soliciting opinions from customers who gathered around and asking one question after another, in rapid sequence. One guy she listened closely to was maybe eighteen or nineteen, with a diamond stud in his ear and a thin beard. He was wearing a Polo baseball cap, a brown leather jacket, and the big, oversized leather boots that are everywhere uptown right now. Baysie would hand him a shoe and he would hold it, look at the top, and move it up and down and flip it over. The first one he didn't like: "Oh-kay." The second one he hated: he made a growling sound in his throat even before Baysie could give it to him, as if to say, "Put it back in the bag — now!" But when she handed him a new DMX RXT — a low-cut run/walk shoe in white and blue and mesh with a translucent "ice" sole, which retails for a hundred and ten dollars — he looked at it long and hard and shook his head in pure admiration and just said two words, dragging each of them out: "No doubt."

Baysie was interested in what he was saying, because the DMX RXT she had was a girls' shoe that actually hadn't been doing all that well. Later, she explained to me that the fact that the boys loved the shoe was critical news, because it suggested that Reebok had a potential hit if it just switched the shoe to the men's section. How she managed to distill this piece of information from the crowd of teenagers around her, how she made any sense of the two dozen shoes in her bag, most of which (to my eyes, anyway) looked pretty much the same, and how she knew which of the teens to really focus on was a mystery. Baysie is a Wasp from New England, and she crouched on the floor in Dr. Jay's for almost an hour, talking and joking with the homeboys without a trace of condescension or self-consciousness.

Near the end of her visit, a young boy walked up and sat down on the bench next to her. He was wearing a black woollen cap with white stripes pulled low, a blue North Face pleated down jacket, a pair of baggy Guess jeans, and, on his feet, Nike Air Jordans. He couldn't have been more than thirteen. But when he started talking you could see Baysie's eyes light up, because somehow she knew the kid was the real thing.

"How many pairs of shoes do you buy a month?" Baysie asked.

"Two," the kid answered. "And if at the end I find one more I like I get to buy that, too."

Baysie was onto him. "Does your mother spoil you?"

The kid blushed, but a friend next to him was laughing. "Whatever he wants, he gets."

Baysie laughed, too. She had the DMX RXT in his size. He tried them on. He rocked back and forth, testing them. He looked back at Baysie. He was dead serious now: "Make sure these come out."

Baysie handed him the new "Rush" Emmitt Smith shoe due out in the fall. One of the boys had already pronounced it "phat," and another had looked through the marbleized-foam cradle in the heel and cried out in delight, "This is bug!" But this kid was the acid test, because this kid knew cool. He paused. He looked at it hard. "Reebok," he said, soberly and carefully, "is trying to get butter."

In the car on the way back to Manhattan, Baysie repeated it twice. "Not better. Butter! That kid could totally tell you what he thinks." Baysie had spent an hour coolhunting in a shoe store and found out that Reebok's efforts were winning the highest of hip-hop praise. "He was so fucking smart."

## 2.

If you want to understand how trends work, and why coolhunters like Baysie and DeeDee have become so important, a good place to start is with what's known as diffusion research, which is the study of how ideas and innovations spread. Diffusion researchers do things like spending five years studying the adoption of irrigation techniques in a Colombian mountain village, or developing complex matrices to map the spread of new math in the Pittsburgh school system. What they do may seem like a far cry from, say, how the Tommy Hilfiger thing spread from Harlem to every suburban mall in the country, but it really isn't: both are about how new ideas spread from one person to the next.

One of the most famous diffusion studies is Bruce Ryan and Neal Gross's analysis of the spread of hybrid seed corn in Greene County, Iowa, in the nineteen-thirties. The new seed corn was introduced there in about 1928, and it was superior in every respect to the seed that had been used by farmers for decades. But it wasn't adopted all at once. Of two hundred and fifty-nine farmers studied by Ryan and Gross, only a handful had started planting the new seed by 1933. In 1934, sixteen took the plunge. In 1935, twenty-one more followed; the next year, there were thirty-six, and the year after that a whopping sixty-one. The succeeding figures were then forty-six, thirty-six, fourteen, and three, until, by 1941, all but two of the two hundred and fifty-nine farmers studied were using the new seed. In the language of diffusion research, the handful of farmers who started trying hybrid seed corn at the very beginning of the thirties were the "innovators," the adventurous ones. The slightly larger group that followed them was the "early adopters." They were the opinion leaders in the community, the respected, thoughtful people who watched and analyzed what those wild innovators were doing and then did it themselves. Then came the big bulge of farmers in 1936, 1937, and 1938 – the "early majority" and the "late majority," which is to say the deliberate and the skeptical masses, who would never try anything until the most respected farmers had tried it. Only after they had been converted did the "laggards," the most traditional of all, follow suit. The critical thing about this sequence is that it is almost entirely interpersonal. According to Ryan and Gross, only the innovators relied to any great extent on radio advertising and farm journals and seed salesmen in making their decision to switch to the hybrid. Everyone else made his decision overwhelmingly because of the example and the opinions of his neighbors and peers.

Isn't this just how fashion works? A few years ago, the classic brushed-suede Hush Puppies with the lightweight crêpe sole – the moc-toe oxford known as the Duke and the slip-on with the golden buckle known as the Columbia – were selling barely sixty-five thousand pairs a year. The company was trying to walk away from the whole suede casual look entirely. It wanted to do "aspirational" shoes: "active casuals" in smooth leather, like the Mall Walker, with a Comfort Curve technology outsole and a heel stabilizer – the kind of shoes you see in Kinney's for $39.95. But then something strange started happening. Two Hush Puppies executives – Owen Baxter and Jeff Lewis – were doing a fashion shoot for their Mall Walkers and ran into a creative consultant from Manhattan named

Jeffrey Miller, who informed them that the Dukes and the Columbias weren't dead, they were dead chic. "We were being told," Baxter recalls, "that there were areas in the Village, in SoHo, where the shoes were selling — in resale shops — and that people were wearing the old Hush Puppies. They were going to the ma-and-pa stores, the little stores that still carried them, and there was this authenticity of being able to say, 'I am wearing an original pair of Hush Puppies.' "

Baxter and Lewis — tall, solid, fair-haired Midwestern guys with thick, shiny wedding bands — are shoe men, first and foremost. Baxter was working the cash register at his father's shoe store in Mount Prospect, Illinois, at the age of thirteen. Lewis was doing inventory in his father's shoe store in Pontiac, Michigan, at the age of seven. Baxter was in the National Guard during the 1968 Democratic Convention, in Chicago, and was stationed across the street from the Conrad Hilton downtown, right in the middle of things. Today, the two men work out of Rockford, Michigan (population thirty-eight hundred), where Hush Puppies has been making the Dukes and the Columbias in an old factory down by the Rogue River for almost forty years. They took me to the plant when I was in Rockford. In a crowded, noisy, low-slung building, factory workers stand in long rows, gluing, stapling, and sewing together shoes in dozens of bright colors, and the two executives stopped at each production station and described it in detail. Lewis and Baxter know shoes. But they would be the first to admit that they don't know cool. "Miller was saying that there is something going on with the shoes — that Isaac Mizrahi was wearing the shoes for his personal use," Lewis told me. We were seated around the conference table in the Hush Puppies headquarters in Rockford, with the snow and the trees outside and a big water tower behind us. "I think it's fair to say that at the time we had no idea who Isaac Mizrahi was."

By late 1994, things had begun to happen in a rush. First, the designer John Bartlett called. He wanted to use Hush Puppies as accessories in his spring collection. Then Anna Sui called. Miller, the man from Manhattan, flew out to Michigan to give advice on a new line ("Of course, packing my own food and thinking about 'Fargo' in the corner of my mind").

A few months later, in Los Angeles, the designer Joel Fitzpatrick put a twenty-five-foot inflatable basset hound on the roof of his store on La Brea Avenue and gutted his adjoining art gallery to turn it into a Hush Puppies department, and even before he opened — while he was still painting and putting up shelves — Pee-wee Herman walked in and asked for a couple of pairs. Pee-wee Herman! "It was total word of mouth. I didn't even have a sign back then," Fitzpatrick recalls. In 1995, the company sold four hundred and thirty thousand pairs of the classic Hush Puppies. In 1996, it sold a million six hundred thousand, and that was only scratching the surface, because in Europe and the rest of the world, where Hush Puppies have a huge following — where they might outsell the American market four to one — the revival was just beginning.

The cool kids who started wearing old Dukes and Columbias from thrift shops were the innovators. Pee-wee Herman, wandering in off the street, was an early adopter. The million six hundred thousand people who bought Hush Puppies last year are the early majority, jumping in because the really cool people have already blazed the trail. Hush Puppies are moving through the country just the way hybrid seed corn moved through Greene County — all of which illustrates what coolhunters can and cannot do. If Jeffrey Miller had been wrong — if cool people hadn't been digging through the thrift shops for Hush Puppies — and he had arbitrarily decided that Baxter and Lewis should try to convince non-cool people that the shoes were cool, it wouldn't have worked. You can't convince the late majority that Hush Puppies are cool, because the late majority makes its coolness decisions on the basis of what the early majority is doing, and you can't convince the early majority, because the early majority is looking at the early adopters, and you can't convince the early adopters, because they take their cues from the innovators. The innovators do get their cool ideas from people other than their peers, but the fact is that they are the last people who can be convinced by a marketing campaign that a pair of suede shoes is cool. These are, after all, the people who spent hours sifting through thrift-store bins. And why did they do that? Because their definition of cool is doing something that nobody else is doing. A company can intervene in the cool cycle. It can put its shoes on really cool celebrities and on fashion runways and on MTV. It can accelerate the transition from the innovator to the early adopter and on to the early majority. But it can't just manufacture cool out of thin air, and that's the second rule of cool.

At the peak of the Hush Puppies craziness last year, Hush Puppies won the prize for best accessory at the Council of Fashion Designers' awards dinner, at Lincoln Center. The award was accepted by the Hush Puppies president, Louis Dubrow, who came out wearing a pair of custom-made black patent-leather Hush Puppies and stood there blinking and looking at the assembled crowd as if it were the last scene of "Close Encounters of the Third Kind." It was a strange moment. There was the president of the Hush Puppies company, of Rockford, Michigan, population thirty-eight hundred, sharing a stage with Calvin Klein and Donna Karan and Isaac Mizrahi — and all because some kids in the East Village began combing through thrift shops for old Dukes. Fashion was at the mercy of those kids, whoever they were, and it was a wonderful thing if the kids picked you, but a scary thing, too, because it meant that cool was something you could not control. You needed someone to find cool and tell you what it was.

## 3.

When Baysie Wightman went to Dr. Jay's, she was looking for customer response to the new shoes Reebok had planned for the fourth quarter of 1997 and the first quarter of 1998. This kind of customer testing is critical at Reebok, because the last decade has not been kind to the company. In 1987, it had a third of the American athletic-shoe market, well ahead of Nike. Last year, it had sixteen per cent. "The kid in the store would say, 'I'd like this shoe if your logo wasn't on it,'" E. Scott Morris, who's a senior designer for Reebok, told me. "That's kind of a punch in the mouth. But we've all seen it. You go into a shoe store. The kid picks up the shoe and says, 'Ah, man, this is nice.' He turns the shoe around and around. He looks at it underneath. He looks at the side and he goes, 'Ah, this is Reebok,' and says, 'I ain't buying this,' and puts the shoe down and walks out. And you go, 'You was just digging it a minute ago. What happened?'" Somewhere along the way, the company lost its cool, and

Reebok now faces the task not only of rebuilding its image but of making the shoes so cool that the kids in the store can't put them down.

Every few months, then, the company's coolhunters go out into the field with prototypes of the upcoming shoes to find out what kids really like, and come back to recommend the necessary changes. The prototype of one recent Emmitt Smith shoe, for example, had a piece of molded rubber on the end of the tongue as a design element; it was supposed to give the shoe a certain "richness," but the kids said they thought it looked overbuilt. Then Reebok gave the shoes to the Boston College football team for wear-testing, and when they got the shoes back they found out that all the football players had cut out the rubber component with scissors. As messages go, this was hard to miss. The tongue piece wasn't cool, and on the final version of the shoe it was gone. The rule of thumb at Reebok is that if the kids in Chicago, New York, and Detroit all like a shoe, it's a guaranteed hit. More than likely, though, the coolhunt is going to turn up subtle differences from city to city, so that once the coolhunters come back the designers have to find out some way to synthesize what was heard, and pick out just those things that all the kids seemed to agree on. In New York, for example, kids in Harlem are more sophisticated and fashion-forward than kids in the Bronx, who like things a little more colorful and glitzy. Brooklyn, meanwhile, is conservative and preppy, more like Washington, D.C. For reasons no one really knows, Reeboks are coolest in Philadelphia. In Philly, in fact, the Reebok Classics are so huge they are known simply as National Anthems, as in "I'll have a pair of blue Anthems in nine and a half." Philadelphia is Reebok's innovator town. From there trends move along the East Coast, trickling all the way to Charlotte, North Carolina.

Reebok has its headquarters in Stoughton, Massachusetts, outside Boston – in a modern corporate park right off Route 24. There are basketball and tennis courts next to the building, and a health club on the ground floor that you can look directly into from the parking lot. The front lobby is adorned with shrines for all of Reebok's most prominent athletes – shrines complete with dramatic action photographs, their sports jerseys, and a pair of their signature shoes – and the halls are filled with so many young, determinedly athletic people that when I visited Reebok headquarters I suddenly wished I'd packed my gym clothes in case someone challenged me to wind sprints. At Stoughton, I met with a handful of the company's top designers and marketing executives in a long conference room on the third floor. In the course of two hours, they put one pair of shoes after another on the table in front of me, talking excitedly about each sneaker's prospects, because the feeling at Reebok is that things are finally turning around. The basketball shoe that Reebok brought out last winter for Allen Iverson, the star rookie guard for the Philadelphia 76ers, for example, is one of the hottest shoes in the country. Dr. Jay's sold out of Iversons in two days, compared with the week it took the store to sell out of Nike's new Air Jordans. Iverson himself is brash and charismatic and faster from foul line to foul line than anyone else in the league. He's the equivalent of those kids in the East Village who began wearing Hush Puppies way back when. He's an innovator, and the hope at Reebok is that if he gets big enough the whole company can ride back to coolness on his coattails, the way Nike rode to coolness on the coattails of Michael Jordan. That's why Baysie was so excited when the kid said Reebok was trying to get butter when he looked at the Rush and the DMX RXT: it was a sign, albeit a small one, that the indefinable, abstract thing called cool was coming back.

When Baysie comes back from a coolhunt, she sits down with marketing experts and sales representatives and designers, and reconnects them to the street, making sure they have the right shoes going to the right places at the right price. When she got back from the Bronx, for example, the first thing she did was tell all these people they had to get a new men's DMX RXT out, fast, because the kids on the street loved the women's version. "It's hotter than we realized," she told them. The coolhunter's job in this instance is very specific. What DeeDee does, on the other hand, is a little more ambitious. With the *L Report*, she tries to construct a kind of grand matrix of cool, comprising not just shoes but everything kids like, and not just kids of certain East Coast urban markets but kids all over. DeeDee and her staff put it out four times a year, in six different versions — for New York, Los Angeles, San Francisco, Austin-

Dallas, Seattle, and Chicago — and then sell it to manufacturers, retailers, and ad agencies (among others) for twenty thousand dollars a year. They go to each city and find the coolest bars and clubs, and ask the coolest kids to fill out questionnaires. The information is then divided into six categories — You Saw It Here First, Entertainment and Leisure, Clothing and Accessories, Personal and Individual, Aspirations, and Food and Beverages — which are, in turn, broken up into dozens of subcategories, so that Personal and Individual, for example, includes Cool Date, Cool Evening, Free Time, Favorite Possession, and on and on. The information in those subcategories is subdivided again by sex and by age bracket (14-18, 19-24, 25-30), and then, as a control, the *L Report* gives you the corresponding set of preferences for "mainstream" kids.

Few coolhunters bother to analyze trends with this degree of specificity. DeeDee's biggest competitor, for example, is something called the *Hot Sheet*, out of Manhattan. It uses a panel of three thousand kids a year from across the country and divides up their answers by sex and age, but it doesn't distinguish between regions, or between trendsetting and mainstream respondents. So what you're really getting is what all kids think is cool — not what cool kids think is cool, which is a considerably different piece of information. Janine Misdom and Joanne DeLuca, who run the Sputnik coolhunting group out of the garment district in Manhattan, meanwhile, favor an entirely impressionistic approach, sending out coolhunters with video cameras to talk to kids on the ground that it's too difficult to get cool kids to fill out questionnaires. Once, when I was visiting the Sputnik girls — as Misdom and DeLuca are known on the street, because they look alike and their first names are so similar and both have the same awesome New York accents — they showed me a video of the girl they believe was the patient zero of the whole eighties revival going on right now. It was back in September of 1993. Joanne and Janine were on Seventh Avenue, outside the Fashion Institute of Technology, doing random street interviews for a major jeans company, and, quite by accident, they ran into this nineteen-year-old raver. She had close-cropped hair, which was green at the top, and at the temples was shaved even closer and dyed pink. She had rings and studs all over her face, and a thick collection of silver tribal jewelry around her neck, and vintage jeans. She looked into the camera and said, "The sixties came in and then the seventies came in and I think it's ready to come back to the eighties. It's totally eighties: the eye makeup, the clothes. It's totally going back to that." Immediately, Joanne and Janine started asking around. "We talked to a few kids on the Lower East Side who said they were feeling the need to start breaking out their old Michael Jackson jackets," Joanne said. "They were joking about it. They weren't doing it yet. But they were going to, you know? They were saying, 'We're getting the urge to break out our Members Only jackets.'" That was right when Joanne and Janine were just starting up; calling the eighties revival was their first big break, and now they put out a full-blown videotaped report twice a year which is a collection of clips of interviews with extremely progressive people.

What DeeDee argues, though, is that cool is too subtle and too variegated to be captured with these kind of broad strokes. Cool is a set of dialects, not a language. The *L Report* can tell you, for example, that nineteen- to twenty-four-year-old male trendsetters in Seattle would most like to meet, among others, King Solomon and Dr. Seuss, and that nineteen- to twenty-four-year-old female trendsetters in San Francisco have turned their backs on Calvin Klein, Nintendo Gameboy, and sex. What's cool right now? Among male New York trendsetters: North Face jackets, rubber and latex, khakis, and the rock band Kiss. Among female trendsetters: ska music, old-lady clothing, and cyber tech. In Chicago, snowboarding is huge among trendsetters of both sexes and all ages. Women over nineteen are into short hair, while those in their teens have embraced mod culture, rock climbing, Tag watches, and bootleg pants. In Austin-Dallas, meanwhile, twenty-five- to thirty-year-old women trendsetters are into hats, heroin, computers, cigars, Adidas, and velvet, while men in their twenties are into video games and hemp. In all, the typical *L Report* runs over one hundred pages. But with that flood of data comes an obsolescence disclaimer: "The fluctuating nature of the trendsetting market makes keeping up with trends a difficult task." By the spring, in other words, everything may have changed.

The key to coolhunting, then, is to look for cool people first and cool things later, and not the other way around. Since cool things are always changing, you can't look for them, because the very fact they are cool means you have no idea what to look for. What you would be doing is thinking back on what was cool before and extrapolating, which is about as useful as presuming that because the Dow rose ten points yesterday it will rise another ten points today. Cool people, on the other hand, are a constant.

When I was in California, I met Salvador Barbier, who had been described to me by a coolhunter as "the Michael Jordan of skateboarding." He was tall and lean and languid, with a cowboy's insouciance, and we drove through the streets of Long Beach at fifteen miles an hour in a white late-model Ford Mustang, a car he had bought as a kind of ironic status gesture ("It would look good if I had a Polo jacket or maybe Nautica," he said) to go with his '62 Econoline van and his '64 T-bird. Sal told me that he and his friends, who are all in their mid-twenties, recently took to dressing up as if they were in eighth grade again and gathering together – having a "rally" – on old BMX bicycles in front of their local 7-Eleven. "I'd wear muscle shirts, like Def Leppard or Foghat or some old heavy-metal band, and tight, tight tapered Levi's, and Vans on my feet – big, like, checkered Vans or striped Vans or camouflage Vans – and then wristbands and gloves with the fingers cut off. It was total eighties fashion. You had to look like that to participate in the rally. We had those denim jackets with patches on the back and combs that hung out the back pocket. We went without I.D.s, because we'd have to have someone else buy us beers." At this point, Sal laughed. He was driving really slowly and staring straight ahead and talking in a low drawl – the coolhunter's dream. "We'd ride to this bar and I'd have to carry my bike inside, because we have really expensive bikes, and when we got inside people would freak out. They'd say, 'Omigod,' and I was asking them if they wanted to go for a ride on the handlebars. They were like, 'What is wrong with you. My boyfriend used to dress like that in the eighth grade!' And I was like, 'He was probably a lot cooler then, too.'"

This is just the kind of person DeeDee wants. "I'm looking for somebody who is an individual, who has definitely set himself apart from everybody else, who doesn't look like his peers. I've run into trendsetters who look completely Joe Regular Guy. I can see Joe Regular Guy at a club listening to some totally hardcore band playing, and I say to myself 'Omigod, what's that guy doing here?' and that totally intrigues me, and I have to walk up to him and say, 'Hey, you're really into this band. What's up?' You know what I mean? I look at everything. If I see Joe Regular Guy sitting in a coffee shop and everyone around him has blue hair, I'm going to gravitate toward him, because, hey, what's Joe Regular Guy doing in a coffee shop with people with blue hair?"

We were sitting outside the Fred Segal store in West Hollywood. I was wearing a very conservative white Brooks Brothers button-down and a pair of Levi's, and DeeDee looked first at my shirt and then my pants and dissolved into laughter: "I mean, I might even go up to you in a cool place."

Picking the right person is harder than it sounds, though. Piney Kahn, who works for DeeDee, says, "There are a lot of people in the gray area. You've got these kids who dress ultra funky and have their own style. Then you realize they're just running after their friends." The trick is not just to be able to tell who is different but to be able to tell when that difference represents something truly cool. It's a gut thing. You have to somehow just know. DeeDee hired Piney because Piney clearly knows: she is twenty-four and used to work with the Beastie Boys and has the formidable self-possession of someone who is not only cool herself but whose parents were cool. "I mean," she says, "they named me after a tree."

Piney and DeeDee said that they once tried to hire someone as a coolhunter who was not, himself, cool, and it was a disaster.

"You can give them the boundaries," Piney explained. "You can say that if people shop at Banana Republic and listen to Alanis Morissette they're probably not trendsetters. But then they might go out and assume that everyone who does that is not a trendsetter, and not look at the other things."

"I mean, I myself might go into Banana Republic and buy a T-shirt," DeeDee chimed in.

Their non-cool coolhunter just didn't have that certain instinct, that sense that told him when it was O.K. to deviate from the manual. Because he wasn't cool, he didn't know cool, and that's the essence of the third rule of cool: you have to be one to know one. That's why Baysie is still on top of this business at forty-one. "It's easier for me to tell you what kid is cool than to tell you what things are cool," she says. But that's all she needs to know. In this sense, the third rule of cool fits perfectly into the second: the second rule says that cool cannot be manufactured, only observed, and the third says that it can only be observed by those who are themselves cool. And, of course, the first rule says that it cannot accurately be observed at all, because the act of discovering cool causes cool to take flight, so if you add all three together they describe a closed loop, the hermeneutic circle of coolhunting, a phenomenon whereby not only can the uncool not see cool but cool cannot even be adequately described to them. Baysie says that she can see a coat on one of her friends and think it's not cool but then see the same coat on DeeDee and think that it is cool. It is not possible to be cool, in other words, unless you are — in some larger sense — already cool, and so the phenomenon that the uncool cannot see and cannot have described to them is also something that they cannot ever attain, because if they did it would no longer be cool. Coolhunting represents the ascendancy, in the marketplace, of high school.

Once, I was visiting DeeDee at her house in Laurel Canyon when one of her *L Report* assistants, Jonas Vail, walked in. He'd just come back from Niketown on Wilshire Boulevard, where he'd bought seven hundred dollars' worth of the latest sneakers to go with the three hundred dollars' worth of skateboard shoes he'd bought earlier in the afternoon. Jonas is tall and expressionless, with a peacoat, dark jeans, and short-cropped black hair. "Jonas is good," DeeDee says. "He works with me on every-thing. That guy knows more pop culture. You know: What was the name of the store Mrs. Garrett owned on 'The Facts of Life'? He knows all the names of the extras from eighties sitcoms. I can't believe someone like him exists. He's fucking unbelievable. Jonas can spot a cool person a mile away."

Jonas takes the boxes of shoes and starts unpacking them on the couch next to DeeDee. He picks up a pair of the new Nike ACG hiking boots, and says, "All the Japanese in Niketown were really into these." He hands the shoes to DeeDee.

"Of *course* they were!" she says. "The Japanese are all into the tech-looking shit. Look how exaggerated it is, how bulbous." DeeDee has very ambivalent feelings about Nike, because she thinks its marketing has got out of hand. When she was in the New York Niketown with a girlfriend recently, she says, she started getting light-headed and freaked out. "It's cult, cult, cult. It was like, 'Hello, are we all drinking the Kool-Aid here?'" But this shoe she loves. It's Dr. Jay's in the Bronx all over again. DeeDee turns the shoe around and around in the air, tapping the big clear-blue plastic bubble on the side – the visible Air-Sole unit – with one finger. "It's so fucking rad. It looks like a platypus!" In front of me, there is a pair of Nike's new shoes for the basketball player Jason Kidd.

I pick it up. "This looks . . . cool," I venture uncertainly.

DeeDee is on the couch, where she's surrounded by shoeboxes and sneakers and white tissue paper, and she looks up reprovingly because, of course, I don't get it. I can't get it. "Beyooond cool, Maalcolm. Beyooond cool."

# Planning the New Business Pitch: A Practical Guide

## By Hart Weichselbaum

*Dr. Weichselbaum is president of The Planning Practice, an ad and brand planning consultancy based in Chicago. He was head of planning at The Richards Group for 13 years, has been an adjunct faculty member at DePaul University's Kellstadt Graduate School of Business, and was a founding member of the organization that became the Account Planning Committee of the 4As. He is executive editor of this book.*

## Introduction

NEW BUSINESS IS THE LIFEBLOOD of every agency, no matter what its size.

Increasingly frequent client turnover is now a nasty fact of agency life and it shows no signs of abating.

It's an old saw in the advertising business, but it has never been more true: for more and more agencies, you're only as good as your last pitch.

The reality of new business development is that agencies have had to compress the analysis and strategy stage of the new business pitch to accommodate the often short-sighted demands of clients eager to find a new partner and launch a new campaign. This challenge is even greater for smaller and mid-sized agencies with limited resources.

So what is a small or mid-sized agency (or an advertising student) with limited resources supposed to do? The well-thought-out systems presented in many large agency pitch books or outlined in textbooks and case histories are not particularly helpful when time and money are in extremely short supply.

# Fast Track Planning

What's needed is an approach that accommodates this reality. Here we propose one we call Fast Track Planning. It's how to do account planning on a limited budget and within the time constraints that clients often impose on the agencies competing for their business.

If I've learned anything in twenty years of working with agencies of all sizes, it's that a lot can be accomplished in a week or two, when the team has a plan, the motivation to succeed, and a realistic notion of which steps can be skipped and which corners can be cut.

Don't misunderstand me: *there is no substitute for careful analysis and a well-thought-out creative strategy.* In fact, one could argue that one of the problems with the advertising business today is that the economic and time pressures have undermined both — much to the detriment of advertising effectiveness. But unless you happen to be dealing with the rare prospective client who understands this, the simple fact is that you're probably going to be going flat out from the moment you get the client's RFP until your team's smiling faces appear before him or her in that conference room.

I think the hardest thing for people new to new business to remember is that it's very different from the day-to-day business of creating advertising and managing an account. In new business, you're not trying to bring him or her *the* perfect solution. Instead, you're trying to demonstrate that you have the right people and the right process to get job done.

So imagine that the new business director (or your advertising professor) comes to you on Tuesday and says, *"The pitch is next Tuesday, we've got no dough, and we don't know squat."*

## What Clients Want

What are clients looking for in a new business pitch? Gone are the days when even a small client just wants to "see some ads."

Now they expect the following:

- familiarity with their category and business situation,
- consumer insight,
- creative ideas for promotions and point-of-purchase,

- strategic justification for the campaign,
- great-looking materials, and last but not least,
- an informed and engaging presentation.

In short, the bar has been raised for what it takes to win an advertising or marketing services account.

Two factors, in particular, have made the competition keener.

First, urged on by their financially driven parents, big agencies are competing with mid-sized agencies for smaller accounts. And what do you think mid-sized agencies are doing? They're chasing the same accounts that smaller agencies once had to themselves.

Second, the installation of strategic planning at even the smallest agencies has raised expectations for the quality of the thinking behind every new business pitch.

Now, every prospective client wants "account planning," whether he or she calls it that or not.

Clients want to know that (a) you have some understanding of their business, (b) you have carefully chosen a creative strategy that makes sense for their customer and brand, and you can explain why that strategy will work, and (c) you are creative people who can present their ideas in a dramatic and imaginative way.

Responsibility for demonstrating these things, as well as for providing the inspiration and consumer insight at the core of the pitch, usually falls to the account planner.

# General Principles

Before we get into the details of saving time and money on consumer research, strategic planning, and presentation development, here are some general thoughts about getting ready for the big day.

## Start with a Reasonable Guess

It's important to start moving on all fronts — business background, consumer research, advertising strategy, creative development, and ideas for the presentation — as soon as you get the client's brief.

This means you have to identify a strategy very early on, before you have all the information you'll need to support it.

Start with intuition and a reasonable guess, and then evolve the strategy as you learn.

## Work Concurrently

Although you may decide to describe your step-by-step development process in your presentation as a way of reassuring your prospect that there is a method to the madness, in a new business pitch you really can't work in a simple linear way. Think of your first creative brief as merely a thought starter, subject to change as the team's thinking progresses. For many, the hardest part is developing the creative strategy and the creative concurrently.

But, when you think about it, even when agencies have all the time in the world, strategy and creative development grow up together and inform each other. The idea that ad strategy develops in an orderly sequential way is rarely true even for ongoing business, and it is much less true in a fast-track pitch.

The diagram below demonstrates the perception we often wish to create about the process and the reality in the fast-track pitch.

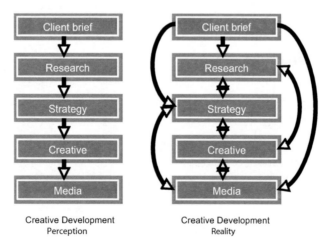

Creative Development
Perception

Creative Development
Reality

## Some Waste Is OK

When it's all done, don't worry about wasted effort. You have to overdo it to get it done. For example, sometimes it's helpful to work against two strategies for a day or two. You can count on the fact that some of your ideas won't make it into the final presentation. This is often true of your research effort as well. You probably have only ninety minutes to present anyway. Every pitch consultant in the world will tell you that agencies try to present too much and that running long is a major problem in new business pitches.

## Good Enough Is Better Than Perfect

Don't worry too much about getting the strategy or the creative idea exactly right for the presentation. Your goal should be to identify the best idea you can and still leave time to produce it for the meeting. After all, even if you win the pitch, you may not produce the idea you presented. The client may have information they haven't shared that leads to modifications of your idea. Or the client may have ideas of his or her own. Remember, even if you win, they'll probably ask you to go back to the drawing board. So enjoy the exhilaration and let your enthusiasm for the client's business and your understanding and respect for their customers show through.

# The Planner's Role

Let's divide the planner's role in preparing for next Tuesday's pitch into three parts: **Understanding**, **Strategy**, and **Presentation**.

## Understanding

How do you get up to speed on a client's brand, business, and key target customer quickly and without spending a lot of money you don't have? In order to gain this understanding, the planner can conduct secondary research (find relevant information that someone else has collected) or primary research (conduct the research yourself by talking to people) – and you will probably want to do both kinds for your pitch. That's right, both kinds – and *fast*.

Here I'll focus on some of the corners you can cut when you don't have much time or money.

## Secondary Research

As in so many aspects of life, the Internet has changed everything. That's particularly true for doing secondary research. No more slogging through old newspaper clippings, calling the 4As or the AMA research library, or scurrying down to the library to get the background information you'll need for the pitch. Now you can often find a fairly perceptive industry overview online in a matter of minutes.

Business magazine and national newspaper sites (forbes.com, businessweek.com, nytimes.com, wsj.com, etc.) are a great place to start.

Look for an article that summarizes the industry situation, identifies recent trends, and (if you're lucky) talks about your client's business.

You may even discover an article that offers deeper insight into the challenges your client or their industry is facing.

Trade publications, industry newsletters, financial information, and analyst web sites are other good places to look, but they frequently charge for their information and analysis.

If you have a little bit of money to invest in the pitch, you can buy an industry overview from one of the many services that make them available online. Buying secondary research is easier than ever, because you have online access to thousands of non-proprietary studies in virtually every imaginable category.

Marketresearch.com is a good place to start, but your favorite search engine can deliver you to numerous competing services. (And a research company called Decision Analyst provides a listing of many sources at www.secondarydata.com.)

Search engine skills have replaced library skills in the planner's contribution to pitch preparation. If you're lucky enough to find a long *New York Times* article on the category or a *Business Week* issue related to your client's business, the Internet can make you an industry "expert" in next to no time.

## Primary Research

Even if your prospect has provided you with background research, you will want to identify some issues they haven't researched and address them. For example, you can use research to learn more about how buyers make their decision, the role advertising plays in the decision, which product features and benefits drive the decision, which advertising proposition is most compelling, or simply as grist for the creative idea mill.

Conducting primary research is enormously important in pitch preparation, but perhaps not for the reasons you might think. Although the directional findings of "quick and dirty" research will add to your confidence when you get up in front of your client to make your case, the fact is that it's almost impossible to get definitive results when you have no time and no money. The most important reason to conduct primary research is the compelling messages it sends to your prospect.

Presenting primary research as part of your pitch communicates the following:

- It says that you believe consumer understanding is at the core of how your agency or team creates successful advertising.

- It shows that you went beyond the assignment by executing research in the very short time available to you.

- In the absence of any client-provided research, it gives the impression that your strategy is based on something more compelling than your own intuition and self-reflection.

Conducting consumer research does one more thing: it gives you an opportunity to add a multimedia dimension to your presentation. You can bring the client's target into the room by showing video or other artifacts of the research you conducted. And, if you acknowledge in your presentation that your results are preliminary and will need to be confirmed in more comprehensive research, it's amazing what you can get away with.

Given the real reasons for conducting primary research, a key objective is creating by-products that can be used in the presentation both to liven it up and to ensure that you get credit for all the hard work you've done.

As you do your research, always be thinking about how you're going to present it in the pitch meeting.

## Collecting the Data

It's virtually impossible to recruit and conduct focus groups or depth interviews in a week, using the standard practice of recruiting anonymous respondents through a facility database. But that shouldn't stop you from talking to people. Here are six things you can do that will cost little more than the price of a few pizzas.

1. **Focus Groups.** Conduct some focus groups with friends or friends of friends. Often they will participate for free or for cheap eats. The important thing is not how you recruited them, but whether they are legitimate prospects for the client's product or service. Don't worry about paying for a facility with a one-way mirror; any well-lit conference room or dining room will do.

   Be sure to video the interviews so you can edit together the relevant parts for the presentation. It takes only a few minutes of carefully edited video from an inexpensive camcorder to convey that you conducted primary research and to offer some insight into the consumer or the brand. Instead of a static, wide shot, have someone operate the camcorder, so he or she can zoom in for compelling close-ups.

2. **One-on-One Interviews.** One-on-one interviews can be even more persuasive. A favored technique is to tape heavy users of the product or service, while they extol its virtues. Not only are you gaining useful information about the product's benefits (compelling creative strategies are often based on the features heavy users find important), but the resulting edited video will make your prospects feel good about their life's work and the wonderful product or service they supply to the world.

3. **Store Visits and Mystery Shoppers.** In-person research can be supplemented with store visits or mystery shoppers for a retail client. (Again, don't forget the camera or camcorder.) Store visits that include shopper and store manager interviews are *de rigueur* for any retail account pitch or for a product where retail distribution is a key issue. For retailers with a wide geographic footprint, it can be impressive to conduct store visits in markets other than your own by asking a favor of planners (or advertising students) in distant cities. You will certainly want to return the favor when they find themselves in a similar situation.

4. **Message Boards and Blogs.** Another increasingly popular technique for gaining consumer input is monitoring web message boards and blogs related to the prospect's product or category. It's a no-cost way to get candid and up-to-the-minute input from people who are often opinion leaders for a product category. Although there are costly professional services that systematically monitor boards and blogs for consumer opinion, many clients don't bother to mine these important sources of insight.

5. **Quantitative Data Collection.** Collecting quantitative data can be even more impressive than conducting in-person interviews. And again, the internet comes to the rescue. Numerous web sites, like surveymonkey.com and zoomerang.com, will let you conduct online quantitative surveys that you design yourself for shockingly little money. Some of them let you sign up for an unlimited number of surveys for one low price (you still have to provide a list to e-mail to or buy one from them). One of these services lets you conduct a ten-item survey of up to 100 people for free.

   One tactic that impresses clients is an overnight poll. Several companies (Synovate, for example) will ask a thousand people one question for $750 and provide results for you the next day. Checking a fact that supports your strategy with a sample of 1000 can give clients the impression that you fielded an enormous national study as part of your diligence in understanding their customer.

The trick is not to attempt too much: it takes time and money to design, field, analyze and report on a consumer survey. It's best to address a small number of specific questions, like who is the best target for the client's product or which bit of message emphasis in the ad copy strategy is most persuasive and believable.

6. **Interviews with Influencers.** Quick and cheap interviews with influencers is another useful approach. If you can't afford to talk to a large number of consumers, talk to a smaller group that has contact with a large number of consumers like sales people in a retail store or people who service the product. When Nigel Carr was at Kirschenbaum & Bond and wanted to find out "what women really think" for a pitch, he interviewed hair stylists because the intimate conversations they have with their customers gives them a unique perspective on personal issues.

Finally, don't forget to visit the store, use the product, sign up for the service, chat with your friends, and visit the web site every chance you get in the days before the pitch. That way you'll have plenty of personal anecdotes to weave into your presentation, and your client will know you have personal experience with their product or service.

## B2B Primary Research – A Special Case

For a business-to-business pitch, the principles are the same, but the challenges of achieving low cost and quick turnaround are a little greater and require a bit more effort. Instead of interviewing consumers, you'll be contacting customers and others in the business's value chain. The client's customers — especially those who do business with other firms — are valuable because they can tell you about your client's strengths and weaknesses on a comparative basis. People in other parts of the value chain can give you a perspective on how the client's business fits into an overall picture of their industry.

It's important to talk to the right people. Business purchases often involve many people in a single company who play different roles in the decision process: information collectors, spec writers, recommenders, influencers, authorizers, and end users. Merely diagramming the decision process and who your marketing tactics will influence can be an insight into a clients business.

Needless to say, it's absolutely necessary to get the client's permission to talk to their customers, and many of them won't want you to for good reasons: the other competing agencies will want to, lack of confidence in your motives and abilities, the possibility of finding out an embarrassing truth, etc.

Occasionally, though, you will find a client who will not only let you talk to their customers, but will collaborate on the research in the hope of finding out something new about themselves. These opportunities for collaboration, rare though they are, are a great way to build rapport with a prospective client and should be diligently pursued.

Unfortunately, without your prospect's help, it's usually too expensive to recruit and pay incentives to B2B customers. And only a few of the methods from B2C are available to you (e.g., finding "experts," reading web boards and blogs). Consequently, if you want to interview category customers, you'll have to rely on friends and friends of friends who work in the industry to provide you with industry knowledge and quotes that lend authority to your pitch. Often, someone's banker or broker will discuss financial services, someone's doctor will discuss health care, etc.

Video is harder to obtain, but quotes in your presentation can be quite compelling. It's easy to promise anonymity to your respondents, because the person's industry and job title are usually as informative as the person's name.

Middle managers in and around the industry will occasionally talk to you, without compensation. (Sometimes you'll get the impression that they aren't asked their opinion very often.) It's important to be up front about the reason for your call and the way the information will be used. While they won't (usually) reveal proprietary or competitive information, you'll sometimes strike a mother lode.

## Strategy

A big part of the planner's job in a pitch is explaining the agency's proposed advertising or brand strategy. This communication can be greatly facilitated by a "model" or visualization of the agency's thinking. The fact is just about every major (and minor) agency these days has a "proprietary" model that illustrates its process or approach. And these models often play an important role when these agencies pitch.

During the years I was at The Richards Group, our approach grew into what we called "Spherical Branding," because "a sphere is the strongest three-dimensional shape." There were a number of reasons that this resonated with our agency culture and capabilities — it also helped us frame our strategies in a relatively unique way.

Proprietary strategy models serve some useful purposes, even though they are, for the most part, very similar. In some cases, they may even be a bona fide point of difference in a pitch among smaller agencies.

Models serve these purposes:

- They provide a common language for discussing advertising and brands.

- They serve as an organizing principle for thinking about the client's business.

- They describe the agency's process in creating marketing communications.

- They can provide a simplified way of describing a complex idea, like an ad development process or a brand.

A process model is especially useful in persuading prospective clients that your efforts are not some whim or ad hoc affair, but rather a disciplined and systematic approach that has delivered results for prior clients, and by implication, will work for this prospective client, too.

In chapter seven of her book, *Goodthinking*, Wendy Gordon presents about a dozen models used in branding and marketing communications. (For example, she describes the BrandWorks™ model, which posits that every brand has a personality, salience, product image, user image, and occasion image. She organizes these concepts into a diamond-shaped diagram: "As flaws are not visible to the naked eye, the diamond can only be valued by looking through a number of facets in turn." Get it?)

Visits to the websites of the largest marketing services companies will provide many more examples. After you have looked at a half-dozen or so, you will have no trouble creating your own proprietary model.

One of my favorites is a simple three-part model that has been used in various forms by a variety of agencies over the years. Its premise is that your brand proposition (and advertising message) lies at the intersection of a consumer need, a brand strength, and a competitive gap. (See diagram.)

As basic as it is, this model has two important uses in a pitch:

- It illustrates good principles of brand communication, because it suggests that good brand messages are important to consumers (relevant), differentiated from competitors (different), and match a product or brand strength (true).

- It organizes your strategy presentation into parts: the consumer, the company (or product), and the competition, and helps your approach and thinking look systematic and well-organized.

As you present your insights in each of the three areas, they can appear in the appropriate place in the diagram. And when you present your big idea (or positioning or brand message or whatever), it can appear in the intersection space, since it will be related to your thinking about the consumer, the brand, and the competition.

A simple example illustrates: Let's say your agency is pitching the Corona Beer business (as we did at The Richards Group in the mid-1990s). You've drawn some interesting insights from your conversations with consumers, your impressions of the brand, and your study of the marketplace. The three-part model can help you put them together to tell a compelling story. Let's say you learned the following:

## *Corona is relaxed and unpretentious

- **Consumer Insight:** Many regular and occasional imported beer drinkers feel that the European imports, like import leader Heineken, taste good, but they also have an elitist aspect that is unappealing to red-blooded American beer drinkers.

- **Competitive Insight:** The product looks unlike anything else on the market. Most beer, domestic or imported, comes in brown or green bottles with printed paper labels. Corona comes in a clear bottle with a painted label. Many imported beers are too heavy and too flavorful for American tastes. Corona has a light, clean taste that is reinforced by the clear bottle.

- **Brand Insight:** Corona is, above all, a Mexican beer. Unlike gloomy Europe, Mexico is a land of beaches and sunshine.

Assembling these pieces into the three-part model enables you to present the brand strategy to your client in a logical and understandable way. In fact, this brand message (or something like it) has been the basis of Corona advertising ever since.

## The Presentation

New business presentations that consist of standing up in a dimly lit room and reciting from PowerPoint slides are a thing of the past.

Successful agencies these days put as much thought and imagination into the presentation of their ideas as they do into the ideas themselves. The pitch meeting is your opportunity to encourage your prospect's hope that you are the most creative people they will ever meet. And, given the amazing array of technology and tools available to even the most inexperienced and cash-strapped agency, there's no reason to disappoint them.

In The Richards Group's final pitch presentation for the Mercedes-Benz business, the client arrived to see three new (rented) competitor vehicles — Lexus, Infiniti, and Acura — in the agency parking lot, with an overhead banner that read "The Competition."

When they left the presentation, they saw three crushed hunks of metal — in the same three colors as the original cars — from the local junk yard.

Now, the banner read: "Crush The Competition." Pretty dramatic.

Dramatic ideas don't have to be so elaborate, or expensive.

Here are some tried and true ideas:

1. **Decor.** Decorate the presentation room in a way that conveys the theme of your presentation. When FCB pitched the Aqua Fina business, the theme of their presentation was "purity." So when the clients arrived, they saw a conference room with white walls, white furniture, and white carpeting. When Goodby & Silverstein pitched the Haggar business, their theme was casual dress. So just before the meeting, they took the client's furniture out of their conference room and replaced it with casual living room furniture — sofas, overstuffed chairs, and so on. The relaxed atmosphere made a point and helped them win. When Richards pitched a chain of daycare centers, we handed the clients crayons instead of pens for note taking during the meeting.

2. **Artifacts.** Use the artifacts of your preparation as evidence of the work you've done to prepare. If you're pitching a restaurant client and have visited all the stores in their chain, take pictures and post them in the presentation room. Profile the target audience in a collage of pictures cut from magazines or printed from the

Internet that shows their demographics, personal values, activities, and interests. Intermingle any research data or statistics you have managed to obtain and present your findings from the collages.

The consumer research you've done is an excellent source of material. Show the materials created in the project exercises from your consumer focus groups (collages, thought bubble cartoons, psychodrawings, etc.). Display the photos or video you shot of your respondents (or they shot of themselves) when they were trying or shopping for the product or service.

3. **Drama.** Find a way to dramatize your creative strategy. Blow your brief up and print it as a big poster, or better yet, write it on the wall in big letters. Make T-shirts or ball caps with your themeline. Video-record interviews with heavy users of the product or service and edit them into a video about what the brand stands for. Or to be even more theatrical, create a ripomatic about the brand: scan still pictures or rip clips from rented or borrowed movies and use them as the visuals for a voiced-over presentation of what you believe the brand stands for.

4. **Online.** Some agencies create custom websites as part of their pitch. It's another opportunity to demonstrate your creativity, and it may allow you to dispense with the pitch document altogether (and save a tree). Google has new tools for site building that even a novice can use to produce amazing results.

Or create a blog that your client can follow in the period leading up to the pitch. Encourage the client to post and engage in a dialogue while the pitch is in development. You can post parts of your customer interviews, any background research, and your insights – anything that your prospect might find interesting and relevant to his or her business.

Form and content are both important in a pitch. But remember that in the pitch situation, unlike an ongoing agency relationship, clients are forced to make quick judgments about ideas presented in a rough or in-complete form, delivered by people they barely know. Given these unreal circumstances, perhaps it's not surprising that form often trumps content when it comes to making the final decision.

## Summing Up

Now you've learned something about how to compress what ought to be an eight- to twelve-week process down to the time that's allowed for many new business pitches. Of course, when you have more time and more money, you can do a lot more: in addition to talking to heavy users of the product or service, you can get the perspective of light and lapsed users, too; instead of fielding one key question in an overnight study, you can construct a real questionnaire and bring more comprehensive learning to the client's business problem, etc. But even when there is more time, many of the ideas presented here about strategy and presentation still apply.

There's a lot more to a successful pitch than putting your planning on a fast track. A more extended treatment of the subject would cover differentiating your agency brand from your competitions', organizing your agency team for new business success, establishing a system for tracking prospects, writing effective responses to RFPs, and optimizing the composition of the pitch team.

Clearly, there's an entire book that needs to be written. Until then, good luck with your pitch!

# The Science of Shopping
### The American shopper has never been so fickle. What are stores, including the new flagship designer boutiques, doing about it? Applying science.

## By Malcolm Gladwell

*Malcolm Gladwell has been a staff writer with the* New Yorker *magazine since 1996. His 1999 profile of Ron Popeil won a National Magazine Award, and in 2005 he was named one of* Time Magazine's *100 Most Influential People. He is the author of two books,* The Tipping Point: How Little Things Make a Big Difference *(2000) and* Blink: The Power of Thinking Without Thinking *(2005), both of which were number one* New York Times *bestsellers. This article originally appeared in the* New Yorker, *November 4, 1996.*

## 1.

Human beings walk the way they drive, which is to say that Americans tend to keep to the right when they stroll down shopping-mall concourses or city sidewalks. This is why in a well-designed airport travellers drifting toward their gate will always find the fast-food restaurants on their left and the gift shops on their right: people will readily cross a lane of pedestrian traffic to satisfy their hunger but rarely to make an impulse buy of a T-shirt or a magazine. This is also why Paco Underhill tells his retail clients to make sure that their window displays are canted, preferably to both sides but especially to the left, so that a potential shopper approaching the store on the inside of the sidewalk – the shopper, that is, with the least impeded view of the store window – can see the display from at least twenty-five feet away.

Of course, a lot depends on how fast the potential shopper is walking. Paco, in his previous life, as an urban geographer in Manhattan, spent a great deal of time thinking about walking speeds as he listened in on the great debates of the nineteen-seventies over whether the traffic lights in midtown should be timed to facilitate the movement of cars or to facilitate the movement of pedestrians and so break up the big platoons that move down Manhattan sidewalks. He knows that the faster you walk the more your peripheral vision narrows, so you become unable to pick up visual cues as quickly as someone who is just ambling along. He knows, too, that people who walk fast take a surprising amount of time to slow down – just as it takes a good stretch of road to change gears with a stick-shift automobile. On the basis of his research, Paco estimates the human downshift period to be anywhere from twelve to twenty-five feet, so if you own a store, he says, you never want to be next door to a bank: potential shoppers speed up when they walk past a bank (since there's nothing to look at), and by the time they slow down they've walked right past your business. The downshift factor also means that when potential shoppers enter a store it's going to take them from five to fifteen paces to adjust to the light and refocus and gear down from walking speed to shopping speed – particularly if they've just had to navigate a treacherous parking lot or hurry to make the light at Fifty-seventh and Fifth. Paco calls that area inside the door the Decompression Zone, and something he tells clients over and over again is never, ever put anything of value in that zone – not shopping baskets or tie racks or big promotional displays – because no one is going to see it. Paco believes that, as a rule of thumb, customer interaction with any product or promotional display in the Decompression Zone will increase at least thirty per cent once it's moved to the back edge of the zone, and even more if it's placed to the right, because another of the fundamental rules of how human beings shop is that upon entering a store – whether it's Nordstrom or Kmart, Tiffany or the Gap – the shopper invariably and reflexively turns to the right. Paco believes in the existence of the Invariant Right because he has actually verified it. He has put cameras in stores trained directly on the doorway, and if you go to his office, just above Union Square, where videocassettes and boxes of Super-eight film from all his work over the years are stacked in plastic Tupperware containers practically up to the ceiling, he can show you reel upon reel of grainy entryway video – customers striding in the door, downshifting, refocusing, and then, again and again, making that little half turn.

Paco Underhill is a tall man in his mid-forties, partly bald, with a neatly trimmed beard and an engaging, almost goofy manner. He wears baggy khakis and shirts open at the collar, and generally looks like the academic he might have been if he hadn't been captivated, twenty years ago, by the ideas of the urban anthropologist William Whyte. It was Whyte who pioneered the use of time-lapse photography as a tool of urban planning, putting cameras in parks and the plazas in front of office buildings in midtown Manhattan, in order to determine what distinguished a public space that worked from one that didn't. As a Columbia undergraduate, in 1974, Paco heard a lecture on Whyte's work and, he recalls, left the room "walking on air." He immediately read everything Whyte had written. He emptied his bank account to buy cameras and film and make his own home movie, about a pedestrian mall in Poughkeepsie. He took his "little exercise" to Whyte's advocacy group, the Project for Public Spaces, and was offered a job. Soon, however, it dawned on Paco that Whyte's ideas could be taken a step further – that the same techniques he used to establish why a plaza worked or didn't work could also be used to determine why a store worked or didn't work. Thus was born the field of retail anthropology, and, not long afterward, Paco founded Envirosell, which in just over fifteen years has counselled some of the most familiar names in American retailing, from Levi Strauss to Kinney, Starbucks, McDonald's, Blockbuster, Apple Computer, AT&T, and a number of upscale retailers that Paco would rather not name. When Paco gets an assignment, he and his staff set up a series of video cameras throughout the test store and then back the cameras up with Envirosell staffers – trackers, as they're known – armed with clipboards. Where the cameras go and how many trackers Paco deploys depends on exactly what the store wants to know about its shoppers. Typically, though, he might use six cameras and two or three trackers, and let the study run for two or three days, so that at the end he would have pages and pages of carefully annotated tracking sheets and anywhere from a hundred to five hundred hours of film. These days, given the expansion of his business, he might

tape fifteen thousand hours in a year, and, given that he has been in operation since the late seventies, he now has well over a hundred thousand
hours of tape in his library. Even in the best of times, this would be a
valuable archive. But today, with the retail business in crisis, it is a gold
mine. The time per visit that the average American spends in a shopping
mall was sixty-six minutes last year – down from seventy-two minutes in
1992 – and is the lowest number ever recorded. The amount of selling
space per American shopper is now more than double what it was in the
mid-seventies, meaning that profit margins have never been narrower, and
the costs of starting a retail business – and of failing – have never been
higher. In the past few years, countless dazzling new retailing temples have
been built along Fifth and Madison Avenues – Barneys, Calvin Klein,
Armani, Valentino, Banana Republic, Prada, Chanel, Niketown, and on
and on – but it is an explosion of growth based on no more than a hunch,
a hopeful multimillion-dollar gamble that the way to break through is to
provide the shopper with spectacle and more spectacle. "The arrogance
is gone," Millard Drexler, the president and CEO of Gap, told me. "Arrogance makes failure. Once you think you know the answer, it's almost
always over." In such a competitive environment, retailers don't just want
to know how shoppers behave in their stores. They have to know. And
who better to ask than Paco Underhill, who in the past decade and a half
has analyzed tens of thousands of hours of shopping videotape and, as a
result, probably knows more about the strange habits and quirks of the
species *Emptor americanus* than anyone else alive?

## 2.

Paco is considered the originator, for example, of what is known in the
trade as the butt-brush theory – or, as Paco calls it, more delicately, *le facteur
bousculade* – which holds that the likelihood of a woman's being converted
from a browser to a buyer is inversely proportional to the likelihood of
her being brushed on her behind while she's examining merchandise.
Touch – or brush or bump or jostle – a woman on the behind when she
has stopped to look at an item, and she will bolt. Actually, calling this a
theory is something of a misnomer, because Paco doesn't offer any explanation for why women react that way, aside from venturing that they are

"more sensitive back there." It's really an observation, based on repeated and close analysis of his videotape library, that Paco has transformed into a retailing commandment: a women's product that requires extensive examination should never be placed in a narrow aisle.

Paco approaches the problem of the Invariant Right the same way. Some retail thinkers see this as a subject crying out for interpretation and speculation. The design guru Joseph Weishar, for example, argues, in his magisterial "Design for Effective Selling Space," that the Invariant Right is a function of the fact that we "absorb and digest information in the left part of the brain" and "assimilate and logically use this information in the right half," the result being that we scan the store from left to right and then fix on an object to the right "essentially at a 45-degree angle from the point that we enter." When I asked Paco about this interpretation, he shrugged, and said he thought the reason was simply that most people are right-handed. Uncovering the fundamentals of "why" is clearly not a pursuit that engages him much. He is not a theoretician but an empiricist, and for him the important thing is that in amassing his huge library of in-store time-lapse photography he has gained enough hard evidence to know how often and under what circumstances the Invariant Right is expressed and how to take advantage of it.

What Paco likes are facts. They come tumbling out when he talks, and, because he speaks with a slight hesitation — lingering over the first syllable in, for example, "re-tail" or "de-sign" — he draws you in, and you find yourself truly hanging on his words. "We have reached a historic point in American history," he told me in our very first conversation. "Men, for the first time, have begun to buy their own underwear." He then paused to let the comment sink in, so that I could absorb its implications, before he elaborated: "Which means that we have to totally rethink the way we sell that product." In the parlance of Hollywood scriptwriters, the best endings must be surprising and yet inevitable; and the best of Paco's pronouncements take the same shape. It would never have occurred to me to wonder about the increasingly critical role played by touching — or, as Paco calls it, petting — clothes in the course of making the decision to buy them. But then I went to the Gap and to

Banana Republic and saw people touching and fondling and, one after another, buying shirts and sweaters laid out on big wooden tables, and what Paco told me — which was no doubt based on what he had seen on his videotapes — made perfect sense: that the reason the Gap and Banana Republic have tables is not merely that sweaters and shirts look better there, or that tables fit into the warm and relaxing residential feeling that the Gap and Banana Republic are trying to create in their stores, but that tables invite — indeed, symbolize — touching. "Where do we eat?" Paco asks. "We eat, we pick up food, on tables."

Paco produces for his clients a series of carefully detailed studies, totalling forty to a hundred and fifty pages, filled with product-by-product breakdowns and bright-colored charts and graphs. In one recent case, he was asked by a major clothing retailer to analyze the first of a new chain of stores that the firm planned to open. One of the things the client wanted to know was how successful the store was in drawing people into its depths, since the chances that shoppers will buy something are directly related to how long they spend shopping, and how long they spend shopping is directly related to how deep they get pulled into the store. For this reason, a supermarket will often put dairy products on one side, meat at the back, and fresh produce on the other side, so that the typical shopper can't just do a drive-by but has to make an entire circuit of the store, and be tempted by everything the supermarket has to offer. In the case of the new clothing store, Paco found that ninety-one per cent of all shoppers penetrated as deep as what he called Zone 4, meaning more than three-quarters of the way in, well past the accessories and shirt racks and belts in the front, and little short of the far wall, with the changing rooms and the pants stacked on shelves. Paco regarded this as an extraordinary figure, particularly for a long, narrow store like this one, where it is not unusual for the rate of penetration past, say, Zone 3 to be under fifty per cent. But that didn't mean the store was perfect — far from it. For Paco, all kinds of questions remained.

Purchasers, for example, spent an average of eleven minutes and twenty-seven seconds in the store, nonpurchasers two minutes and thirty-six seconds. It wasn't that the nonpurchasers just cruised in and out: in those two minutes and thirty-six seconds, they went deep into the store and examined an average of 3.42 items. So why didn't they buy? What, exactly, happened to cause some browsers to buy and other browsers to walk out the door?

Then, there was the issue of the number of products examined. The purchasers were looking at an average of 4.81 items but buying only 1.33 items. Paco found this statistic deeply disturbing. As the retail market grows more cutthroat, store owners have come to realize that it's all but impossible to increase the number of customers coming in, and have concentrated instead on getting the customers they do have to buy more. Paco thinks that if you can sell someone a pair of pants you must also be able to sell that person a belt, or a pair of socks, or a pair of underpants, or even do what the Gap does so well: sell a person a complete outfit. To Paco, the figure 1.33 suggested that the store was doing something very wrong, and one day when I visited him in his office he sat me down in front of one of his many VCRs to see how he looked for the 1.33 culprit.

It should be said that sitting next to Paco is a rather strange experience. "My mother says that I'm the best-paid spy in America," he told me. He laughed, but he wasn't entirely joking. As a child, Paco had a nearly debilitating stammer, and, he says, "since I was never that comfortable talking I always relied on my eyes to understand things." That much is obvious from the first moment you meet him: Paco is one of those people who look right at you, soaking up every nuance and detail. It isn't a hostile gaze, because Paco isn't hostile at all. He has a big smile, and he'll call you "chief" and use your first name a lot and generally act as if he knew you well. But that's the awkward thing: he has looked at you so closely that you're sure he does know you well, and you, meanwhile, hardly know him at all. This kind of asymmetry is even more pronounced when you watch his shopping videos with him, because every movement or gesture means something to Paco — he has spent his adult life deconstructing the shopping experience — but nothing to the outsider, or, at least, not at first. Paco had to keep stopping the video to get me to see things through his eyes before I began to understand. In one sequence, for example, a camera mounted high on the wall outside the changing rooms documented a man and a woman shopping for a pair of pants for what appeared to be their daughter, a girl in her mid-teens. The tapes are soundless, but the basic steps of the shopping dance are so familiar to Paco that, once I'd grasped the general idea, he was able to provide a running commentary on what was being said and thought. There is the girl emerging from the changing room wearing her first pair. There she is glancing at her reflection in the mirror, then turning to see herself from the back. There is the mother looking on. There is the father — or, as fathers are known in the trade, the "wallet carrier" — stepping forward and pulling up the jeans. There's the girl trying on another pair. There's the primp again. The twirl. The mother. The wallet carrier. And then again, with another pair. The full sequence lasted twenty minutes, and at the end came the take-home lesson, for which Paco called in one of his colleagues, Tom Moseman, who had supervised the project. "This is a very critical moment," Tom, a young, intense man wearing little round glasses, said, and he pulled up a chair next to mine. "She's saying, 'I don't know whether I should wear a belt.' Now here's the salesclerk. The girl says to him, 'I need a belt,' and he says, 'Take mine.' Now there he is taking her back to the full-length mirror." A moment later, the girl returns, clearly happy with the purchase. She wants the jeans. The wallet carrier turns to her, and then gestures to the salesclerk. The wallet carrier is telling his daughter to give back the belt. The girl gives back the belt. Tom stops the tape. He's leaning forward now, a finger jabbing at the screen. Beside me, Paco is shaking his head. I don't get it — at least, not at first — and so Tom replays that last segment. The wallet carrier tells the girl to give back the belt. She gives back the belt. And then, finally, it dawns on me why this store has an average purchase number of only 1.33. "Don't you see?" Tom said. "She wanted the belt. A great opportunity to make an add-on sale . . . lost!"

## 3.

Should we be afraid of Paco Underhill? One of the fundamental anxieties of the American consumer, after all, has always been that beneath the pleasure and the frivolity of the shopping experience runs an undercurrent of manipulation, and that anxiety has rarely seemed more justified than today. The practice of prying into the minds and habits of American consumers is now a multibillion-dollar business. Every time a product is pulled across a supermarket checkout scanner, information is recorded, assembled, and sold to a market-research firm for analysis. There are companies that put tiny cameras inside frozen-food cases in supermarket aisles; market-research firms that feed census data and behavioral statistics into algorithms and come out with complicated maps of the American consumer; anthropologists who sift through the garbage of carefully targeted households to analyze their true consumption patterns; and endless rounds of highly organized focus groups and questionnaire takers and phone surveyors. That some people are now tracking our every shopping move with video cameras seems in many respects the last straw: Paco's movies are, after all, creepy. They look like the surveillance videos taken during convenience-store holdups — hazy and soundless and slightly warped by the angle of the lens. When you watch them, you find yourself waiting for something bad to happen, for someone to shoplift or pull a gun on a cashier.

The more time you spend with Paco's videos, though, the less scary they seem. After an hour or so, it's no longer clear whether simply by watching people shop — and analyzing their every move — you can learn how to control them. The shopper that emerges from the videos is not pliable or manipulable. The screen shows people filtering in and out of stores, petting and moving on, abandoning their merchandise because checkout lines are too long, or leaving a store empty-handed because they couldn't fit their stroller into the aisle between two shirt racks. Paco's shoppers are fickle and headstrong, and are quite unwilling to buy anything unless conditions are perfect — unless the belt is presented at exactly the right moment. His theories of the butt-brush and petting and the Decompression Zone and the Invariant Right seek not to make shoppers conform to the desires of sellers but to make sellers conform to the desires of shoppers. What Paco is teaching his clients is a kind of slavish devotion to the shopper's every whim. He is teaching them humility. Paco has worked with supermarket chains, and when you first see one of his videos of grocery aisles it looks as if he really had — at least in this instance – got one up on the shopper. The clip he showed me was of a father shopping with a small child, and it was an example of what is known in the trade as "advocacy," which basically means what happens when your four-year-old goes over and grabs a bag of cookies that the store has conveniently put on the bottom shelf, and demands that it be purchased. In the clip, the father takes what the child offers him. "Generally, dads are not as good as moms at saying no," Paco said as we watched the little boy approach his dad. "Men tend to be more impulse-driven than women in grocery stores. We know that they tend to shop less often with a list. We know that they tend to shop much less frequently with coupons, and we know, simply by watching them shop, that they can be marching down the aisle and something will catch their eye and they will stop and buy." This kind of weakness on the part of fathers might seem to give the supermarket an advantage in the cookie-selling wars, particularly since more and more men go grocery shopping with their children. But then Paco let drop a hint about a study he'd just done in which he discovered, to his and everyone else's amazement, that shoppers had already figured this out, that they were already one step ahead – that families were avoiding the cookie aisle. This may seem like a small point. But it begins to explain why, even though retailers seem to know more than ever about how shoppers behave, even though their efforts at intelligence-gathering have rarely seemed more intrusive and more formidable, the retail business remains in crisis. The reason is that shoppers are a moving target. They are becoming more and more complicated, and retailers need to know more and more about them simply to keep pace. This fall, for example, Estée Lauder is testing in a Toronto shopping mall a new concept in cosmetics retailing. Gone is the enclosed rectangular counter, with the sales staff on one side, customers on the other, and the product under glass in the middle. In its place the company has provided an assortment of product-display, consultation, and testing kiosks arranged in a broken circle, with a service desk and a cashier in the middle. One of the kiosks is a "makeup play area," which allows customers to experiment on their own with a hundred and thirty different shades of lipstick. There are four self-service displays – for perfumes, skin-care products, and makeup — which are easily accessible to customers who have already made up their minds. And, for those who haven't, there is a semiprivate booth for personal consultations with beauty advisers and makeup artists. The redesign was prompted by the realization that the modern working woman no longer had the time or the inclination to ask a salesclerk to assist her in every purchase, that choosing among shades of lipstick did not require the same level of service as, say, getting up to speed on new developments in skin care, that a shopper's needs were now too diverse to be adequately served by just one kind of counter. "I was going from store to store, and the traffic just wasn't there," Robin Burns, the president and CEO of Estée Lauder U.S.A. and Canada, told me. "We had to get rid of the glass barricade." The most interesting thing about the new venture, though, is what it says about the shifting balance of power between buyer and seller. Around the old rectangular counter, the relationship of clerk to customer was formal and subtly paternalistic. If you wanted to look at a lipstick, you had to ask for it. "Twenty years ago, the sales staff would consult with you and tell you what you needed, as opposed to asking and recommending," Burns said. "And in those days people believed what the salesperson told them." Today, the old hierarchy has been inverted. "Women want to draw their own conclusions," Burns said. Even the architecture of the consultation kiosk speaks to the transformation: the beauty adviser now sits beside the customer, not across from her.

## 4.

This doesn't mean that marketers and retailers have stopped trying to figure out what goes on in the minds of shoppers. One of the hottest areas in market research, for example, is something called typing, which is a sophisticated attempt to predict the kinds of products that people will buy or the kind of promotional pitch they will be susceptible to on the basis of where they live or how they score on short standardized questionnaires. One market-research firm in Virginia, Claritas, has divided the entire country, neighborhood by neighborhood, into sixty-two different categories — Pools & Patios, Shotguns & Pickups, Bohemia Mix, and so on — using census data and results from behavioral surveys. On the basis of my address in Greenwich Village, Claritas classifies me as Urban Gold Coast, which means that I like Kellogg's Special K, spend more than two hundred and fifty dollars on sports coats, watch "Seinfeld," and buy metal polish. Such typing systems — and there are a number of them — can be scarily accurate. I actually do buy Kellogg's Special K, have spent more than two hundred and fifty dollars on a sports coat, and watch "Seinfeld." (I don't buy metal polish.) In fact, when I was typed by a company called Total Research, in Princeton, the results were so dead-on that I got the same kind of creepy feeling that I got when I first watched Paco's videos. On the basis of a seemingly innocuous multiple-choice test, I was scored as an eighty-nine-per-cent Intellect and a seven-per-cent Relief Seeker (which I thought was impressive until John Morton, who developed the system, told me that virtually everyone who reads The New Yorker is an Intellect). When I asked Morton to guess, on the basis of my score, what kind of razor I used, he riffed, brilliantly, and without a moment's hesitation. "If you used an electric razor, it would be a Braun," he began. "But, if not, you're probably shaving with Gillette, if only because there really isn't an Intellect safety-razor positioning out there. Schick and Bic are simply not logical choices for you, although I'm thinking, you're fairly young, and you've got that Relief Seeker side. It's possible you would use Bic because you don't like that all-American, overly confident masculine statement of Gillette. It's a very, very conventional positioning that Gillette uses. But then they've got the technological angle with the Gillette Sensor. . . . I'm thinking Gillette. It's Gillette."

He was right. I shave with Gillette — though I didn't even know that I do. I had to go home and check. But information about my own predilections may be of limited usefulness in predicting how I shop. In the past few years, market researchers have paid growing attention to the role in the shopping experience of a type of consumer known as a Market Maven. "This is a person you would go to for advice on a car or a new fashion," said Linda Price, a marketing professor at the University of South Florida, who first came up with the Market Maven concept, in the late eighties. "This is a person who has information on a lot of different products or prices or places to shop. This is a person who likes to initiate discussions with consumers and respond to requests. Market Mavens like to be helpers in the marketplace. They take you shopping. They go shopping for you, and it turns out they are a lot more prevalent than you would expect." Mavens watch more television than almost anyone else does, and they read more magazines and open their junk mail and look closely at advertisements and have an awful lot of influence on everyone else. According to Price, sixty per cent of Americans claim to know a Maven.

The key question, then, is not what I think but what my Mavens think. The challenge for retailers and marketers, in turn, is not so much to figure out and influence my preferences as to figure out and influence the preferences of my Mavens, and that is a much harder task. "What's really interesting is that the distribution of Mavens doesn't vary by ethnic category, by income, or by professional status," Price said. "A working woman is just as likely to be a Market Maven as a nonworking woman. You might say that Mavens are likely to be older, unemployed people, but that's wrong, too. There is simply not a clear demographic guide to how to find these people." More important, Mavens are better consumers than most of the rest of us. In another of the typing systems, developed by the California-based SRI International, Mavens are considered to be a subcategory of the consumer type known as Fulfilled, and Fulfilleds, one SRI official told me, are "the consumers from Hell — they are very feature oriented." He explained, "They are not pushed by promotions. You can reach them, but it's an intellectual argument." As the complexity of the marketplace grows, in other words, we have responded by appointing the most skeptical and the most savvy in our midst to mediate between us and sellers. The harder stores and manufacturers work to sharpen and refine their marketing strategies, and the harder they try to read the minds of shoppers, the more we hide behind Mavens.

## 5.

Imagine that you want to open a clothing store, men's and women's, in the upper-middle range — say, khakis at fifty dollars, dress shirts at forty dollars, sports coats and women's suits at two hundred dollars and up. The work of Paco Underhill would suggest that in order to succeed you need to pay complete and concentrated attention to the whims of your customers. What does that mean, in practical terms? Well, let's start with what's called the shopping gender gap. In the retail-store study that Paco showed me, for example, male buyers stayed an average of nine minutes and thirty-nine seconds in the store and female buyers stayed twelve minutes and fifty-seven seconds. This is not atypical. Women always shop longer than men, which is one of the major reasons that in the standard regional mall women account for seventy per cent of the dollar value of all purchases. "Women have more patience than men," Paco says. "Men are more distractible. Their tolerance level for confusion or time spent in a store is much shorter than women's." If you wanted, then, you could build a store designed for men, to try to raise that thirty-per-cent sales figure to forty or forty-five per cent. You could make the look more masculine — more metal, darker woods. You could turn up the music. You could simplify the store, put less product on the floor. "I'd go narrow and deep," says James Adams, the design director for NBBJ Retail Concepts, a division of one of the country's largest retail-design firms. "You wouldn't have fifty different cuts of pants. You'd have your four basics with lots of color. You know the Garanimals they used to do to help kids pick out clothes, where you match the giraffe top with the giraffe bottom? I'm sure every guy is like 'I wish I could get those, too.' You'd want to stick with the basics. Making sure most of the color story goes together. That is a big deal with guys, because they are always screwing the colors up." When I asked Carrie Gennuso, the Gap's regional vice-president for New York, what she would do in an all-male store, she laughed and said, "I might do fewer displays and more signage. Big signs. Men! Smalls! Here!" As a rule, though, you wouldn't want to cater to male customers at the expense of female ones. It's no accident that many clothing stores have a single look in both men's and women's sections, and that the quintessential nineties look — light woods, white walls — is more feminine than masculine. Women are still the shoppers in America, and the real money is to be made by making retailing styles more female-friendly, not less. Recently, for example, NBBJ did a project to try to increase sales of the Armstrong flooring chain. Its researchers found that the sales staff was selling the flooring based on its functional virtues – the fact that it didn't scuff, that it was long-lasting, that it didn't stain, that it was easy to clean. It was being sold by men to men, as if it were a car or a stereo. And that was the problem. "It's a wonder product technologically," Adams says. "But the woman is the decision-maker on flooring, and that's not what's she's looking for. This product is about fashion, about color and design. You don't want to get too caught up in the man's way of thinking."

To appeal to men, then, retailers do subtler things. At the Banana Republic store on Fifth Avenue in midtown, the men's socks are displayed near the shoes and between men's pants and the cash register (or cash/ wrap, as it is known in the trade), so that the man can grab them easily as he rushes to pay. Women's accessories are by the fitting rooms, because women are much more likely to try on pants first, and then choose an item like a belt or a bag. At the men's shirt table, the display shirts have matching ties on them – the tie table is next to it – in a grown-up version of the Garanimals system. But Banana Republic would never match scarves with women's blouses or jackets. "You don't have to be that direct with women," Jeanne Jackson, the president of Banana Republic, told me. "In fact, the Banana woman is proud of her sense of style. She puts her own looks together." Jackson said she liked the Fifth Avenue store because it's on two floors, so she can separate men's and women's sections and give men what she calls "clarity of offer," which is the peace of mind that they won't inadvertently end up in, say, women's undergarments. In a one-floor store, most retailers would rather put the menswear up front and the women's wear at the back (that is, if they weren't going to split the sexes left and right), because women don't get spooked navigating through apparel of the opposite sex, whereas men most assuredly do. (Of course, in a store like the Gap at Thirty-ninth and Fifth, where, Carrie Gennuso says, "I don't know if I've ever seen a man," the issue is moot. There, it's safe to put the women's wear out front.)

The next thing retailers want to do is to encourage the shopper to walk deep into the store. The trick there is to put "destination items" – basics, staples, things that people know you have and buy a lot of – at the rear of the store. Gap stores, invariably, will have denim, which is a classic destination item for them, on the back wall. Many clothing stores also situate the cash/wrap and the fitting rooms in the rear of the store, to compel shoppers to walk back into Zone 3 or 4. In the store's prime real estate – which, given Paco's theory of the Decompression Zone and the Invariant Right, is to the right of the front entrance and five to fifteen paces in – you always put your hottest and newest merchandise, because that's where the maximum number of people will see it. Right now, in virtually every Gap in the country, the front of the store is devoted to the Gap fall look – casual combinations in black and gray, plaid shirts and jackets, sweaters, black wool and brushed-twill pants. At the Gap at Fifth Avenue and Seventeenth Street, for example, there is a fall ensemble of plaid jacket, plaid shirt, and black pants in the first prime spot, followed, three paces later, by an ensemble of gray sweater, plaid shirt, T-shirt, and black pants, followed, three paces after that, by an ensemble of plaid jacket, gray sweater, white T-shirt, and black pants. In all, three variations on the same theme, each placed so that the eye bounces naturally from the first to the second to the third, and then, inexorably, to a table deep inside Zone 1 where merchandise is arrayed and folded for petting. Every week or ten days, the combinations will change, the "look" highlighted at the front will be different, and the entryway will be transformed.

Through all of this, the store environment – the lighting, the colors, the fixtures – and the clothes have to work together. The point is not so much beauty as coherence. The clothes have to match the environment. "In the nineteen-seventies, you didn't have to have a complete wardrobe all the time," Gabriella Forte, the president and chief operating officer of Calvin Klein, says. "I think now the store has to have a complete point of view. It has to have all the options offered, so people have choices. It's the famous one-stop shopping. People want to come in, be serviced, and go out. They want to understand the clear statement the designer is making."

At the new Versace store on Fifth Avenue, in the restored neoclassical Vanderbilt mansion, Gianni Versace says that the "statement" he is making with the elaborate mosaic and parquet floors, the marble façade and the Corinthian columns is "quality – my message is always a scream for quality." At her two new stores in London, Donna Karan told me, she never wants "customers to think that they are walking into a clothing store." She said, "I want them to think that they are walking into an environment, that I am transforming them out of their lives and into an experience, that it's not about clothes, it's about who they are as people." The first thing the shopper sees in her stark, all-white DKNY store is a video monitor and café: "It's about energy," Karan said, "and nourishment." In her more sophisticated, "collection" store, where the walls are black and ivory and gold, the first thing that the customer notices is the scent of a candle: "I wanted a nurturing environment where you feel that you will be taken care of." And why, at a Giorgio Armani store, is there often only a single suit in each style on display? Not because the store has only the one suit in stock but because the way the merchandise is displayed has to be consistent with the message of the designers: that Armani suits are exclusive, that the Armani customer isn't going to run into another man wearing his suit every time he goes to an art opening at Gagosian.

The best stores all have an image — or what retailers like to call a "point of view." The flagship store for Ralph Lauren's Polo collection, for example, is in the restored Rhinelander mansion, on Madison Avenue and Seventy-second Street. The Polo Mansion, as it is known, is alive with color and artifacts that suggest a notional pre-War English gentility. There are fireplaces and comfortable leather chairs and deep-red Oriental carpets and soft, thick drapes and vintage photographs and paintings of country squires and a color palette of warm crimsons and browns and greens — to the point that after you've picked out a double-breasted blazer or a cashmere sweater set or an antique silver snuffbox you feel as though you ought to venture over to Central Park for a vigorous morning of foxhunting. The Calvin Klein flagship store, twelve blocks down Madison Avenue, on the other hand, is a vast, achingly beautiful minimalist temple, with white walls, muted lighting, soaring ceilings, gray stone flooring, and, so it seems, less merchandise in the entire store than Lauren puts in a single room. The store's architect, John Pawson, says, "People who enter are given a sense of release. They are getting away from the hustle and bustle of the street and New York. They are in a calm space. It's a modern idea of luxury, to give people space."

The first thing you see when you enter the Polo Mansion is a display of two hundred and eight sweaters, in twenty-eight colors, stacked in a haberdasher's wooden fixture, behind an antique glass counter; the first thing you see at the Klein store is a white wall, and then, if you turn to the right, four clear-glass shelves, each adorned with three solitary-looking black handbags. The Polo Mansion is an English club. The Klein store, Pawson says, is the equivalent of an art gallery, a place where "neutral space and light make a work of art look the most potent." When I visited the Polo Mansion, the stereo was playing Bobby Short. At Klein, the stereo was playing what sounded like Brian Eno. At the Polo Mansion, I was taken around by Charles Fagan, a vice-president at Polo Ralph Lauren. He wore pale-yellow socks, black loafers, tight jeans, a pale-purple polo shirt, blue old-school tie, and a brown plaid jacket – which sounds less attractive on paper than it was in reality. He looked, in a very Ralph Lauren way, fabulous. He was funny and engaging and bounded through the store, keeping up a constant patter ("This room is sort of sportswear, Telluride-y, vintage"), all the while laughing and hugging people and having his freshly cut red hair tousled by the sales assistants in each section. At the Calvin Klein store, the idea that the staff – tall, austere, sombre-suited – might laugh and hug and tousle each other's hair is unthinkable. Lean over and whisper, perhaps. At the most, murmur discreetly into tiny black cellular phones. Visiting the Polo Mansion and the Calvin Klein flagship in quick succession is rather like seeing a "Howards End"/"The Seventh Seal" double feature.

Despite their differences, though, these stores are both about the same thing – communicating the point of view that shoppers are now thought to demand. At Polo, the "lifestyle" message is so coherent and all-encompassing that the store never has the 1.33 items-per-purchase problem that Paco saw in the retailer he studied. "We have multiple purchases in excess – it's the cap, it's the tie, it's the sweater, it's the jacket, it's the pants," Fagan told me, plucking each item from its shelf and tossing it onto a tartan-covered bench seat. "People say, 'I have to have the belt.' It's a lifestyle decision."

As for the Klein store, it's really concerned with setting the tone for the Calvin Klein clothes and products sold outside the store – including the designer's phenomenally successful underwear line, the sales of which have grown nearly fivefold in the past two and a half years, making it one of the country's dominant brands. Calvin Klein underwear is partly a design triumph: lowering the waistband just a tad in order to elongate, and flatter, the torso. But it is also a triumph of image – transforming, as Gabriella Forte says, a "commodity good into something desirable," turning a forgotten necessity into fashion. In the case of women's underwear, Bob Mazzoli, president of Calvin Klein Underwear, told me that the company "obsessed about the box being a perfect square, about the symmetry of it all, how it would feel in a woman's hand." He added, "When you look at the boxes they are little works of art." And the underwear itself is without any of the usual busyness – without, in Mazzoli's words, "the excessive detail" of most women's undergarments. It's a clean look, selling primarily in white, heather gray, and black. It's a look, in other words, not unlike that of the Calvin Klein flagship store, and it exemplifies the brilliance of the merchandising of the Calvin Klein image: preposterous as it may seem, once you've seen the store and worn the underwear, it's difficult not to make a connection between the two.

All this imagemaking seeks to put the shopping experience in a different context, to give it a story line. "I wish that the customers who come to my stores feel the same comfort they would entering a friend's house – that is to say, that they feel at ease, without the impression of having to deal with the 'sanctum sanctorum' of a designer," Giorgio Armani told me. Armani has a house. Donna Karan has a kitchen and a womb. Ralph Lauren has a men's club. Calvin Klein has an art gallery. These are all very different points of view. What they have in common is that they have nothing to do with the actual act of shopping. (No one buys anything at a friend's house or a men's club.) Presumably, by engaging in this kind of misdirection designers aim to put us at ease, to create a kind of oasis. But perhaps they change the subject because they must, because they cannot offer an ultimate account of the shopping experience itself. After all, what do we really know, in the end, about why people buy? We know about the Invariant Right and the Decompression Zone. We know to put destination items at the back and fashion at the front, to treat male shoppers like small children, to respect the female derrière, and to put the socks between the cash/wrap and the men's pants. But this is grammar; it's not prose. It is enough. But it is not much.

## 6.

One of the best ways to understand the new humility in shopping theory is to go back to the work of William Whyte. Whyte put his cameras in parks and in the plazas in front of office buildings because he believed in the then-radical notion that the design of public spaces had been turned inside out – that planners were thinking of their designs first and of people second, when they should have been thinking of people first and of design second. In his 1980 classic, "The Social Life of Small Urban Spaces," for example, Whyte trained his cameras on a dozen or so of the public spaces and small parks around Manhattan, like the plaza in front of the General Motors Building, on Fifth Avenue, and the small park at 77 Water Street, downtown, and Paley Park, on Fifty-third Street, in order to determine why some, like the tiny Water Street park, averaged well over a hundred and fifty people during a typical sunny lunch hour and others, like the much bigger plaza at 280 Park Avenue, were almost empty. He concluded that all the things used by designers to attempt to lure people into their spaces made little or no difference. It wasn't the size of the space, or its beauty, or the presence of waterfalls, or the amount of sun, or whether a park was a narrow strip along the sidewalk or a pleasing open space. What mattered, overwhelmingly, was that there were plenty of places to sit, that the space was in some way connected to the street, and – the mystical circularity – that it was already well frequented. "What attracts people most, it would appear, is other people," Whyte noted:

If I labor the point, it is because many urban spaces still are being designed as though the opposite were true – as though what people liked best were the places they stay away from. People often do talk along such lines, and therefore their responses to questionnaires can be entirely misleading. How many people would say they like to sit in the middle of a crowd? Instead, they speak of "getting away from it all," and use words like "escape," "oasis," "retreat." What people do, however, reveals a different priority.

Whyte's conclusions demystified the question of how to make public space work. Places to sit, streets to enjoy, and people to watch turned out to be the simple and powerful rules for park designers to follow, and these rules demolished the orthodoxies and theoretical principles of conventional urban design. But in a more important sense — and it is here that Whyte's connection with Paco Underhill and retail anthropology and the stores that line Fifth and Madison is most striking — what Whyte did was to remystify the art of urban planning. He said, emphatically, that people could not be manipulated, that they would enter a public space only on their own terms, that the goal of observers like him was to find out what people wanted, not why they wanted it. Whyte, like Paco, was armed with all kinds of facts and observations about what it took to build a successful public space. He had strict views on how wide ledges had to be to lure passersby (at least thirty inches, or two backsides deep), and what the carrying capacity of prime outdoor sitting space is (total number of square feet divided by three). But, fundamentally, he was awed by the infinite complexity and the ultimate mystery of human behavior. He took people too seriously to think that he could control them. Here is Whyte, in "The Social Life of Small Urban Spaces," analyzing hours of videotape and describing what he has observed about the way men stand in public. He's talking about feet. He could just as easily be talking about shopping:

> Foot movements . . . seem to be a silent language. Often, in a schmoozing group, no one will be saying anything. Men stand bound in amiable silence, surveying the passing scene. Then, slowly, rhythmically, one of the men rocks up and down; first on the ball of the foot, then back on the heel. He stops. Another man starts the same movement. Sometimes there are reciprocal gestures. One man makes a half turn to the right. Then, after a rhythmic interval, another responds with a half turn to the left. Some kind of communication seems to be taking place here, but I've never broken the code.

# Section IV: Future

In the 21st Century, account planning has evolved with the changing nature of the advertising business.

Now, agencies provide their clients with integrated communications programs, of which traditional TV and print ads may be the smallest part.

Simultaneously, planners have taken on new roles. They have become more specialized within agencies and moved outside to work in other kinds of organizations.

Meanwhile, agencies have become increasingly global to reflect the needs of their increasingly global clients.

This last group of readings looks at the present and near future of account planning as it continues to evolve.

# Above and Beyond Advertising Planning

## By John Griffiths

*John Griffiths has been a communications planner for (gulp) 24 years. Since 2000, he's had over 70 clients. The vast majority of projects involve solving problems very fast and thinking outside of the box. He has been a planning director twice - which was quite enough! By way of additional interesting background, he was born in Singapore and brought up in Japan, spent a year of his life on a sheep farm in New Zealand, plays in a band (guitar, keyboards, whatever), has a degree in philosophy and English and still dabbles in both from time to time. Most important, for most of us, he supervises the delightfully informative website, planningaboveandbeyond.com — do visit.*

ACCOUNT PLANNING HAS BEEN in existence for over 40 years, and despite the different styles typified by advertising agencies such as BMP and JWT, that have been so instrumental in its development, there is now an accepted core of theory and practice.

However, virtually all of this lies in the area of advertising. In the last ten years the majority of the top 20 direct marketing, sales promotion, and design agencies have either started an account planning department, have a planning director on the board, or claim to offer planning as one of their services. In spite of this, there is virtually no written account of how planning functions in these areas: the second edition of *How to Plan Advertising*[1] contains a single chapter on the subject. As I will show, account planning needs to be adapted to work with disciplines other than advertising.

The first discovery made by a planner crossing the border between advertising and other disciplines is that much has to be unlearned. Planning developed specifically for advertising has a number of assumptions as a consequence, due to its specific needs. And, before planning can work in a multi-disciplinary framework, it is essential that the planner service each communication discipline effectively on its own terms.

## Planning and Other Disciplines

Planning is not essential to the production of ads, so it plays a qualitative role in adding value to what is made. To function well outside advertising, planning has to add value to what is being produced, and it needs to align itself with the business model for the appropriate discipline – because they all make money differently.

Taking two weeks to write a creative brief, two weeks to bond with the creative team, plus another two weeks to write up the results at the end of the campaign is the quickest way to get fired in any agency other than an ad agency! In the majority of agencies not directly involved in advertising, the planner's time is charged directly by the hour, and has to be accounted for.

## So What Is the Business Model?

Exhibit 1

| How Each Discipline Makes Its Money | | |
|---|---|---|
| **Discipline** | **Making Money** | **Making Profit** |
| Advertising | Media commission/fees related to media spend | Biggest accounts |
| Direct Marketing | Construction and operation of bespoke medium: account handling/targeting | Complex accounts |
| Sales Promotion | Construction and operation of bespoke mechanic: account handling | Complex mechanics (any size) |
| Public Relations | Through labor of account handling | Biggest accounts |
| Sponsorship | Fee proportionate to size of sponsorship | Biggest accounts |
| Web Based | Construction and operation of bespoke medium: account handling/targeting | Complex accounts |

Advertising makes its money through commission or fees still linked, however distantly, to the media spend. The larger the account, the more profitable — theoretically. In fact, large accounts subsidise smaller ones, which may offer greater creative possibilities (Exhibit 1).

Direct marketing makes its money by constructing its own medium, rather than renting somebody else's. Every campaign requires the creation, operation, and dismantling of a medium. That is why DM agencies have larger account teams, why account handlers present strategy, and why the headcount and the hours spent on the account are critical. In DM, complexity, rather than size, is profitable, since size can provide economies of scale but complexity carries its own mark-up. The planner has to contribute to the effectiveness of this medium, whose success derives from much more than the construction of the message.

Sales promotion earns its income from implementing one of a basic range of mechanics, in a sufficiently attention-grabbing way, to ensure that the mechanic is effective. The choice of mechanic is the greatest contributor to the success of the promotion. The scale of the promotion and its complexity create profits.

Sponsorship is often used as a more cost-effective way to increase salience without paying for the space outright as in advertising. The fee is proportionate to the size of the sponsorship. Profitability comes from scale, but also from the implementation of tie-ins.

PR, like advertising, borrows media, but can only influence what is written through direct briefings and event management. Income derives from the size of account, the number of handlers required to service it and, to an extent, the complexity of the account.

Web-based communications are also constructing a medium rather than borrowing one, although its distribution costs are massively lower. It generates income (and maybe even profit) through complexity.

## How Is Value Added to Each Discipline?

Advertising adds value through great creative: the same space can achieve disproportionate results simply through the power of an idea. Advertising

Exhibit 2

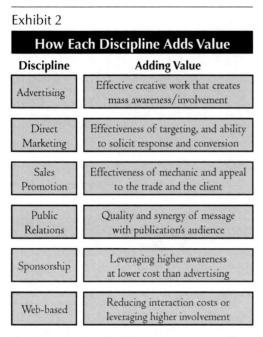

| Discipline | Adding Value |
|---|---|
| Advertising | Effective creative work that creates mass awareness/involvement |
| Direct Marketing | Effectiveness of targeting, and ability to solicit response and conversion |
| Sales Promotion | Effectiveness of mechanic and appeal to the trade and the client |
| Public Relations | Quality and synergy of message with publication's audience |
| Sponsorship | Leveraging higher awareness at lower cost than advertising |
| Web-based | Reducing interaction costs or leveraging higher involvement |

is also still the cheapest way to create awareness and involvement with a mass audience. Unsurprisingly, advertising planners have a lot to do with creative work. (See Exhibit 2.)

Direct marketing also depends on good creative. But targeting is all-important. An indifferent execution sent to the right people will generate more response and pay back quicker than a brilliant mailing to the wrong audience. So from the timesheets of a DM agency you will see much more time allocated to targeting and implementation than to creative development. The benefit goes straight to the bottom line. Planners in a DM agency do better to devote their time to more effective targeting – spending too much time polishing the creative product may win awards but will not necessarily improve the ROI.

In sales promotion the planner's job is particularly difficult. The account handlers are perfectly capable of selecting the right mechanic. However, they appreciate planning support in tailoring the concept to the target audience, ensuring the mechanic delivers a branded rather than a generic benefit (when did you last remember a promotion?), and building arguments to sell the promotion to the client and then the trade. There may also be a need for research that generates insights into how people will interact with the mechanic and so improve the effectiveness of implementation.

In sponsorship the trick is to secure high awareness at a lower cost than through advertising. In broadcast sponsorship the relationship between programming and the brand can trigger audiences into reconsidering the brand and their relationship with it. So planning's role will be much closer to audience research and insight than writing surgically accurate briefs for programme 'bookends'.

In PR, value is added by maximising the value of the audience of a particular medium. By understanding the overlap between the medium audience and the brand audience, and by providing insights into how the audience for each publication sees the brand and the category, the planner can help to provide tailored briefs for each publication. These are likely to be more effective than divvying up the by-lines and handing them to different feature writers as 'exclusives'.

On the web, value is added through reducing the cost of communicating with particular audiences or creating high involvement with a niche audience. Here the planner will make a contribution, not just by understanding these audiences and what they want from the web, but by understanding how they interact with the internet as a medium. Web sites that don't change behaviour don't pay. New media planners have to be behaviourists through and through.

## And Now to Integration…

The nightmare for the planner who works with a multi-disciplinary team can now be seen in its full horror. How can the planner with limited time ever be expected to add value to the aggregated account team? The one refuge (often tried) is to fall back on the certainties of advertising planning. This, for reasons already given, guarantees that the planner won't deliver, and will only frustrate the rest of the team, who will have to attempt to adapt the planning product themselves (if they have the patience).

> **Advertising planning assumptions that don't work for other disciplines**
>
> - Planning adds value by improving the quality of creative work.
> - Strategic development is about the construction of a message.
> - The overarching task of the communication is to strengthen the values of the brand.
> - Brand personality needs to be consistent.
> - The communications objective is to increase salience or to change attitudes.
> - The mass audience can be divided into those who get it (purchasers and considerers) and those who don't (non-considerers), which is largely how they are researched.
> - Measurement is something of a black box and is quite difficult.

Integrated communication itself needs to be understood in terms of the business model and how value is added. In summary, agencies field integrated campaigns so that the most profitable elements subsidise the most visible. Every agency wants the advertising, but many have started to offer other disciplines to subsidise it.

The account planner needs to add value to every discipline, the whole has to work together and each part needs to perform effectively within its own framework – advertising needs a strong creative idea, DM needs effective targeting, and so on.

## A model playing field for the IMC planner

Enter yet another planning triangle (Exhibit 3). This considers three fundamental manifestations of a brand that all communication disciplines address, one way or another. It works as a playing field for the planner. When you know what discipline you are working with, it tells you what position to play to make a contribution. It saves time and heartache because it ensures the planner is always in a position to provide the right support.

Brands have three manifestations: as promise, where the communications tell you what it will be like to buy and use the product; as an experience, when the product actually performs what it is supposed to do and the consumer interacts with the retailer or client organisation; and as a medium, because every brand has a medium – that is to say an audience that uses it, or does not use it, but more than half believe in it.

Around 30 years ago there were three types of company: product-based companies that used advertising to make promises about themselves; service-based companies that no one could see the point of advertising; and media where ads appeared. Now, virtually every company makes products (and promises about them), is a service business that engages with its customers

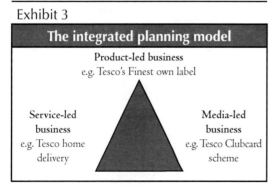

Exhibit 3

**The integrated planning model**

Product-led business
e.g. Tesco's Finest own label

Service-led business
e.g. Tesco home delivery

Media-led business
e.g. Tesco Clubcard scheme

and is trying to increase the size of its audience/medium (Exhibit 4). Ad agencies add value to the brand as promise; DM and CRM programmes add value by generating income efficiently out of the audience medium and

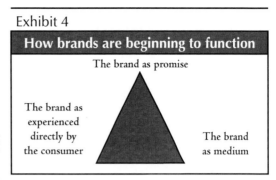

Exhibit 4

**How brands are beginning to function**

The brand as promise

The brand as experienced directly by the consumer

The brand as medium

increasing its size/value; sales promotion and internet agencies add value by changing behaviour.

The planner who works with the brand as promise will get into the mindset of the consumer. The planner who works with the brand as medium will think like a management accountant – adept at quantifying audiences, and calculating the value of communicating with them and the financial returns. The planner who works with the brand as experience will be a private investigator, expert in watching consumer behaviour and knowing how to create patterns and addictions that will make a mechanic more effective.

## Planning and the Integrated Development Process

The planner within a multidisciplinary team needs to harness the considerable skill-set within the team. Planners can't do it by themselves, which is why, when developing the brand as promise (using a brand template, essence, onion or whatever), there needs to be a core brand-promise team, probably dominated by advertising people who ensure that the promise is articulated in a way the entire team can use.

Likewise, there needs to be a targeting team, drawn from media and data planning, who ensures that the audience is understood, quantified, and that the same definitions are used across all disciplines. They also ensure the campaign is evaluated in terms of the value generated out of that audience. The two teams are there to ensure that both brand elements and audience remain consistent (Exhibit 5, next page).

The output of the teams needs to be checked to ensure that it fulfils the brand promise and effectively addresses the audience. One failing of

Exhibit 5

**A new way of organizing the team**

Core brand promise team
(advertising-led)

Line members of
team function
first as **specialists**,
then as **generalists**
to agree strongest
blend of elements

Planner as
team integrator

Core brand
team
(targeting-led)

multidisciplinary campaigns is that they concentrate the budget on a subset of the audience – often the heaviest purchasers. Part of the responsibility of the targeting team is to ensure an appropriate level of spend to each proportion of the audience, based on likely return.

In all this, the planner plays an integrative role. Once the brand promise is defined, there is no reason in principle why the team has to wait for an advertising creative team to come up with an idea that everyone else has to adapt. The brand promise should be capable of being delivered through all channels. And the most brilliant campaign concept is useless if there is insufficient budget, or the idea only works on TV.

## Specialist-Generalists

Within a multidisciplinary team everyone is simultaneously a specialist and a generalist, a specialist in their own particular discipline and a generalist in their understanding of the other disciplines and how audiences consume them. A persistent weakness in the development of multimedia campaigns is that so much of the strategy is developed by advertising specialists and what they produce can't easily be translated.

At the other end of the spectrum, a favourite complaint against integrated campaigns is that they are less effective because generalists produce them. Getting effective work out of an integrated team entails harnessing the specialists, ensuring that no specialism is allowed to dominate and that each member of the team is encouraged to think beyond the boundaries of their own discipline. I believe the planner is ideally placed to ensure that all the specialists get a consistent and thorough brief, and then to draw out the generalist skills of the team to produce work that fits together.

[1] Cooper: *How to Plan Advertising.* Continuum Int Publishing Group, 2001.

# Your Next Job Description: What Clients Think

## By Scott Lukas & Stephen Walker

*Scott Lukas is head of Dosage, a brand strategy, communications planning and research company based in New York. Dosage co-developed an approach to positioning and integrated communications planning for Lowe Worldwide, now implemented in over 40 offices worldwide. Prior to Dosage, Scott worked at Chiat/Day, Fallon McElligott Berlin, and helped start Berlin Cameron.*

*Stephen Walker is President of Headmint, a planning consultancy based in New York. After 10 years planning for London creative "hotshops," such as BBH, he joined Chiat/Day in 1993, where he worked with Scott Lukas. In 1997, he co-founded Red Spider, a global, virtual consultancy that made account planning available outside the agency environment. In 2000, he moved on to co-found a second trans-Atlantic consultancy, Headmint, specializing in providing strategic guidance to global clients such as Ford, Nestlé, and Coca-Cola. Headmint also provides strategic planning training to various types of communications agencies*

*This article is adapted from a presentation by Lukas and Walker at the 2003 AAAA Planning Conference.*

## Cooling Ardor?

BEFORE WE GET INTO WHAT CLIENTS told us they wanted from planning, it's worthwhile taking a few minutes to describe the background to this survey. Another appropriate title for this could have been "Why Jeff Goodby Is Kind of Right." We had recently begun to notice some mixed signals about the value and role of planning.

Certainly from what we'd been reading and hearing through the grapevine, planning was losing some of its former luster. In under 10 years, planning seemed to have gone from nowhere, to superstardom, and then back to its apparently perennial state of questionable value.

## Value Capped?

Going straight for the jugular, we figured if this was in any way true, it would show up in the nitty gritty of salaries. We had heard stories about depressed planning salaries and decided to try get hold of what data we could. We'd like to thank Ada Alpert for her help with the numbers here. Ada's numbers don't paint the rosiest of pictures. [Ada Alpert is founder and president of Alpert Executive Search, specializing in placing account planning and brand consultancy professionals. —Ed.]

Within the agency environment at least, a senior planner's value now appears to max out at the top end below those of the other two disciplines for which we could get data. Senior planning salaries in particular also appear to be slipping further in the downturn. So while younger planners might outpace their account service counterparts initially, over the long haul, planners don't do as well.

When asked for her conclusions on the data she said, "You can't fire the creative people because you have to do ads, and you can't fire the account people because they have the relationships – and that leaves planning vulnerable."

Yet there were also other, more positive signs for planning – clients are hiring planners, pitch consultants require them, even a hard core of creatives support and want them – kind of.

At this stage, rather than doing what planners normally do – that is, huddle together with the usual suspects on the APG committee for some serious navel gazing, or worse, go ask creatives if they still like us – we decided to go find out some more from the most important, but to our knowledge previously un-consulted, source: the clients.

We wanted to understand how clients view planning, and how they would like to see it develop in the future. Based on the good and the bad news floating around about planning, we created a number of initial hypotheses, both positive and negative, and got on the phone.

On the positive side, we speculated that the definition and role, and corresponding value, of planning has grown – from "voice of the consumer" feedback within ad development, to a broader based consultancy role providing advice regarding the health/growth of the brand overall and a deeper understanding of the business overall.

On the negative side, we speculated that planners are a dying breed. As marketing dollars spread across more tactics, organizations, and people, planners are marginalized as "nice to have," not "need to have" in the grand mix. Clients are either less aware of or less interested in planning than ever before or buy it from independent consultant sources.

## The Client Perspective

As far as we know this is an unprecedented survey of US client satisfaction with planning. Between us, we conducted 30 one-on-one interviews with senior advertising clients, drawn from some of the country's largest ad spenders. We deliberately selected "experienced" users of planning. Interestingly, we found that many of these clients had previously worked on the agency side.

Aside from these interviews, we felt that no up-to-date audit of clients views on planning today would be complete without broader context – both in terms of where planning has grown from and where it appears headed

We spent time reviewing the history and seminal points of the development of planning, trawling back over key papers, essays, memos, and articles. We dredged up notes from Fred Goldberg to Lee Clow and Jay Chiat, bitching about planning and its lack of consistency from as way back as 1987, and a spirited and rousing reply from Rob White.

We even found pictures of Jon Steel with hair.

As luck would have it, we also found that Jane Newman, who as planning mythology has it, is the mother of planning in America, was in New York resting from her work with the poor in Africa. Jane kindly spent several sessions with us reviewing our findings and discussing how they compared and contrasted with the not-so-distant beginnings of planning in the States. We owe Jane our deepest thanks for her support, time, and insights.

We also wanted more input regarding the future direction of planning from the agency perspective, and not least, planners' reactions to some of our findings.

So we also spoke to ten Planning Directors around the country to get a sense from them on how they see planning developing.

## Implications

We think there are a number of important implications raised by this feedback — some of which may confirm what we might have already suspected, some of which we think are new and maybe worthy of further thought.

Certainly, it seems that some of the founding principles of planning may have been eroded, compromised, or confused over the last ten years. High demand means planning's role and definition have diverged — it's being pulled in many different directions.

We wonder how important it is that not once did we hear clients suggest that the planner's role was to champion the agency's underlying beliefs about creativity and effectiveness, when this was all Jane and Stanley [Pollitt] ever seemed to talk about?

Do we care about our clients' apparent loss of trust in the objectivity and independence of the planner? Does our image seem a little tarnished?

Is it significant that planning used to be defined very much as a process as opposed to a particular person on the account team? What about the fact that the process demanded the involvement of all key players in the development of strategy — even clients?

How important is it, we wonder, that planning was never conceived to be an additional profit center for the agency? Yet, quite clearly, this is implicit within most planning department functions today. At the very least, planning departments have to pay their own way.

## Opposite Worlds

What's interesting about the timing of this audit is that the industry conditions that initially created planning in the '60s, are totally the reverse of those we find today.

Agencies in Pollitt's day were moving from being generalist marketing advisors to ad development specialists. Simply put, planners were needed to help make creative advertising more relevant for consumers and more reliable for clients. Conversely today, as we all know, agencies are headed in the opposite direction, towards a more general, multidisciplinary provision of marketing and communication ideas and execution.

As a result, it is perhaps hardly surprising that planning is being stretched across an ever broader canvass. It is also, therefore, not surprising to see planning apparently under pressure in some places, yet thriving in others. The key questions are: How do we avoid any mine fields ahead? Are there any critical breaking points – babies that shouldn't get thrown out with the bath water?

## Former Champion of Agency Beliefs

Talking to Jane Newman, we were reminded of that anecdote that goes something like this – When I was 16, I couldn't believe how stupid my father was. But by the time I got to be 30, I was really surprised at how much he'd learned.

Talking with Jane about planning for the first time in 10 years was a similarly enlightening experience for us.

On the topic of the apparent loss of trust in planners and, in particular, their objectivity revealed by our interviews, Jane reminded us that back then, planning, especially at Chiat and BMP, symbolized an agency's fundamental beliefs in the relationship between effectiveness and creativity, and the agency's desire to do the right thing for the client at all times. She made the point that, today, clients and agencies appear more and more to assume that creative advertising and effective advertising are at the opposite end of a spectrum, rather than two points on a circle that are, in her mind, inseparable.

Perhaps planning needs to re-emphasize its belief in the link between creativity and effectiveness. Or maybe we don't believe it's that simple anymore. Have we come to think "well you can have the good stuff, or you can have the stuff that works?"

Jane also reminded us that planning was never considered as a profit center, but as an added-value service to the client, to the extent that it was the agency, and not the client, who paid for any focus groups in connection with creative development. It certainly seems that, as far as clients are concerned, the connection of planning to the agency's culture and, in particular, in its role embodying the need for objective, informed, and untainted input into the highly subjective and unpredictable process of creative development has been diluted or forgotten altogether.

For a long time now "the voice of the consumer" role has been maligned and jettisoned by planners. Importantly, however, while this has been abandoned, it seems for many clients this source of credibility, authority, and expertise of the planner, apparently, has not been replaced with much – making planning for some a service choice they don't value or feel they can get elsewhere.

Perhaps it is time to re-evaluate the relationship planners have with the consumer and with the agency.

Clients also seem pretty convinced that most planners and planning departments now prioritize their creativity over their objectivity. Jane got really fired up on this one, noting that today many more planners seem to want to define their role as the third member of the creative team, seeing their job as helping the creative be even more creative, as opposed to applying strategic creativity and insights to help make creative work more effective work.

## Creativity, then Objectivity

Clients were clear in their response to this – while a planner's ideas and creativity can inform entire companies and brand strategies, it also means that they appear to be kowtowing to the agency's creative department and its self-serving agenda to make award-winning advertising, rather than the right advertising. Placed in this position, planners run the risk of being seen as vacuous, slick ad salesmen and pitchsters, rather than the objective conscience of the agency's creativity.

Jane talked about the passionate and frequent screaming matches between she and her planners and a long list of star creative directors. We wonder whether there ought to be more tension again between the planners and the creatives. Or maybe if we're all going to be brand strategists anyway, we should be less interested in tweaking the ads. It seems a reasonable hypothesis that the further planners define their role away from the traditional function of planning, the less welcome or relevant they will become to the creative department.

## A Process, Not a Person

Doing the research highlighted for us the extent to which, historically, planning was defined and explained as a process and not as a person on the account team. Lee Clow still says today that anyone can do planning: it isn't exclusive to the planners.

Jane reminded us that when Jay hired her, he mandated that she write the creative brief with the creative teams, a critical difference from UK planning practice at the time.

This meant that planners became equal partners and the drivers of a more professional ad development process. Planners weren't solely responsible for the entire brief, strategic presentation, positioning recommendation or pitch the way they are today – they were equal partners in getting these things right with the account person and the creative and media departments. In other words, planning was a way of making advertising, not a department or an individual. Today, this does not seem to be as much the case – planning seems to be increasingly personified and defined by the individual planner. And, as we have seen, the quality and value can vary immensely.

Of course while planning was defined more as a consistent process, this didn't mean that the planners were homogeneous. The opposite has always been true. Planners have always had to be able to rapidly adapt their skills and style to a variety of different conditions, agency cultures, and audiences.

## Different Types of Planning

But perhaps we need to consider further the fragmentation and diversity of planning reported by clients. Of course, there's nothing new about different styles of planners. If this conference were the Crufts dog show, we'd see that there has always been a healthy, diverse mix of breeds.

Planners have always prided themselves on being an eclectic bunch. But today, different remuneration standards and holding company business models have forced more emphasis on planning paying its way, or even turning a profit. In response, planners have proved themselves highly adaptable in fitting into the culture and business conditions in which they are trying to operate.

We think planners have proven themselves to be cockroaches rather than chameleons: they're indestructible. In ten years or so, planning in the States has achieved what Jane and the first and second waves of planners had to work so hard for: more broad acceptance, management recognition and value, a growing client appetite, and even their own revenue streams.

In doing so, however, the mutation has been considerable. We think that what's important about this is that clients have reported not just that they are witnessing different types of planners, but also that they are recognizing, and buying or rejecting, different types of planning.

## Planning is Mutating

In stark contrast to the first Account Planning Group (APG) conference we attended with Jane 10 years ago, where there was pretty much just one breed that mattered – "English planner." Analysis of attendees' job titles this year revealed just how many versions of planning there are now in the US. A more appropriate analogy for this conference today might be an agricultural show – a place where you come to see the new versions and offspringings of planning – the 20-foot chickens from Wieden or the self-milking cows from Ogilvy.

Planning is a Petri dish, apparently constantly capable of creating new variants and new value. While approximately 20 percent of the attendees here today are still defined on their business cards by the standard pedigree of "account planner," we also see that there are many more exotic and different breeds thriving today, such as the brand strategist, as well as some other truly remarkable new hybrids, such as "Director of Insightment."

We think these titles fundamentally imply different roles for planning than the one we struggled to explain and justify less than 10 years ago. Planning as Jane Newman and Stanley Pollitt used to know it is fragmenting. Clients are reporting strengths and weakness across these different new variants. These new mutations have to compete with external sources more than traditional planning ever had to.

This raises critical questions. We have to be sure that we don't let the exploding universe of planning confuse us, our clients, our departments, or our agency managers and creatives. We probably have to be extra careful to define and explain the specific role we see planning fulfilling at our shops. As well as what role or roles individual planners play within that planning function.

In order to survive and thrive in this more complex and diversified environment, planners may have to rethink their jobs, their career development paths, and even where they should go work next.

## Not Sucking

One of the most powerful insights revealed by the audit is that not sucking as a planner is generally what clients want.

As planning mutates and explodes and we add our millionth ingredient, the feedback raises issues about the credibility of planning and the need for clarity, focus, and discipline in directing one's energies as a planner or planning director. Quite clearly what has always been a broad role is getting bigger — what used to be called "the job without walls" could now be called the job without borders. Even when planning's role was relatively focused upon making advertising better, there were gripes about consistency and quality. Today, this problem seems set to grow further as the job and the potential roles for a planner expand.

This begs the questions: How much can we take on before we start to suck? How big can planners get before they get bad?

While, on the whole, we think this genetic diversity of planning ultimately is a sign of its strength and future longevity, if planning was a brand we were asked to fix, our first conclusion would be that it needed to refocus.

It seems to be getting a little out of control.

Quite clearly the growing demand for planning is sometimes forcing, and sometimes inviting, planning to evolve and stretch its capabilities – often, according to clients, to places where planners look under-qualified, inexperienced, and shallow.

To Jane's mind this threatened the planning discipline more clearly than any other factor – placing planners in situations where they don't know what they are talking about simply serves to undermine planning's role and the planning individual completely.

We wonder how exposed planners today feel in some of the areas they are being asked to take on. Net net, in the future, not sucking as a planner will mean being honest about your qualifications, clearly setting expectations, and being diligent about growing your skill base.

## "One Planner Does It All" Is Over

It also appears that clients (as well as, we suspect, many of the other people who sit around the integrated communications conference table) are now at a point where the claim that every planner in the department is equally capable and qualified across this exploding palette of required skills is over.

And if it's not possible or credible for each planner to be an expert in all the things clients or more integrated agencies demand, then departments may increasingly need to be structured differently, more as a group of planning specialists, teams of narrower, deeper experts on which different accounts draw, on an as-needed basis. Otherwise, the dangers of becoming shallow generalists – fraudulent communications jacks-of-all-trades – are more than apparent in the client feedback.

Obviously, such a different departmental approach and structure would represent a significant departure from today's scenario of dedicated planners for individual accounts. Not least, we think that the process and benefits of planning versus the individual planner would once again become the resource clients are provided with and asked to pay for. A process and team rather than an individual marketing or advertising guru.

## Your Next Job Description

Your next job description? Being in "planning" won't be specific enough.

Earlier, Stephen distinguished the role for planning (what the agency delivers to clients) from the role of planners. You're going to have to think about your role in delivering planning for your agency.

So, the question becomes: what role do you want to have? We think there are a number of different possibilities and opportunities for planners. Some exist today. Some might in the future.

The real trick will be finding the one that beats those salary averages we talked about in the beginning. It's a dog eat dog world.

Here are seven options.

### Option One: The "Back to the Future" Planner

One option is to buck the trend and rededicate to advertising. Many believe that mass communication is still going to be the greatest slice of the pie. Clients will always need to communicate efficiently to a large number of people. So advertising and agencies will remain at the forefront.

Clients certainly want this from planners. They want their agency to get the ads right more of the time. And they want ads made more efficiently.

The back-and-forth created by the development of unclear, uninspired, and ineffective advertising causes a serious drain on time and money. Good planning can help with all those things.

To be successful we'll have to invest in more training and better working processes to increase our consistency. We know "working processes" sounds about as uncreative and un-fun as something can be. But like a band that knows what key they are playing in, having a mutual understanding of what everyone is doing can make jamming a whole lot better. And be it either re-establishing that famous "voice of the consumer" role or replacing it with something else, we must re-establish a sense of objectivity.

## Option Two: Up

Another option is moving upstream to become brand strategists. Given the increased emphasis on brands and integrated communications, this seems like a natural evolution. It seems bigger than, but inclusive of, advertising. It opens up opportunities for work outside advertising and communications, because the planners can define themselves in whatever capacity is needed. And that'll help bring money in through the planning department. From what we heard from planning directors, this is probably the best description of how most planners spend their time these days.

When we talked to Jane Newman about this she said this isn't account planning. She believed that the brand strategy role dilutes planning's definition. She said break off and charge for it. Many of the planning directors we spoke to are trying to do exactly that. Others see this as a natural evolution of the job and what clients are already paying for.

Be careful, though. If we were creative director and saw the planners moving away from a position of advertising focus and expertise, we'd tell them to stop messing with our work.

## Option Three: Up Up

David Metcalf, a copywriter and friend, once stated that only two people in an organization can say "yes" to anything important, but everyone can say "no." So the trick is getting to those two "yes" people and working at that level — all the action is there.

Management consultants are particularly good at this because they talk the language of business. In an effort to reclaim a larger role as partner, planning departments and agencies are offering this kind of expertise as well.

Some agencies have hired business planners or developed distinct departments or subsidiaries that help clients (and help the agency) with the "hard" side of business and brand strategy, that has traditionally been known as the domain of the management consultants.

The challenge for most of us is that this job description demands an entirely different set of skills, and it will be difficult for us to credibly graduate to this role. It is most likely that agencies will poach classic consultants who can blend the "hard" and "soft" side of business and brand strategy, or those "hard siders" who culturally fit well with us on the "soft" side.

The good news is that we haven't heard of too much success. "Hard siders" are generally not good with brands, are uncreative, and are not linked and used to working with people who execute things. This door is still open for us.

## Option Four: Client-Side

Or, "if you can't beat 'em, join 'em."

Client side is also an option. More and more we've heard of planners working within client organizations. That's certainly one way for clients to ensure quality control and total dedication to the brand and business.

We think the jury is still out on whether this will succeed. On one hand, it makes sense that the traditional client and client planner could operate similarly to the AE/Planner partnership.

On the other hand, it is difficult enough to try to make planning work with a little distance from the clients. Being inside a client organization probably is the worst place for planning to deliver the perspective and objectivity clients want. One ex-agency client we interviewed said that we would never believe the blinders put on you when working client-side.

And would we all go crazy working on one thing all the time?

When thinking about the need for our discipline, he was thinking about human nature. How the nature and closeness of relationships impact how we work. We wonder if those palpable pressures within the client organization will tempt client-side planners into expediency as well.

## Option Five: Deep and Specialized

One of the clearest things we heard from clients about the future and integration was the desire for specialist planners in all areas of their marketing.

Usually matched with some "master brand" planner, clients envisioned a world where four or five "pedigree" planners helped the team plan how to use different areas of communications.

Listening to clients, it sounded like meetings are going to get bigger and bigger. Boy, that'll be fun. Four planners in a meeting. Where are all these planners going to come from? And who is going to pay for them? Clients want 'em, but will they pay? Do PDs have to flip the bill?

## Option Six: Wide

Another evolution of planning is to spread it wide. This role would be to apply consumer learning and expertise across an increasingly wide spectrum of communications and marketing activity. This job description is often called "connection planning" and relies heavily on an expertise that blends traditional account planning and media planning.

We couldn't help but ask ourselves: Who has all this knowledge and skill? How would you acquire them? Could you find enough of these people to put one on every account?

It seems the issue here would be credibility, being a jack-of-all-trades.

That said, this might be *the* job description for the next generation. There is still a lot more fun, money, competitive differentiation and credibility for planners in execution than consultancy. And once you have expertise and experience in a wide range of disciplines you'd be plenty useful. If you're young enough, you might want to think differently about your career path.

Like the *New York Times*' Thomas Friedman, who decided the best way to be an expert in the emerging story of globalism was to rotate through reporting gigs on all its influences (politics, economics, technology, culture, etc.), the best development path for planning's young-un's might be a rotation through each of these disciplines rather than growing up through an advertising agency alone.

## Option Seven: A New Role?

Our last possibility for planners is once again connected to the challenges of integration, and the demands clients and agencies have for clearer leadership and successful working methods in this area. The two top challenges clients have are:

- devising integrated strategy, and
- ensuring its execution.

Planners have always been part of a string quartet: Planner, Account person, Creative Director, and Media Director. All four played together and made music for the client.

In an integrated world, the inclusion of all disciplines has turned the quartet into a full orchestra. And while we believe that at least one planner should remain in the orchestra, we envision a different planner in a different role as well.

Think of this new role as a conductor who sits separate from the rest. A conductor's role is to get the best music out of the orchestra. He doesn't have to be able to play every instrument. In fact, he doesn't play any, but he does need to know the music better than anyone. And, without him, it would be a big mess.

So, rather than being the central "vessel" of all knowledge on the brand and its communication across an increasingly wide set of activities, planners could become the owners and managers of the task of forming the best links across these different disciplines – planners as leaders of the strategic integration process.

Not a leader by virtue of knowledge, but by process. Responsible for getting the best out of the expanded team of specialist experts. Not the source of knowledge, but the expert in effectively using that knowledge.

This job description isn't as different as it might sound.

## The Best Definition

The best definition of planning we've ever heard was "helping the agency get it right more of the time." Planning's new role doesn't stray from that. Infusing consumer-informed thinking into the communications development and decision-making process is what planners have always done. The "what" doesn't change.

What's changed is *how* planners can do it. As we have seen from its birth, planning was synonymous with process. It was the way a group of people went about making ads. Planning was closer to being a process than a person. Planners were the ones to help make it happen. In this role, planners will lead the process again.

This role will need you to take a couple of leaps that some of you may not be able to take. First, that a group of people, if guided correctly, can be harnessed to be strategically creative and great. That "all of us are smarter than one of us." It's going to take some humility. You're not going to be a rock star. In her bio from last year's conference, Anne Bologna of Fallon described herself as a "silent planner." She's got it right.

The other leap is to be open to the idea that a process can be a fun and creatively freeing way to work. Looking back at the history of successful planning organizations, it was surprising how prevalent process was. We had mythologized the creativity of the strategies and the resulting work but had forgotten how they got there. Having proven tools and processes is the bedrock of a good planner.

You think anyone would throw themselves into Iron Planning (a planner competition) without the confidence of knowing ways to go about thinking about a problem? At this point it may be intuitive, but it's there.

As for those consultants that we always talk about? Read *The McKinsey Mind*. It's all about their process to approaching problems. We need to codify this thinking so it is more widely used and understood.

When we spoke with clients we were surprised how natural a fit this mutation was with planners. Many of the clients thought this role would be that of an experienced account manager, purely from the perspective of coordination and who was perceived to be most senior and in control. But when asked to react to this potential role, clients immediately saw the value. Planners were leaders in strategy. They got people to think differently. They respected consumers. They had moderating and people skills.

Clients also saw the potential for planners to shake loose from their advertising dedication most easily. Like it or not, clients see consumers as the territory of planners.

Many planners are already positioned as brand people, not advertising people. It seems more feasible for a planner to move to a more neutral position of integration than for an advertising account person or creative director.

When we spoke with Jane Newman about it, she was excited by the idea. She saw planning's core role and way of working evolved for a new world. To Jane's credit, we wanted her to talk about the past. She only wanted to talk about the future.

## How Could This Happen?

What tools would you use? How would you involve consumers?

How cool would it be to get the client and all the marketing partners working together?

And how much more smoothly could you generate and sell ideas because people would be involved?

Well there you have it: some options for your next job description. They aren't mutually exclusive. Reality will dictate some morphing. The trick, though, will be clearly defining what you do and not taking on too much.

While we've answered some questions, we've probably raised quite a few more.

- Who do you want to be?
- What scope of responsibilities best fits your skills?
- How do you want work?

- Where do you want to work?
- What skills should you acquire?
- What's your best career path?
- In which role can you best help your account or your agency?
- What pays the best?

This raises some questions for your department as well.

- Who should be in a department?
- What mix of skills, roles, and responsibilities should your department have?
- How should the planning function best be delivered?
- Should we think differently about how the department is deployed? Does a team approach make the most sense?
- Does every business need a dedicated planner?
- What's the basis of our credibility? And is it all the same?
- Will planning functions add value or create profit?
- Could some do one and some do the other?

# ALL EUROPEANS ARE NOT ALIKE
### But the global marketers have come up with a new strategy to get around it.

## By John Heilemann

*John Heilemann is a special correspondent for* Wired *and a former staff writer for the* New Yorker *and the* Economist. *He is the author of* Pride Before the Fall: The Trials of Bill Gates and the End of the Microsoft Era *and is finishing* The Valley, *which will be available in September of 2009. He lives in San Francisco. This article originally appeared in the* Annals of Style *section of the* New Yorker, *May 5, 1997.*

AMONG ADVERTISING PEOPLE – a breed so convinced their vocation is as much art as commerce that they hold their own film festival every summer in Cannes – the dusty pages of the *Harvard Business Review* are not normally considered a must-read. But back in 1983, when Theodore Levitt, a professor of business administration at Harvard, published a widely noted article on the dawn of globalization, people in the ad business got all excited. Levitt declared that the age of the multinational firm, which was forever customizing its products and its advertising in dozens of ways for dozens of different markets, was over. In the new age of global markets – or, at least, regional markets, covering entire continents – the companies that would prosper, he argued, were those with products, like Coca-Cola and Levi's, whose ingredients *and* images were the same everywhere. Levitt's article was more polemic than reportage, but it was a portent of what, by the end of the decade, many multinationals would be demanding of their ad agencies: global advertising.

The demand was most fervent in Europe, where the arrival of the single market after 1992 promised to bring about just the sort of situation Levitt had described. Among the most powerful clients – mainly American corporations, such as Procter & Gamble and Gillette, but also

European ones, such as Unilever — the new catchphrase was "the pan-European campaign": an ad that could run, more or less identically, in all twelve markets of the European Community. These clients contended that tastes were converging, and cultural differences eroding, throughout the region: "the Euroconsumer" was a concept much in vogue. Ad agencies, too, joined the euphoric chorus. In Britain, the brothers Saatchi, who had used Levitt's article to justify the acquisition binge that built their far-flung network, pointed to their global campaign for British Airways ("The World's Favourite Airline"), while McCann-Erickson touted its international work for Coke.

Today, the aim is the same, but the euphoria has faded. For much of the nineties, multinationals have been harmonizing their products' designs and packaging and manufacturing across Europe, but when it comes to advertising, the task has been incomparably more difficult. Differences in tastes and habits and language and life styles have proved to be stubborn. Nearly two years ago, the advertising agency Leo Burnett began work on two projects that turned out to make all this abundantly clear. The clients could hardly have been more different — Johnnie Walker Red Label and McDonald's — nor could the particulars of the campaigns. Yet from the two projects a lesson emerged that few admen, and even fewer clients, are prepared to admit: fourteen years after Levitt's article, and five after the dizzy utopianism of 1992, the Euroconsumer remains a rare, if not a mythical, beast — and one that continues to elude even the world's cleverest marketers.

Leo Burnett is certainly one of those. Based in Chicago, with seventy-nine offices around the world, Burnett has created some of the most durable icons in modern advertising — the Jolly Green Giant, the Pillsbury Doughboy, Tony the Tiger — and it is behind three of the most potent global brands: Marlboro, McDonald's, and Kellogg. Triumphs of this sort are not easily replicated, however. The Marlboro Man wasn't originally intended for foreign consumption, but the cowboy turned out to be a powerful symbol of America in country after country. And a similarly un-planned rollout took place with Kellogg's Tony the Tiger. Unfortunately, today's clients don't want to take such chances. They want campaigns that travel from Day One, and this has spurred people in Adland to develop hyperrational approaches to what is, at bottom, an irrational art.

In a corner office in Leo Burnett's European headquarters, in London, sits Helena Rubinstein, a cheerful, dark-haired Englishwoman (no relation to the late cosmetics magnate) who is the mother of a technique that has become a central part of the way Burnett tackles pan-European assignments. What Rubinstein does, in her words, is "deconstruct brands," and if you visit her she can show you a breathtaking array of charts and diagrams that illustrate how she hacks a product's image down to its irreducible core – to what she calls "the DNA of the brand." As she explains it, "In regional projects, you always get the same response: 'That's all very well, but it's different in my country.' So the question is what elements are common to the brand that can be applied everywhere." To figure this out, Rubinstein guides the client's marketing officials and the admen through a two-day workshop, using reams of qualitative and quantitative research to identify in detail various aspects of the brand – its "personality," its "functions, its "differentiators," and its "source of authority" – and arrive at a concise statement of what the brand should stand for in market after market. The statement can boil down to two or three words. It is, in Burnett parlance, the brand's "essence."

Brand audits, as exercises of this sort are called, are a growing trend in international advertising. Norman Berry, the European creative director of Ogilvy & Mather, says that a brand audit led his agency to realize that its client, IBM, sells not machines but "solutions," and hence to create the global campaign "Solutions for a Small Planet." At the London agency Bartle Bogle Hegarty, the auditing process – there called "brand vision" – inspired a pan-European campaign for Polaroid. "Polaroid's problem was that they kept thinking of themselves as a camera," John Hegarty, B.B.H.'s chairman and creative director, told me. "But the 'vision' process taught us something: Polaroid is *not* a camera – it's a social lubricant. So you don't present it as a camera, or take pictures of happy families, or talk about how it's a record of the moment. Pox to all that! What Polaroid is really about is enjoying yourself." In one of the campaign's ads, a beautiful girl gets the attention of a rock star by flinging a picture of herself onto the stage; in another, a Japanese worker sends a scandalous photograph to a female boss who has humiliated him. The tag line: "Live for the moment."

In July of 1995, Burnett won a chance to put Rubinstein's brand-essence approach into practice in grand style when it was awarded the Johnnie Walker account by United Distillers, the spirits arm of the British drinks conglomerate Guinness P.L.C. Johnnie Walker Red is the world's most popular Scotch, and the source of close to sixty per cent of U.D.'s profits. Yet in Europe the brand was in some trouble. Its market share was falling in a number of countries, and — what was more worrying — it was failing to attract the twenty-to-thirty-year-old drinkers vital to any alcohol brand's long term survival. U.D. asked Burnett to create a pan-European campaign, led by a commercial that was designed to run in every market where liquor ads are allowed on television, with the goal of luring those young drinkers.

In Northern Europe — in Germany and the UK, especially — Scotch has an aging profile," Goff Moore, who is Burnett's worldwide account director for U.D., explained. Sharp-featured and sharp-tongued, with a double-breasted suit and a raffish air, Moore is a Brit who knows his liquor. When I asked him how various spirits were perceived in Europe, he riffed: "Gin is young and trendy and exciting, except in the UK, where it's a stuffy old drink that majors and bishops and retired members of the Tory Parry drink. Vodka is the party drink of Europe. Bourbon is sexy and imported — the whiskey of the new generation. Tequila is 'Let's get pissed.' And rum — well, Bacardi is the product of its advertising. Bacardi is escape." What about Scotch? "In Greece and Italy, it's a hip drink." And everywhere else? "It's 'my father's drink.'"

To unearth the essence of Red Label, a team from the London office, including its creative director, Gerard Stamp, and an account planner, Lucy Edge, went to Scotland on what they called "a journey of discovery." There they met Red Label's master blender and toured other distilleries on the "whiskey trail." Edge also delved into the research that had been done on the brand and on "young transitionals" in Europe in the previous five years. She found, she said, that the crumbling of the institutions of old Europe had left young people "full of uncertainty" and looking for new ways "to be their own heroes." At the workshop to settle on an essence, Edge presented her findings to a U.D. marketing team led by Jenny Vaughan, the worldwide brand director for Johnnie Walker. Red Label, everybody agreed, was a strong, fiery drink, and after hours of discussion the essence emerged: "impassioned empowerment."

I asked Moore what this meant, and he began by drawing an analogy with another U.D. brand: Gordon's gin. "There's something about the way a gin-and-tonic performs that's unlike any other drink," he said. Warming to his subject, he went on, "We call it 'potent effervescence.' When you drink a G. and T., it refreshes not only your palate but your mind – it sets you up!" Now he was rolling. "There's a wonderful Leo Burnett/Chicago ad for Dewar's that went, 'You never solved the world's problems over a glass of white wine.' There's something more serious about Scotch, more reflective. You go to the bar in the evening and you have a glass of Johnnie Walker, and you suddenly see things more clearly. You start thinking about what your life is going to be like. You don't necessarily have to get assholed. Drink is a social facilitator – it's an enabler – and when it's Scotch it's very much an empowerer. It empowers you to think in a much more positive way about what you want to do with your life."

Translating all this into a commercial was up to Stamp and his creative underlings. Working from the brief "Red Label fires your spirit," they produced two rough ads, one called "Water of Life" and the other called "It All Started with a Red Label," and presented them to Jenny Vaughan. In "Water of Life" – a literal translation of the Gaelic for whiskey – the hero attends the running of the bulls in Pamplona and, after he narrowly escapes being trampled, celebrates with a glass of Red Label. In "It all started," two friends agree, over a glass of Johnnie Walker, to go on a jungle adventure, which takes a comic wrong turn. Vaughan, who is thirty-four and Australian, with a sober demeanor that contrasts pleasingly with the prodigious liquor cabinet in her London office, liked both ads. "'It all started' was appealing because it was about the concept of the drink inspiring you to do something you've always dreamed of," she said. "'Water of Life' was about the idea that you should do great things in life, and not just the easy ones — like drinking Scotch instead of something reasonably tasteless." She paused. "Like vodka."

Vaughan had the two ads tested in every European market, and it was instantly clear that "It all started" was doomed. "Instead of thinking, 'They had the courage to fulfill their dreams,' people thought, 'Oh, God, they've gone and got pissed and done something stupid,'" she said. (This, she observed, is the danger with any liquor ad that begins, rather than ends, with a drink.) "Water of Life" had troubles, too, but these seemed fixable. The main problem was that the Pamplona setting raised hackles, "People said 'The Spanish don't know anything about whiskey,'" Vaughan said. More to the point, the ad bombed in Germany. According to Stamp, "The Germans didn't like it because it seemed reckless. Also, because of the German animal-rights campaigners, you can't show a goldfish in a goldfish bowl on German television, so a bull run was just not on."

Stamp went back to work, and soon he and his team came up with a new near-death experience to build an ad around. Called "Logs," the spot had its hero working on a construction project deep in the jungle. A storm breaks, triggering a chain reaction that sends an enormous log hurtling toward him. In a flashback, he sees all his life's most vibrant moments — birth, family, school, sex — and then, at the last instant, the log misses him, and he goes off and has a Red Label. Like virtually all pan-European ads, this one would avoid language barriers, not by dubbing (which is cheesy) but by avoiding dialogue. During the flashback, there would be a line of printed copy — "When your life flashes before you, make sure it's worth watching" — which could be translated market by market.

While all this was happening, a rival Burnett team, in Chicago, was developing an ad of its own. Called "Walk the Walk," the spot was a montage of shots of the "striding man" — Johnnie Walker Red's symbol — come to life and striding, as it were, alongside real people, to the beat of a pop soundtrack. Vaughan and the rest of the U.D. team weighed the two options. "Walk the Walk" had several things in its favor — most obviously, its use of the "striding man" and of the mnemonic association between the product and the slogan, both of which "would do a hell of a thing for branding," Vaughan thought. But "Walk the Walk" also struck her less as a campaign than as a single ad ("What would we do next?"), and less as an ad than as "an MTV video." Besides, the phrase "walk the walk" was an Americanism: nobody in Europe would have a clue what it meant.

So "Logs" it would be — although there were still cross-cultural hitches. To begin with, "Water of Life," which was being used as the tag line in "Logs," was baffling in many languages — "People thought it meant watered-down whiskey," Vaughan said — and so it was replaced with "Taste Life." Then there was the nightmare of translation posed by "When your life flashes before you, make sure it's worth watching." In market after market, either the words literally made no sense or the meaning was lost — presaging acute difficulties for the print version of the campaign. "A proverb in English isn't a proverb in Czech or Greek," Vaughan said, "and that's something we'd never really anticipated." In Portugal and Turkey, among other countries, the line had to be modified; in Italy no line runs at all; and in Germany attempts at translation were so maddening that the line was discarded and replaced with "Live every day as if it were your last." (Vaughan: "Basic words: 'live,' 'day,' 'last' — every language has those.)

Last August, "Logs" began its rollout across Europe, and in Australia and South Africa as well. A lavishly produced spot with the look — and the budget — of a John Boorman film, it is a hit with U.D.; the verdict of the marketplace will take at least a year to gauge. "We know we're going to get some older consumers saying they don't see Scotch this way, and that's fine by us," Goff Moore told me. "Because unless we can bring that twenty-to-thirty-year-old group into Scotch in a big way, those older drinkers will die off and there won't be anyone to replace them." (Not for nothing are the Johnnie Walker and the Marlboro accounts situated on the same floor of the Burnett building in Chicago; the admen call it the "sin floor.")

But when I visited Stamp in London he expressed reservations about his creation. The idea behind the campaign was plainly universal, he said, but to find an execution that would work everywhere required significant compromises. "I wonder if by making it cross borders, it's weaker than it would have been if we'd made it for one specific market," Stamp mused. He pointed out that, in tests, the Australian market had loved the version of the ad featuring the bull run, which Stamp himself had always preferred. "Logs," on the other hand, was "aspirational for Germans and Italians" but seemed to Australians at once too familiar and too full of echoes of white imperialism and all that.

I asked Stamp about the wisdom of pan-European campaigns in general. "They can work, at times very well, but they by no means work on all briefs, and I don't think they should," he said. "Advertising that forces itself across borders just ends up being resented. The French resent it enormously when there's a British or an American influence – you can be fined there for advertising in English – and I don't blame them, actually. The assumption that the ideal would be, at some point hence, for all advertising to be able to work everywhere is to me a very depressing prospect."

Depressing or not, in the past decade the quest for pan-European ads on the order of "Logs" has become, for many major clients, like the search for the Holy Grail. Recently, though, some large companies have decided that, while their advertising should have a uniform strategy and theme across the region, the ads themselves – the "executions" – can differ substantially from place to place, adjusting to the quirks of each local market. Which of these two approaches makes sense depends on a range of variables, but a critical factor is the type of product being sold.

For instance, food is intensely resistant to the single-execution approach. Eating habits seem to be the most locally rooted consumer habit of all, and the few firms that have managed to establish brands that reach across Europe have tweaked their advertising to take account of this. Arguably, the most successful pan-European food brand is Kellogg. To the untrained eye, Kellogg's advertisements for Frosties – as Frosted Flakes are called in Europe – seem to be exactly alike from market to market: there's Tony the Tiger, the kids, the sports, the sugar rush. But AJ Roehl, Burnett's worldwide account director for Kellogg's, told me I'd missed the nuances. Because of the different breakfast habits in Northern and

Southern Europe – for example, Germans are brought up eating muesli, while breakfast in Italy is, he said, "dominated by biscotti" – the Frosties ads that run in Southern Europe include a few shots to "educate the consumer": the cereal being put in the bowl, the fruit being added, and, finally, what Roehl called "the milk-pour." (Burnett also deploys the milk-pour widely in Eastern Europe.)

Probably nobody has thought more about such matters than Donald Gunn, Burnett's director of creative resources, whose job is basically to look at more ads than anybody else alive. Each year, Gunn, a fifty-eight-year-old Scotsman with an affable manner and a musical voice, surveys maybe eight thousand television and print ads produced by Burnett and other agencies around the world. From this vast crop he culls the best and files them in something called the Great Commercials Library – a huge, elaborately cross-indexed archive kept in the Burnett building in Chicago (though Gunn works out of London).

There are twenty-three product categories and two hundred and fifty-seven subcategories in the Library, and when it comes to their aptness for pan-European advertising Gunn seems to have opinions about all of them. "Badge" products, like liquor or cigarettes, are ripe for single-execution campaigns, because they target a group whose tastes are definitely converging throughout Europe – conspicuous consumers. Functional products, like razors or detergents, are well suited to this approach, too, and so are products with images associated with a particular country, especially if the country happens to be America (Levi's, Coke, etc.) or, at least, isn't in Europe (with the exception of France, for perfume). Cars, on the other hand, are a lot like food: "A Mercedes has enormous cachet in Britain, but in Germany it's a taxi," Gunn says. He admires Volkswagen, which has taken the route of a European strategy with local executions. In Italy, a crew of battered, talking crash-test dummies marvel at a healthy Volkswagen dummy jogging by. In France a patient taking a Rorschach test sees every pattern as a leak under his car, until he's presented with the VW logo, and he's mystified: "It's a banana?" "The Volkswagen driver is always the hero," Gunn notes. "But the French ad is very French. It works by making someone else look stupid."

Gunn can go on and on like this. One day when I was visiting him in London, he told me he had developed a presentation based on his conclusion that all great ads employ one of twelve "master formats." As Gunn took me through the presentation, he offered a running commentary on why many of the formats were ill-suited for crossing borders. Celebrity endorsements, for instance, are hard, unless the star is on the Michael Jordan scale. Testimonials are impossible, since they require dubbing. Pan-European ads often use voice-overs — with the voice customized for each country — and this, Gunn said, is one reason that the master formats involving narrative with dialogue tend not to travel well. Another reason, he argued, is that "stories are about characters, and the most resonant characters are culturally specific."

In the presentation, and in several other lengthy sessions in front of his VCR, Gunn showed me what he considers the best ads that have run Europe-wide in the past few years. There was a spot for Pirelli tires with Carl Lewis racing through New York with treads on his feet. There was a spot for Dunlop tires in which a rotund, nipple-ringed demon ambushes a car with a falling grand piano, a river of soapsuds, a carpet of ball bearings, and a Velvet Underground soundtrack — to no effect. There was a spot for Tag Heuer watches that had a swimmer racing a shark, a hurdler leaping an oversized razor blade, and a relay runner grabbing a dynamite baton — all mind games that athletes play to juice their performance. There were two spots for Smirnoff in which peering through the bottle mimics the vodka effect: a necklace becomes a snake, a fat man becomes a walrus, a staircase becomes piano keys. There was a spot for Nike in which soccer stars, portrayed in giant murals, come to life and send the ball zooming around the world. And there was the Levi's campaign — a series of retro vignettes that, as their creator, B.B.H.'s John Hegarty, says, "'sell the land where the teenager was born."

What was striking about these ads, as Gunn pointed out, was that in important respects they were much alike. They were highly visual and were frequently symbolic; they focussed not on the consumer but on the product; and they were often aimed at one of the two audiences that market researchers agree really are turning into Euroconsumers — the young and the rich. To me, what all this suggested was how daunting it was to create an ad for the whole of Europe, and Gunn agreed that it was so. "The debate used to be very polarized, between those who vehemently said that going pan-European was always right, and those who said it was always wrong," he said. "Now people have realized that sometimes it's right, but often — in a majority of cases — it's wrong."

I asked whether he thought the change had something to do with people growing less Panglossian about European union In general. "No," he said. "It has something to do with people in advertising having learned better sense."

In the summer of 1995, right around the time that Burnett was winning the Johnnie Walker account, the agency was immersed in the search for another brand's essence: the essence of McDonald's. In McDonald's, unlike United Distillers, Burnett has a client that strives to maintain a consistent image in Europe (and, indeed, in the world) but whose marketing is distinctly local. Thom Kettle, McDonald's vice-president for international marketing, told me flatly, "We've never commissioned a pan-European ad, and we probably never will."

For McDonald's, marketing in Europe is a function of its history. Unlike most multinationals, which expanded across Europe in a more or less orderly fashion, McDonald's sprouted like Topsy. The company has been in England for twenty-two years, but in France there was no McDonald's organization — only a scattered set of franchisees — until 1981, and as recently as a year ago there were just thirty-eight of its restaurants in the whole of Italy. With its businesses in Europe at such disparate stages of development, and contending with different competitors and eating habits, Kettle explained, it seemed natural to the executives at McDonald's headquarters, in Oak Brook, Illinois, to let those businesses decide about their own advertising.

Among laypersons, of course, the common perception is that McDonald's is selling the same thing everywhere in Europe — that, like Marlboro and Coke, it is selling "Americanness." But when I suggested this to Florence Waterman, Burnett's European account director for

McDonald's, she smiled a weary smile. Waterman is clever and well read, with a penchant for citing Derrida and Foucault to discuss, say, the first ad ever to feature Ronald McDonald. (He was played, with panache, by a young Willard Scott.) An American, she has been working on the McDonald's account in Europe since 1981. "To have the level of frequentation that McDonald's is seeking, it has to be in the fabric of everyday life," she said. Unlike Marlboro or Coke, she went on, "McDonald's isn't really a product. It may be a ubiquitous American brand, but what you have are hundreds of retail establishments around Europe, many of them decorated in local styles, to suit local tastes, and run and serviced by local people. What's left may come from America, but it's got to become very familiar and wholesome in terms of the local culture, and if it's American food that's an interesting accident."

Waterman is a believer in culinary localism. She can speak endlessly about the regional food splits in Europe — about the pasta belt and the wheat belt and the rice belt, and about the olive-oil belt and the butter belt and the pork-fat belt — and about how these splits affected the development of what is known in the trade as the Q.S.R. (quick-service restaurant) habit in each market. But she knows that, gradually, tastes in Europe *are* converging: "The real outré traditional foods are all in decline. Haggis is a tourist curiosity in Scotland now, and don't get me started on real French cheeses — or real Stilton, for that matter." She also knows that McDonald's is on its way to being an unremarkable presence everywhere in Western Europe, and that the company is working furiously toward this goal.

A couple of years ago, Waterman and Mike Allen, Burnett's international account director for McDonald's, began to worry. The advertising was inconsistent and sometimes themeless, designed mainly to drive up short-term sales rather than foster long-term growth. Worse, in too many places the ads positioned McDonald's as fashionable and exotic instead of wholesome. As an example, Waterman showed me several ads from the early nineties. One ad, produced by Burnett's Spain office, was a quick, highly generic rush of smiling faces and upbeat music. In another ad, created in Burnett's artsy Norway office, the proprietors and the staff of a Chinese restaurant taunt their customers — "No hamburger!" — while they devour a McDonald's feast in the kitchen. "None of this was bad advertising," Allen says, half convincingly. "It just wasn't the best expression of what McDonald's is really about."

So in July of 1995 Waterman and Allen called a meeting of the account directors and creative directors then working on the McDonald's account in all the European countries where the agency handled the brand — Britain, Belgium, Spain, Sweden, Switzerland, and Norway. The meeting took place over three days, in Paris, and its purpose was to agree on a brand essence that could be a basis for the ad campaigns around the region. Sheerly as a practical matter, this would prove difficult. The Swiss creative director hardly spoke English, and one of the Spanish admen needed to translate for his colleague.

Led by Helena Rubenstein, the group parsed McDonald's positive qualities: its appeal as a "family place," its appeal to kids, its speed of service, its "tasty food," and the McDonald's "magic." It also parsed the brand's negative qualities: "patronizing," "smiling but not genuine (faceless)," "unhealthy (not a real barrier but used as an excuse due to lack of information)," and the perception in Europe of the company as "Big Brother."

The group came up with mock job titles for the workers at McDonald's: "human-craving manager," "active fun-food entrepreneur," "guaranteed hunger satisfier." As the hours passed, a consensus began to form, with the account director from Norway as the sole dissenter: he insisted that none of the group's conclusions applied to his country. "I thought the Swiss creative director would be the most difficult," Waterman recalls. "But when I saw him trying, in broken English, to convince the Norwegian, I knew we were home." The essence of McDonald's, the group decreed, was "a trusted friend."

This was the simple part. Whether the exercise had worked or not would become apparent only when Burnett's European agencies began producing new McDonald's ads. Waterman had no illusions. "We were asking these people to reinvent locally something that a pure multinational, like Coke, would do once, from its headquarters, and then roll out all over the world," she said, and one day when I visited her in her London office, she showed me the results.

First, Waterman played an ad from Belgium, in which a small boy, obviously distraught because he has new eyeglasses, is taken by his mother to McDonald's, sees how the glasses seem to magnify the hamburgers, flirts with a little girl, and cheers up. In an ad from Sweden, a working mother who schemes to get out of a business meeting, only to have her boss cancel it, takes her daughter to McDonald's and sees the boss there with his son. In a British ad called "The Go-Between," a boy maneuvers his father into taking him to McDonald's, where the dad runs into his estranged wife and chats sweetly with her — to their son's delight. Finally, Waterman showed me a new ad from the avant-gardists in Norway: a stunning, elegiac black-and-white spot in which a boy is led by his grand-mother through a city full of strange sights — long-haired, shouting men, Asian glam rockers, a girl with studs in her tongue — and arrives safely, in the end, at McDonald's.

Waterman is convinced that all these ads share a certain wholesome feeling, an intimation that "this is not a trendy place, this is a family place, this is a *safe* place, a place where you can be intimate — and then there's the food promise." In style and substance, though, they illustrate the point that, in advertising, narrative is inherently local. Burnett's of-fice in Norway had considered running the Swedish ad since the people look alike, but discovered that it "jarred," Waterman said, because of the perception that "family units are more intact in Norway." Similarly, the "Go-Between" would be awkward in Ireland, because divorce had only just been legalized there." And a new British spot, which never shows either a McDonald's restaurant or a single bit of McDonald's food, probably couldn't run anywhere else in Europe, because nowhere else is the level of familiarity high enough to risk it.

Such constraints are not strictly a European phenomenon. One recent McDonald's ad in Britain was called "Birds and Bees." It was written by Gerard Stamp, and was based on a conversation he'd had one day with his daughter. In the ad, a little girl is potting a plant. She looks up and asks her father where babies come from. After hemming and hawing, he tries to distract her by offering to take her to McDonald's. She happily accepts and then, as the father sighs with relief, she announces that they can talk about babies over Big Macs. By playing on a father's unease in discussing sex, the ad, Stamp said, "is quintessentially British." Mike Allen told me that he considered importing the spot to America, but the television networks objected. "Oh, yes, that's right," Stamp said, with a grin. "You don't *have* sex in America, do you?"

"Nothing reflects a country and an age better than its advertising," Jean-Marie Dru, chairman of the French agency B.D.D.P., writes in his new book, *Disruption*, and this certainly seemed true at Britain's Creative Circle Awards, in March. The Creative Circle dinner is the first of the year's big European advertising-awards shows — an event at which six hundred or so of London's most prominent young art directors and copywriters drink vodka, eat steak-and-ale pie, smoke cigars, and congratulate themselves on their creativity. Donald Gunn had invited me to the dinner, and we sat at a table in the back of the hall, taking note of which of the "films," as the European admen like to call them, had run throughout Europe. But there was not much to take note of. In a long reel of winners, only two ads were pan-European.

By the law of averages, as the sheer number of such ads rises the number of compelling ones is bound to increase. And the over-all number is rising fast. Among the mega-clients, some of the giddiness about the single market is no doubt gone. A European design consultant told me, "In the late eighties, companies were saying they wanted their colors to be blue and gold, because those were the colors of the European Community flag. But now they're the colors of bureaucracy, and nobody wants any part of them." Yet if the conceit of a 'United States of Europe' has disappeared among the big marketers, the impulse behind that conceit *is* more powerful than ever. With manufacturing, research, packaging, and design all being consolidated and centralized, why should advertising be different?

Ad agencies, of course, think that advertising is very different, yet they have little choice but to go along – seeking the brand essence and the brand vision and all the rest. But this has done precious little to change their view that some of the sharpest insights come not from what consumers share but from what sets them apart – from the differences that, in Europe, have proved to be not only stubborn but, at times, a source of pride.

The winner of the top prize at this year's Creative Circle Awards, and one of the most talked-about ads in London of late, was a commercial for a drink called Blackcurrant Tango. The ad opens in Tango's headquarters, where the firm's "spokesperson" strides purposefully across the room, reading a letter from "Sebastian," a French exchange student, who tried a Blackcurrant Tango and didn't think much of it. The spokesman sneers: "You're an exchange student, aren't you, Sebastian? All hair gel and fancy loafers?" Faster and faster, the Tango man heads outdoors and through the parking lot, stripping off his clothes to reveal a robust belly and purple boxing trunks, and issues an indignant rebuke – "You're one dissenting voice in a billion, Johnny French" – that turns into a challenge to settle things in the ring. By the end, the challenge has turned into an attack on all things Euro, and the Tango man stands in a field at the edge of the white cliffs of Dover, surrounded by cheering English fans, ready to fight.

# Writing Creative Briefs

## By Hart Weichselbaum

*Dr. Weichselbaum is president of The Planning Practice, an ad and brand planning consultancy based in Chicago. He was head of planning at The Richards Group for 13 years, has been an adjunct faculty member at DePaul University's Kellstadt Graduate School of Business, and was a founding member of the organization that became the Account Planning Committee of the 4As. He is executive editor of this book.*

IN MOST AGENCIES, THE DEFINING ROLE of the account planner is leading the development of the creative brief. In fact, it's often the most tangible output of the planner's work. Part of learning to be a good planner is learning to write good briefs.

The creative brief is a document that distills and summarizes the agency's strategic thinking and conveys it to the creative team. Usually no more than a page or two, it's the end result of a larger process that includes strategic business analysis, brand and target audience understanding, refinement and debate with the client and other agency players, and planning and conducting the meeting in which the brief is presented to creatives. Concisely and cogently, the brief has to engage the team responsible for creating the ads and inspire them to do great work.

Creative briefs can be written for any kind of strategic communication – not just for traditional TV, radio, magazine, billboard, and newspaper ads, but also for direct mail, banner ads, viral ads, mobile ads, sales promotion programs, brand names, logos, and websites. The length and amount of detail in the brief will vary, but the basic principles remain the same. A brief for an infomercial may have a lot of factual information and supporting material, while one for a billboard had better be quite short. (At The Richards Group, a brief longer than one page required special dispensation from Stan Richards himself.)

In this chapter, we'll discuss why we have creative briefs, how to write a good one, what questions they answer, and how to maximize their impact on the process of ad creation. We'll end with a little food for thought about where it's all headed. But right now, let's focus on some basics.

## Why Do We Have Briefs?

Simply put, we have briefs because they increase the probability that we will get the ads right. We increase our chances of success by:

- thinking through who the target is and why the message is important to them,

- making sure the message addresses advertising objectives, and

- considering alternative directions and debating them with the other members of the team.

Not only do we increase our chances of getting the ads right, but the process of brief writing also increases our chances of getting them right *the first time*. If you can get the rest of the team to buy into your thinking, you reduce the number of times the creative team brings you ads you have to send back. Good briefs actually save everybody's time, because they prevent the false starts that burn hours and demoralize the team.

Planners should become more like shepherds guiding gently and tending patiently, rather than some sort of master strategist managing with the all-knowing brief. And, in fact, first briefs are often just the first step in a process of refinement that occurs as creative output is developed and critiqued.

Briefs are neither written in stone nor chalk. On the one hand, the brief often evolves in the course of creative development. Creatives sometimes come up with new and compelling ideas in the course of concepting, and sometimes the strategy implicit in their work will cause us to change the brief.

On the other hand, there is the understanding that if the team agreed to a brief ahead of time, there shouldn't be a change without a good reason for that change. Any new solution that is come upon along the way has to fit the evidence that led to the brief in the first place.

## A Division of Labor

Although the planner is usually the one to put the words on paper, he or she doesn't write the creative brief alone. In practice, the planner manages the process of getting input from other members of the agency team (and the client) and distilling their thinking. The planner plays this central role because he or she is the one who understands consumer behavior, follows consumer trends, has studied the latest market research, understands the competitive context, has talked to the product manager, and most important, has the greatest experience in performing this essential task.

The planner chooses from among all the things that might be said and picks the ones that he or she believes will be most effective, while the creative team chooses how to say it. It's a division of labor that allows specialists to do what they do best. In writing the brief, the planner provides the bridge between strategic thinking and the creative work.

## A Contract With Creatives

The brief is a kind of contract between the creative team and the people who develop the strategy. While the brief should guide and stimulate the process, it also has to be flexible enough to allow the creative team to express their creativity. Then, when the ads are being evaluated, the judgment should be about whether the objectives have been met, the audience has been addressed, and the key thought communicated, not the exact way those things were accomplished.

By the way, if the planner doesn't make those decisions, the creative team will make them. They will create something whether they get specific direction or not. While they probably won't bother to write down their brief, their ads will nonetheless have an imagined target, main idea, tone of voice, etc.

## An Ad To Creatives

Thinking of the brief as an ad to creatives is a good guide for creating them. When you think about it, good briefs and good ads have many things in common. Here's some good advice for both.

**Be brief.** At its most basic level, the creative brief tells the creative team what to do. It functions as a work order that specifies the objective, target, and main message of the communication — all the essential information they need to do their job.

Because the amount of information you could put in a brief is potentially very large — there are usually dozens of things you can possibly say about any product or service — often the toughest decisions are about what to leave out.

Like a good ad, good briefs get their point across in a concise and compelling way. A common mistake in brief writing is giving the creative team too much information. (Why do you think they call it a "brief"?) Unnecessary or distracting information makes their job more difficult and forces them to make choices they may be ill-prepared to make. This is sometimes called understanding the importance of what's important.

**Avoid jargon.** Good ads speak in the language of their audience and so do good briefs. Since the target audience for the brief is your creative team, it makes sense to write it in language they can understand. Marketing is rife with jargon that marketers hide behind. Sometimes the planner's task is to take the client's brief to the agency, trim out the unnecessary information, and translate the jargon into everyday English.

**Inspire your audience.** The brief is your chance to provide creatives with your best, most original thinking. If the brief is fresh and insightful, you improve the chances that the ads will be, too. Here is where much brief writing falls short. It doesn't go that extra step of expressing the idea in a compelling way.

There's a big difference between an unfocused proposition like "Corona is a great tasting beer from Mexico" and something more specific and provocative like "Unlike the posturing, self-conscious brown-bottled beers it competes with, Corona is relaxed and unpretentious." Which one do you think it would be easier to write ads to?

# What Questions Do They Answer?

Most briefs answer four basic questions. This is true whether they are for TV ads, websites, sales promotion programs, or whatever. In addition, many agencies have their own "proprietary" formats for the creative brief. No doubt, these can be very useful in highlighting the agency's distinctive approach to creative development. At the end of this chapter, we'll describe one distinctive set of questions used by Crispin Porter + Bogusky. But for the moment, let's cover the four basics.

## 1. What Are We Trying To Accomplish?

The goal here is to convey the objectives of the communication as specifically and straightforwardly as possible.

Ads do more than raise awareness or get people to buy. Often the real objective of advertising is to create a new occasion for use, or justify a higher price or boost the morale of the people who serve customers, or just to get people talking about the brand. Starbuck's 2007 holiday advertising had as its primary goal to evoke warm feelings in its audience with the hope those feelings would transfer to Starbucks and translate into sales of gift cards for family and friends.

The ultimate goal of communications may be to increase sales, but that is far too distant a goal to be useful in a brief, and more important, it doesn't help creatives. The real question is: *How* will sales be increased? By getting customers to buy more often? By attracting new customers? By changing perceptions? Or by getting regular customers to purchase a gift card?

If you are at a loss about finding a sufficiently specific objective, check out the 4A's book called *One Hundred Reasons to Advertise*. It's a little dated, but it's a handy reference for thinking about all the things ads can do.

One more thing: Clients are sometimes wildly optimistic about what communications can achieve. Ads can accomplish wonderful things, but in most business situations they don't make the sale alone. By being honest about what the ads will achieve, you can save yourself some trouble down the road when the sales figures or tracking study results come in.

For example, the goal of the Motel 6 advertising, a very successful radio campaign that has been running since the 1980s, was to make guests feel comfortable about staying in a low-priced chain motel. Many worried they'd be perceived as too poor or too cheap to stay anywhere else. So the advertising had to create another reason for staying there, one that transcended merely saving money.

## 2. Who Are We Talking To?

This part of the brief tells creatives what they need to know about the target audience in order to write ads to them. Thus, the question is sometimes posed as "What do we know about the target audience that can help us?" or "What is the consumer insight that will drive the work?"

The demographic definition of the target audience should be only a starting point. "Adults 18-64" really doesn't help the creative team much in their search for a solution. This is the place to tell the team how and where consumers use the product, how it relates to their life goals or their lifestyle, how it relates to their psychology or culture, why they stop or start using it, how they use advertising in the category – anything that will help the creative team envision who they are writing to and give them a way into consumers' lives.

Another feature of the description is that it must link in some way to the proposition presented in the next section. There are many interesting things about any target audience, but only a few offer an insight that will be useful to creatives.

Motel 6 knew a lot about the segments of travelers it appealed to: young couples on a budget, retirees seeing the country, per diem business travelers – their demographics, travel habits, likes, and dislikes. But the most important thing about them was that they all needed reassurance they would still get a clean, comfortable room even though they were spending less.

## 3. What Is the Single Most Persuasive Idea We Can Convey?

This section contains the focal point for the communication. Sometimes it's called the Main Thought or the Proposition. This is the idea we want the target to accept, and it's usually the single most motivating and differentiating thing we can say about the brand.

Ideas can come from anywhere, though often they are grounded in our knowledge of what the brand's strengths are, what's really motivating to people, and some aspect of what the product or service is or does.

If the communication is to be single-minded (and for most kinds of short-form advertising, that's the only kind that has a prayer of being noticed and remembered), it has to be focused.

Let's say the ad needs to generate interest in a new mobile phone. Should it focus on the phone's quality, reliability, famous brand name, low price, or one or more of its new and unique features? Or, maybe the most important message isn't about the product at all. Perhaps it's some practical customer benefit like keeping track of your kids or succeeding in business or being able to leave your camera or your PDA at home. Or maybe the thing to emphasize is an emotional benefit like being the first to have it or being cooler than your classmates or having a phone to capture embarrassing moments so you can tease your friends.

Choosing among these alternatives depends on good product knowledge, recognition of the brand's strengths and weaknesses, and a deep understanding of the target's needs and motivations.

Not only is there a lot of work in choosing the one most important thing to say, but there is also the challenge in saying it in a provocative way. Try to state the proposition as imaginatively and succinctly as possible. The agency for Motel 6 could have chosen a proposition like "Really low prices." Instead they chose "A smart choice because you don't pay for what you don't need." A good proposition points the way to a solution and has in it the seeds of good creative executions.

## 4. Why Should They Believe It?

Sometimes a proposition requires factual support to change attitudes or behavior. Sometimes it's the way the proposition is stated or the attitude it projects that supports the main idea. One thing is certain: the amount of support must be appropriate for the media you are planning to use. If it's a 30-second TV spot, one support point is often enough (and some think one is too many). Thus, briefs for outdoor advertising tend to be short; those for infomercials or websites are much longer.

As Mike Hall says in his chapter in this book, all kinds of things can make advertising persuasive: offering a functional benefit or unique selling proposition, communicating brand values that resonate, identifying the right call to action, or simply making the brand stand out from the crowd.

Sometimes the ad's attitude or tone of voice can make it more persuasive. If the planner has a point of view about tone of voice, it should go here. Should the ad be authoritative, humorous, factual, emotional, spiritual? What will work best with this audience?

## Some Tips on the Process

Brief creation doesn't occur in a vacuum. Although the planner leads the team, strategy development is usually a collaborative enterprise. Here are some tips for increasing the odds of having maximum impact.

- Make sure you have the facts.

  Although the amount of information you will have in any particular situation will vary greatly, the brief should be based on the best information available. It's amazing how often a client has an untested hunch about what to say in advertising that bears no relationship to the target's reality. And the agency team certainly isn't immune to personal prejudice or wishful thinking. Fortunately there's usually a set of facts that has to be accommodated. And the planner is often in the position to recommend additional research to settle differences.

- If you can, write multiple briefs.

Multiple briefs often clarify the advertising problem. So if there's time, it's usually a good idea to write briefs organized around several propositions. Planners and account service people can compete to produce the best solution. "Dueling briefs" create useful debate and elucidate the strengths and weaknesses of different approaches. Not only does this create better briefs, but it also generates more conviction in presenting your case.

- Involve others.

  Brief writing is a team sport. Everybody brings something to the party. Try to involve your client because he or she has a lot of experience with the product or service being advertised. Try to involve creatives because they are the best writers and are, well, creative. In any case, creatives must be involved somewhere along the way because only they can tell you whether the brief makes sense to them and provides a starting point for an interesting creative execution.

- Plan the briefing.

  If a brief fell in the forest would anyone hear it? The brief is only part of the task. Having a meeting or meetings to communicate the brief to creatives is far more effective than slipping it under the door. The briefing is not an afterthought but an opportunity to provide additional information and make the brief come alive for the creative team. Often the most useful part of the briefing is the supplemental materials and ideas the planner brings to it. Music, images, ads, and other artifacts of the consumer – anything to bring the brief to life – are all fair game.

- Stay humble.

  Never lose sight of the fact that the brief is merely a means to an end. Ad agencies are in the business of creating memorable and effective advertising. So our briefs are only as good as the ads that come out of them. As one advertising sage remarked, "You don't have a great brief until you have a great ad."

# Where Briefs Are Headed

Life was simpler in the days before agencies had such a broad arsenal of new media to choose from. Because marketing is being asked to do more things in more ways, many of the old formulations – including the questions asked in the creative brief – are changing in response to changing times.

Crispin Porter & Bogusky is an advertising agency that has had some rather spectacular success recently – in a world where advertising success is no easy task. Their unique ads for Burger King, beautifully designed work for the Mini, clever "Man Laws" for Miller Beer, and "Truth" anti-smoking campaign seemed to hit the right note in a cynical world.

CP+B is also a perfect example of an agency that has created a brief that reflects both the new roles advertising has been asked to take and the agency's unique approach to creative communication. Their brief addresses each of the four basic questions discussed above; but it does so in a way that evolves and elaborates their meaning.

First, let's look at how these questions are similar, yet different, from what we've been discussing. My comments are in italics.

## The CP+B Creative Brief

- **At-a-Glance.** What is the most relevant and differentiating idea that will surprise consumers or challenge their current thinking or relationship with the brand?

  *In an over-communicated world, it's important to boil the issues down to something quick and simple. The CP+B brief instructs us to reduce our complicated idea to its essence.*

- **Tension.** What is the psychological, social, categorical, or cultural tension associated with this idea?

  *CP+B believes that engaging stories (and engaging communications in general) are based on tension between opposing forces. Is the brand an upstart in an established category? Can the brand be a "good guy" to a competitor's "bad guy," or vice versa? Tension creates emotion, drama, and suspense. Often it begs for resolution, causing people to act.*

- **Question.** What is the question we need to answer to complete this assignment?

    *The communications problem can often be solved by identifying — and then answering — a key question. Charles Kettering said, "A problem well-stated is half-solved."*

- **Talk Value.** What about the brand could help us to start a dialogue between the brand and our target, among our target and/or within popular culture in general? It could be the little rationalizations that people use to support their emotional decision.

    *As much as any other US agency, CP+B has found ways to multiply the impact of their work — and extend their clients' communications budgets — by getting people to talk about it. Their 2004 viral campaign "Subservient Chicken" for Burger King generated 20 million hits as it was passed around the world.*

In many ways, the CP+B brief points the way to where briefs are heading.

1. Rather than describing merely the business context, it places the communications problem in a larger social and cultural context.

2. It acknowledges that people are consuming media in new ways and that what people tell each other about the ad may have more impact than the ad itself.

3. It reflects a unique model of how advertising works by advising creatives to exploit the inherent tension in the brand's situation.

4. It uses language that is "media neutral," that is, it makes no assumptions about what kinds of communications will be needed to solve the problem.

As communications problems and media options become more complex, there will be an increasing need to strategize, prioritize, and distill until we have a document that helps the creative team get it right.

In brief, we'll always need some kind of brief.

# Index

# BOOKS FROM **THE COPY WORKSHOP**

adbuzz.com | 773-871-1179 | FAX 773-281-4643 | thecopyworkshop@aol.com

We publish some of the leading books in advertising and marketing. Our authors are leading educators and industry professionals. These books are designed for those with jobs in the creative department.

## DESCRIPTION

## INFORMATION

This is the #1 book on copywriting. Agencies use it as a training resource. It's used by universities, art schools, and the American Management Association (it's the basic book for their copywriting seminar). The Really New Edition features more great examples of ads that work, a practical approach to integrated communication - The MarCom Matrix - and new chapters on Sales Promotion, Direct, and "MPR" (Marketing Public Relations). Also available in Chinese and Korean.

**The Copy Workshop Workbook**
by Bruce Bendinger

440 pages, $37.50

ISBN# 978-1-887229-12-8

From the Beetle to the Mini. From "Eat Mor Chikin" to the AFLAC Duck. From "Think Different" to "Got Milk." This completely revised and expanded 2nd edition includes life lessons from 18 of advertising's most important talents.

**How To Succeed In Advertising When All You Have Is Talent**
by Laurence Minsky

480 pages, $47.50

ISBN# 978-1-887229-20-3

The search in Market Research is often the search for new insight. Professor Durgee's book combines practical experience for top marketers and ad agencies with his own unique insights into what it takes to find the path to actionable insights. Today, leading-edge writers and researchers such as Gladwell and Rapaille note the power of insight. Durgee offers practical steps on the road to discovering them.

**Creative Insight:**
*The Researcher's Art*
by Jeffrey F. Durgee

233 pages, $29.95

ISBN# 978-1-887229-26-5

This is a book about and by *"The Socrates of San Francisco,"* Howard Gossage, the copywriter who introduced the world to Marshall McLuhan, helped start Friends of the Earth and brought interactivity to his unique brand of advertising.
He was 30 years ahead of his time, so the world may be ready.
The Second Edition also features **The Disc of Gossage** - packed with extras; a radio address, an ad gallery, and more.

**The Book of Gossage**
by Howard Luck Gossage
Introduction by Jeff Goodby, w. Stan Freberg, Kim Rotzoll, John Steinbeck, and Tom Wolfe.

2nd Edition - Includes the Disc of Gossage. 400 pages. $50.00

ISBN# 978-1-887229-28-9

We are pleased to present Professor Elaine Wagner's clear and reader-friendly book clarifying the often complicated process of preparing computer-based graphic files for printing or for sending to a publication.
This is a critical issue and Professor Wagner, with the assistance of printing professional Amy Desiderio, makes this complicated area crystal clear with principles that apply while technology evolves.

**From File To Finish:**
*A Prepress Guide*
by Elaine Wagner &
Amy Desiderio

282 pages, $37.50

ISBN# 978-1-887229-32-6

For more information and to Save 20% on these titles, go to the Book Shop at www.adbuzz.com

# BOOKS FROM **THE COPY WORKSHOP**

adbuzz.com | 773-871-1179 | FAX 773-281-4643 | thecopyworkshop@aol.com

We publish some of the leading books in advertising and marketing. Our authors are leading educators and industry professionals. These books are designed for those in research, media, and account management.

## DESCRIPTION

## INFORMATION

Agencies need to do for themselves what they do for their clients: build a distinctive brand. But they are usually so eager to be a "full-service integrated agency" that they try to stand for everything. Take a Stand for Your Brand shows how agencies can develop a clear positioning that builds on the agency's unique strengths, differentiates the agency in the marketplace, and makes the agency more intensely appealing to prospective clients.

**Take A Stand For Your Brand:**
*Building A Great Agency Brand From The Inside Out*
by Tim Williams

213 pages, $29.95

ISBN# 978-1-887229-25-8

A smart book about one of the most challenging jobs in business - account management.
Use as a core text for a management course, or as a supplement for your student agency. The 2nd Edition includes a new chapter on Account Management in the Era of IMC, featuring contributions from top professionals in a variety of fields.

**The New Account Manager, 2nd Ed.**
by Don Dickinson

524 pages, $47.50

ISBN# 978-1-887229-37-1

The Consumer Insight Classic.
Clear and engaging - written by one of the top professionals in consumer insight. The book takes you through the process step by step - from Data to Information to Insight to Inspiration.
This book is used worldwide by both students and professionals.

**Hitting the Sweet Spot:**
*How Consumer Insights Can Inspire Better Marketing and Advertising*
by Lisa Fortini-Cambell

257 pages, $29.95

ISBN# 978-1-887229-09-8

Welcome to the world of media - the $300 billion business end of the ad business. Learn how it works from some of media's top professors and professionals. This is a book in touch with today —packed with genuine substance and contemporary best practices in a clear, easy-to-read format. A student workbook is available FREE on the MediaBuzz Web site.

**Strategic Media Decisions, 2nd Ed:**
*Understanding The Business End Of The Advertising Business*
by Marian Azzaro, w. Carla Lloyd, Mary Alice Shaver, Dan Binder, Robb Clawson, and Olaf Werder
524 pages, $67.50

ISBN# 978-1-887229-33-3

Years ago, top ad agency executive Norm Macmaster wrote a guide for beginning account executives.
It became legendary - with copies handed down from generation to generation. With the author's permission, we bring this underground classic to light - clear and practical, it provides beginners with the information they need to do the job.

**What Do You Mean I Can't Write?**
*A Practical Guide To Business Writing For Agency Account Managers*
by Norm MacMaster

74 pages, $11.75

ISBN # 978-1-887229-29-6

For more information and to Save 20% on these titles, go to the Book Shop at www.adbuzz.com